General Editor
Simon Braund

THE GREATEST MOVIES
YOU'LL NEVER SEE

First published in the United Kingdom in 2013 by
Aurum Press Limited
74-77 White Lion Street
London N1 9PF
www.aurumpress.co.uk

A catalogue record for this book is available from the British Library.

ISBN 978 1 78131 075 5

10 9 8 7 6 5 4 3 2 1
2017 2016 2015 2014 2013

This book was designed and produced by
Quintessence
230 City Road
London EC1V 2TT

Project Editor   Bruno MacDonald
Designer   Alison Hau
Picture Researchers   Sara di Girolamo, Helena Baser
Production Manager   Anna Pauletti
Editorial Director   Jane Laing
Publisher   Mark Fletcher

Colour reproduction by ChromaGraphics Pte Ltd.

Printed and bound in China by 1010 Printing International Ltd.

CONTENTS

INTRODUCTION

In the summer of 1974, Universal executive Sid Sheinberg paid a visit to the set of one of the studio's movies, shooting on location off the coast of Cape Cod. He was not expecting a pleasant trip. The movie in question was in deep trouble, well on the way to tripling its $3.5 million budget and already alarmingly behind schedule. With a young, relatively untested director at the helm, it was limping along slowly, enduring frantic script revisions, an increasingly rebellious crew, a truculent cast who couldn't stand each other and who had no faith in the project ('A piece of shit', was one lead actor's verdict) and ruinously expensive special effects that refused to work. Even the director, a twenty-seven-year-old college dropout with only one feature film to his credit, admitted he had considered throwing himself down a flight of stairs to avoid accepting the assignment.

With furious studio heads breathing down his neck, Sheinberg was under pressure to fire the director and pull the plug. Instead, swayed by Steven Spielberg's belief in the film and his determination to finish it on his own terms, he decided to stand by him. It was a wise decision. *Jaws* (1975) became not only one of the most profitable films of all time, but it also ushered in the era of the modern blockbuster, changing for ever the way Hollywood makes and markets movies. History, however, is littered with films, many of them less deserving of the axe than *Jaws*, that were not so lucky.

Given the multitude of factors that must fall into place before a film can get made – decent script, adequate financing, distribution network, cast scheduling, technical crew, appropriate director, acceptably luxurious trailer for the star and so on – it's a wonder any actually make it to the screen at all. Of course, a great many do – inexplicably so in some cases; *The Godfather Part III* (1990), the *Police Academy* sequels and the late canon of Eddie Murphy spring to mind. But scores of others, for one reason or another, fall by the wayside, mostly unmissed and unlamented. It's a simple fact that the majority of abandoned movies fail to launch because someone had the good sense to realize that actually making them would be a waste of time, effort and invariably a great deal of money. However – as the title of this book may have already alerted you – the loss (or rather non-existence) of a number of others, derailed by the vagaries of the film-making process, is keenly felt, either because they represent thwarted artistic ambition or the kind of goggle-eyed folly that can only be gazed on in mesmerized wonder – both of which are reason enough to mourn their absence.

Consider, for instance, Stanley Kubrick's monumental biopic of Napoleon, a film he obsessed over for years, amassing a colossal archive of Napoleonic artefacts and reams of background material, but which he could not, in the end, commit to celluloid. Widely regarded as a lost masterpiece, it has become a potent piece of cinematic mythology, the paragon of movie what-ifs. At the more whacked-out end of the spectrum there's Chilean maestro Alejandro Jodorowsky's heroically demented plans for an adaptation of Frank Herbert's sci-fi classic *Dune*, an epic flight of fancy that bore only scant relation to the original book. What, you wonder, might a collaboration between the director of *El Topo*, a head-spinning psychedelic Western that merges the best of Sergio Leone with a bad acid trip, Pink Floyd, H.R. Giger and a cast comprising Mick Jagger, Orson Welles, Gloria Swanson and Salvador Dalí have yielded? Sadly, we'll never know – although it's safe to assume it would have made David Lynch's 1982 attempt to capture the novel look like an episode of *The Jetsons*.

In a crowded field, competition for the 'What Were They Thinking?' (WWTT) top spot is fierce. Among the front-runners though is Jerry Lewis's jaw-droppingly tasteless Holocaust mawk-a-thon *The Day the Clown Cried* (1972), in which Lewis, a comic actor not noted for understated pathos (or understated anything for that matter), plays a circus clown whose antics are employed to lure children into the gas chamber. And yes, 'plays' is right: the film was made but never released – and unless you have access to Lewis's private vault, in which he keeps a closely guarded VHS version, your chances of seeing it are not much better than those of seeing any other film detailed in the pages to come. Still, a monumentally misguided vanity project though it was, *The Day the Clown Cried* made it past the drawing board stage. Others in the WWTT category did not, including a proposed collaboration between Salvador Dalí and the Marx Brothers, a sequel to *Casablanca* (1942) and an attempt by Russian auteur Sergei Eisenstein to chronicle the history of Mexico without adequate financing, a coherent script or any clear idea of how he was going to pull it off. An added impediment was Uncle Joe Stalin, in a purging frame of mind, hot on his case for desertion of the motherland. (Whatever tribulations Spielberg faced on the set of *Jaws*, a mass-murdering despot keen to throw him in the Gulag was not among them.)

Beyond the simple pleasure of imagining how these movies might have turned out, is the opportunity to speculate on the extent to which, had they been made, they might have affected the careers of those involved and, in turn, the history of cinema itself. Take Kubrick's *Napoleon*. This was set to be an enterprise of huge proportions. It would have occupied him for most of the early 1970s, meaning 1971's *A Clockwork Orange*, a film that had serious ramifications in his personal and professional life and which exerted a powerful influence on the tenor of popular culture, might never have seen the light of day. Similarly, had Charlie Chaplin realized his own biopic of Napoleon in the 1930s, he may not have been so inclined to take on Hitler in *The Great Dictator* (1940).

You could fill an entire book with projects Orson Welles tried and failed to get off the ground in his post-Hollywood career. Whether he left Tinseltown in an artistically frustrated huff, or was (as mythology has it) exiled after *Citizen Kane* (1941) brought down the wrath of press baron William Randolph Hearst on his and his paymasters' heads, Welles wandered the wilderness for decades trying to raise money for an assortment of ventures, most of which, tragically, died a long, slow death. The point is, any one of them could have been the critical and commercial hit he needed to restore major investors' confidence in him. Who knows what would have resulted from that – imagine *Spartacus* (1960) or *The Sweet Smell of Success* (1957) in Welles's hands.

More recently, if Steven Spielberg had not had a change of heart in 1979 and pressed on with his dark alien invasion movie *Night Skies* we would have been denied *E.T.* (1982), a film whose poetic charm and sense of childlike wonder set the tone for much of his output during the following decade. By the same token, Darren Aronofsky and Frank Miller's radical re-imagining of the Caped Crusader in *Batman: Year One* presents an interesting dilemma. Most fans would give their right arm to see Aronofsky and Miller collaborate on a *Teletubbies* movie, let alone get a peek at what they cooked up for Batman. But lamentations over the fate of *Batman: Year One* must be measured against the fact that had it come to fruition, Christopher Nolan's *Dark Knight* trilogy would never have left the Batcave. (Read the fascinating details on page 188 and decide for yourself whether that would have been an acceptable trade-off.)

In a sense, the films you're about to encounter represent an alternative history of cinema, or certainly the skeleton of one. It's an impression immeasurably enhanced by the posters, dreamed up by a team of talented artists, to accompany every entry. The posters add a vividness to each movie that highlights another aspect of their appeal: although none of them will ever grace a cinema screen, receive a Blu-ray release or appear on your Netflix queue, they *do* exist. They exist on the pages of this book and, even as you immerse yourself in the story of each one's demise, they exist in the imagination, viewed through the projector of the mind's eye. In this way, they play just as you want them to: perfect, unsullied by asinine script revisions, meddling studio brass, vicious re-cuts, bad casting, lacklustre performances, fired directors or any of the myriad other factors that can intervene on the journey from heated artistic ambition to cold reality. Viewed like this, the book becomes a phantom film festival of the mind.

'Making a movie is like getting on a stagecoach,' Steven Spielberg once said, no doubt with *Jaws* uppermost in his mind. 'At first you're hoping for a pleasant journey. After a while you're just praying you get there.' Here, then, are the ones that didn't make it. The ones that went into the ditch, that ploughed over the cliff or were fatefully diverted onto the endless backroads of development hell. The ones, in short, where the wheels came off, leaving us to pick over the debris and to ponder the question of what might have been if they'd reached their final destination.

A NOTE ON INFORMATION

• In estimating a project's budget, we've generally trusted *Variety* as the most reliable source.

• For Country, we've indicated where the film was produced, rather than where it was shot.

• For Year, we've used (or guesstimated) the date when the film would have been released, rather than when it originated.

• For Starring, we've stuck to actors who were legitimately attached to the film, rather than those rumoured to be involved. The same goes for Director.

CHAPLIN

RETURN FROM ST. HELENA

directed and produced by Charles Chaplin

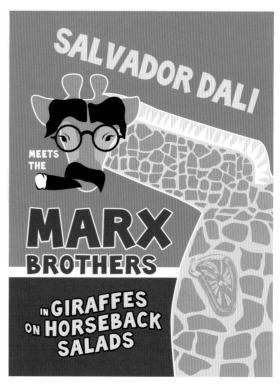

SALVADOR DALI

MEETS THE

MARX BROTHERS

IN GIRAFFES ON HORSEBACK SALADS

¡QUE VIVA MEXICO!

A Sergei Eisenstein Film

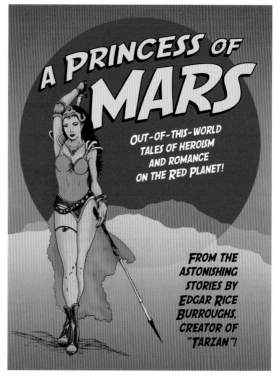

A PRINCESS OF MARS

OUT-OF-THIS-WORLD TALES OF HEROISM AND ROMANCE ON THE RED PLANET!

FROM THE ASTONISHING STORIES BY EDGAR RICE BURROUGHS, CREATOR OF "TARZAN"!

Chapter 1
The Twenties –
The Fifties

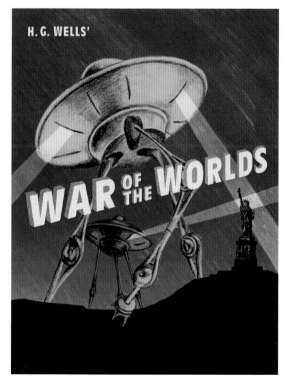

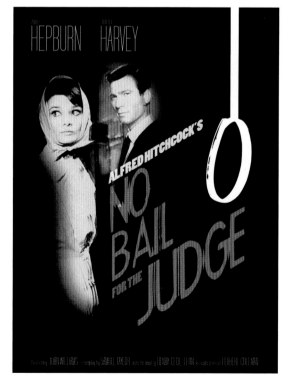

RETURN FROM ST. HELENA

Director Charlie Chaplin **Starring** Charlie Chaplin **Year** 1920s–1930s **Country** US **Genre** Comedy **Studio** United Artists

CHARLIE CHAPLIN

'The happiest moments were when I was on the set and I had an idea or just a suggestion of a story, and I felt good, and then things would happen,' the star (above, as Napoleon) told *Life*. 'It was the only surcease that I had.'

Exiled from the United States in 1952, Charlie Chaplin settled in Vevey, Switzerland, a small village on the shore of Lake Geneva, and lived in a well-appointed villa. Among the staff was an antiques expert whose duties included the conservation of four trunks of Napoleonic memorabilia: uniforms, hats, stirrups, gloves, silverware, letters and so on – a collection Chaplin had been stashing since the early 1920s. The memorabilia, however, was not all he harboured: thoughts of a Napoleon biopic – with himself in the title role and his preeminent leading lady (and one-time real-life love interest) Edna Purviance as the Empress Josephine – had lingered for decades.

ADULATION OF MILLIONS

It's tempting to think that in the 1920s Chaplin's fame and the adulation of millions had gone to his head. A comic genius he was, without doubt. But a dramatic actor with the range to play Napoleon? The Little Tramp as The Little Corporal? In fact, Chaplin was serious, and although the project never came to fruition, it was one that fascinated him for the best part of twenty years.

His fascination with Napoleon was not born of movie-star hubris but had roots in the Dickensian streets of London and his poverty-stricken childhood in the 1890s. 'I hardly remember a father and do not remember him having lived with us,' he wrote in his 1964 autobiography. 'Mother said he looked like Napoleon.' His mother, he recalled, had a mild obsession with the Empress Josephine and would act out scenes from Napoleon's life for him and his brother Sydney. Decades later, having formed United Artists with Mary Pickford, Douglas Fairbanks and director D.W. Griffiths in 1919, Chaplin was casting around for a project and Napoleon once again raised his head – although, initially, he was thinking not of himself but of Purviance.

At twenty-eight, Purviance had grown too 'matronly' to qualify as his love interest either on-screen or off-screen. With her career on the slide, her self-confidence shattered and a burgeoning alcohol problem, she needed a boost. Perhaps out of guilt over jilting her, both professionally and personally, Chaplin sought to provide one. 'Before starting on my first film for United Artists,' he recalled, 'I wanted to launch Edna in a starring role.' Rejecting an adaptation

CHAPLIN
RETURN FROM
ST. HELENA
directed and produced by Charles Chaplin

EMPRESS LITA?

With Edna Purviance out of contention, in the late 1920s Chaplin toyed with casting his then-wife Lita Grey (above right) as Josephine. However, two events of 1927 put paid to that: the release of Abel Gance's epic *Napoléon* and his divorce from Grey.

of *The Trojan Women* by classical Greek playwright Euripides (and you thought Napoleon was a stretch), he fixated on the Empress. Unfortunately for Purviance, the role was beyond her capabilities, and the more Chaplin delved into Josephine's story, the less interest he had in her and the more he had in Napoleon.

In 1931, on a publicity tour for *City Lights*, an assistant recommended Chaplin read a romantic novel by Jean-Paul Weber about Napoleon on St Helena – the island to which the French military leader was exiled in defeat. At the urging of his brother Sydney, who thought it would make a terrific domestic comedy, the star attempted to buy the film rights. He was further encouraged to do so by none other than Winston Churchill, whom he met on the tour. A great admirer of Napoleon, Churchill was intrigued by the film's comic possibilities, especially a scene of its subject taking a bath.

A CHILLING THING TO SEE

Back in Hollywood, the rights secured, Chaplin began working on the script with Alistair Cooke. Famous in the UK for his *Letter from America* broadcasts, and in the United States for hosting *Masterpiece Theatre*, Cooke was a journalist who had secured an interview with Chaplin that led to a lasting friendship. At the start of their collaboration, Cooke took photographs and filmed Chaplin in character. 'He pulled his hair down into a ropey forelock, slipped one hand into his breast pocket and slumped into a wistful emperor,' he recalled. 'He started to talk to himself, tossing in names strange to me – [French generals] Bertrand, Montholon – and then took umbrage, flung an accusing finger at me and, having transformed his dreamy eyes into icicles, delivered a tirade against the British treatment of him on "the little island". His face was now a hewn rock of defiance. I have it still on film, and it is a chilling thing to see.' (In 2010, six years after Cooke's death, an eleven-minute home movie of Chaplin – shot in 1933, the year he started on the Napoleon script – was found among the journalist's possessions. Sadly, it did not contain the footage described here.)

'MADE IT MA, EMPEROR OF FRANCE!'

In the 1930s, it seems Chaplin considered relinquishing the role of Napoleon to another actor. His choice was surprising: James Cagney (right), better known for playing tough guys and gangsters than iconic European autocrats. In his 1974 autobiography *Cagney by Cagney*, the star of *The Public Enemy* (1931) remembers a call from Chaplin, eager to 'talk over business matters and have a pleasant day'. Curious, Cagney accepted an invitation to lunch and tennis. 'I have never seen a guy pour on the charm as relentlessly as he did,' he remembered. 'And I have never been so god-damned bored in my life.' Chaplin told him about the script and asked if he would be interested. 'I told him politely that, no, I wouldn't – thinking to myself that I'd be interested in Napoleon just about as much as I'd be interested in playing Little Lord Fauntleroy.'

According to Cooke, the script was progressing well when, out of the blue, Chaplin told him, 'By the way, the Napoleon thing. It's a beautiful idea – for someone else.' He and Cooke never wrote another word or spoke of it again.

But the star couldn't leave it alone. In 1936, he began his most concerted effort to create a workable screenplay. As a collaborator, he employed British politician and writer John Strachey – who, as the author of *Workers' Control in the Russian Mining Industry* and *The Nature of Capitalist Crisis*, must have brought something interesting to the table. Their script – which leaned heavily on Weber's book – is as far from a straight biopic as can be imagined. Napoleon escapes St Helena by coercing a double to remain on the island in his place. He returns to Paris, but not to rally support and once again seize the reins of power. It seems that, in exile, Napoleon has morphed into a devout pacifist with dreams of uniting Europe; not as a totalitarian superstate with himself as absolute ruler, but as a utopian Neverland of peace and harmony.

DANGEROUS TYRANT

Chaplin and Strachey completed the script in 1937 and the former intended to play both Napoleon and his double. 'The real Napoleon lived on in Paris tending a bookstall near the Pont de l'Alma [a bridge across the Seine],' Chaplin explained in a 1957 interview, published by *Encounter* magazine in 1978. 'He gave up his earnings to the widows and children of war veterans. One day on St Helena – 5 May 1821 – Napoleon died. His double, that is. And the body, as you know, was brought back by the British Navy and given over to the French for burial at Les Invalides [a military site in Paris where the real Napoleon is buried]. All Paris turned out for the state obsequies. It's a great crowd scene. In fact, it is my opening scene.'

'The real Napoleon? Well, you see, he is busy as usual at that bookstall of his; business was very good that day. As the cortège barge on the Seine slowly sails by – pan for close-up – he murmurs: "The news of my death is killing me!"' Apparently, Chaplin laughed immodestly at this gag – one can see why his *métier* was silent comedy. Although he says 'is my opening scene' rather than '*was* my opening scene', it's unlikely that, as late as 1957, Chaplin still had aspirations to bring Napoleon to the screen. He was too old to play the role, and had found a good reason to abandon the project two decades earlier, or certainly modify it out of existence. In 1938, Chaplin turned his attention to another more dangerous tyrant – and, this time, he was highly motivated to get the film made. Executing what he described as a 'switcheroo', he kept the doppelgänger conceit of Napoleon and applied it to *The Great Dictator* (1940). **SB**

WILL IT EVER HAPPEN?

1/10   There are echoes of Chaplin's Napoleon in Alan Taylor's 2001 movie *The Emperor's New Clothes*, starring Ian Holm as both Bonaparte and his double. And a version of Chaplin and John Strachey's script exists in the Chaplin Archive in Bologna, Italy. But as Chaplin died in 1977, the chances of it reaching the screen as he intended are slim to none.

WHAT HAPPENED NEXT. . .

Facing opposition from studio heads, Chaplin was determined to mount an attack on Hitler and Nazi anti-Semitism. It's likely that a viewing of Leni Riefenstahl's *Triumph of the Will* (1935) – not, as critic André Bazin speculated, pique at Hitler for stealing his moustache – sealed his resolve to make *The Great Dictator* (1940, below). In the Napoleon project, he already had the seeds of the plot – notably a tyrant (Adenoid Hynkel) with a double (a meek Jewish barber) whose identities are mistaken.

SALVADOR DALI

MEETS THE

MARX
BROTHERS

in GIRAFFES
on HORSEBACK
SALADS

GIRAFFES ON HORSEBACK SALADS

Director Salvador Dalí **Starring** The Marx Brothers **Year** 1930s **Country** US **Genre** Comedy **Studio** MGM

I n 1937, Salvador Dalí visited Harpo Marx at his Hollywood home. The latter ensured the meeting would be a memorable one. 'He was naked, crowned with roses, and in the center of a veritable forest of harps,' wrote Dalí. 'He was caressing, like a new Leda, a dazzling white swan, and feeding it a statue of the Venus de Milo made of cheese, which he grated against the strings of the nearest harp.' There may be a hint of exaggeration here. Harpo wasn't shy of making a stir by showing up in the buff, but the cheese Venus really wasn't his style. What is not in question is that Dalí *did* visit Harpo and the two enjoyed a friendship of sorts. They had met and expressed mutual admiration at a party in Paris in 1936. As a Christmas gift, Dalí sent Harpo a harp, strung with barbed wire and festooned with forks and teaspoons, a nod to the Marx brother's trademark gag in which stolen silverware cascades from his sleeve. In return, Harpo sent Dalí a photograph of himself playing the harp with bandaged fingers – and an invitation to drop by if he was ever in LA.

JUST ANOTHER NAME

Harpo was among the most beloved screen comedians, but also a barely educated New York street urchin and vaudeville refugee; hardly the obvious confidante of a preeminent surrealist painter. However, in the 1920s and 1930s, he was a member of the famed Algonquin Round Table, whose alumni included Dorothy Parker, George S. Kaufman and Tallulah Bankhead. And through his friend, the flamboyant critic Alexander Woollcott, he came to count among his acquaintances George Bernard Shaw, Somerset Maugham, Arnold Schoenberg and Noël Coward. Dalí was just another name on his dance card.

The artist adored the Marx Brothers, particularly Harpo – seeing in their anarchic comedy the very essence of surrealism. 'In art there is nothing to understand, just as there is nothing to understand in a comedy film,' he wrote. He saw movies as the natural habitat of surrealism – indeed, his 1929 film collaboration with Luis Buñuel, *Un Chien Andalou*, gained him entry into the surrealists' inner circle. A lifelong fascination with the medium had begun.

In 1937, Dalí was in Los Angeles, hoping to insinuate surrealist art into the mainstream. 'I'm in Hollywood, where I've made contact with the three

SALVADOR DALÍ
On the surrealist master's union with Hollywood comic legends the Marx Brothers, their biographer Joe Adamson quotes Groucho: 'It would have been a great combination. Dalí didn't speak much English and neither did Harpo.'

US surrealists: Harpo Marx, Disney and Cecil B. DeMille, he wrote to the movement's founder, André Breton. I believe I've intoxicated them suitably and hope that the possibilities for surrealism here will become a reality.' He was convinced that Harpo, whose antics delighted him, was an ally. Among his portraits of him, one (below left) depicts Harpo seated at the harp, an apple and a lobster on his head, and a severed tongue lolling over the harp frame.

HARVESTING DWARFS

The artist – not content to allow others to spread the surrealist creed by proxy – set about writing scenarios for a Marx Brothers movie. The result, *Giraffes on Horseback Salads*, must have caused Groucho's pasted-on eyebrows to rise an extra inch and for Harpo's famous bug eyes to goggle even further. It may even have distracted Chico from his pinochle, so outlandish was its content. Apart from the three Marx Brothers, the script featured characters called 'The surrealist Woman' and a Spanish businessman named Jimmy. Short on plot but high on outrageous imagery, it boasts scenes of burning giraffes wearing gas masks, Harpo harvesting dwarfs in a huge butterfly net and Groucho – as 'the Shiva of the business world' – answering a slew of telephones with multiple arms. A typical sequence, written by Dalí in English, reads:

```
The surrealist Woman is lying in the middle of a great
bed, sixty feet long, with the rest of the guests
seated around each side. Along the bed, as decorations,
are a group of dwarfs caught by Harpo. Each is
supported on a crystal base, decorated with climbing
flowers. The dwarfs stay as still as statues, holding
lighted candelabras, and change their positions every
few minutes. While love tears at Jimmy's heart, Groucho
tries to crack a nut on the bald head of the dwarf in
front of him. The dwarf, far from looking surprised,
smiles at Groucho in the most amiable way possible.
Suddenly in the middle of dinner, thunder and lightning
begin inside the room. A squall of wind blows the
things over on the table and brings in a whirl of dry
leaves, which stick to everything. As Groucho opens his
umbrella, it begins to rain slowly.
```

HARPO IN *HARPER'S*

Dalí sketched Harpo for *Harper's Bazaar* magazine – a portrait that evoked the eighteenth-century style of French painter Antoine Watteau's *L'Embarquement pour Cythère*. Harpo, Dalí said, was the sun of Hollywood, and Greta Garbo the moon.

Duck Soup it was not – and that's without mention of the dead ox or flock of marauding sheep. The grand finale, a 'great fête' organized by the Marx Brothers, calls for four acres of desert to be cleared of vegetation and levelled like a tennis court, with the undergrowth piled up as a perimeter fence and set alight. Inside the blazing arena, a competition takes place to see who can ride a bicycle the slowest with a stone balanced on their head. All contestants must also grow a beard. Overseeing proceedings from a lofty tower fashioned like the prow of a ship, Groucho reclines on a couch, smoking lazily; while Harpo plays the harp 'ecstatically, like a modern Nero', with Chico accompanying him

While the Marx Brothers continued a triumphant march into posterity, Dalí fared dismally in Hollywood. His hopes of infusing mainstream movies with surrealism largely came to nothing. He created a dream sequence for Alfred Hitchcock's 1945 thriller *Spellbound* (left) but, much to his dismay, it was heavily cut. He also designed a less celebrated dream sequence for 1950's *Father of the Bride*, starring Spencer Tracy. Despite his proposals for a film starring a wheelbarrow, and another featuring rat-gnawing children, that was the last Hollywood project with which he was involved. However, in 2003, fourteen years after his death, *Destino* – a retelling of the Chronos legend he had worked on with Walt Disney in the late 1940s – was nominated for the Academy Award for Best Animated Short Film.

on the piano, attired in a diving suit. 'Scattered across the gangway leading to the tower,' the script concludes, 'an orchestra plays the theme song with Wagnerian intensity as the sun sinks under the horizon.'

It was a far from stealthy attempt to inject Dalí's artistic manifesto into the Tinseltown machine. This was a full-frontal assault on Hollywood, Dalí on an epic scale, and he must have known it had no chance of getting made – or maybe not, given his gargantuan ego. Harpo's reaction is not recorded, but it seems he was less enamoured of Dalí than Dalí was of him. He makes no mention of their alliance in his 1961 autobiography and, according to Marx Brothers biographer Joe Adamson, stuck the barbed-wire harp in a remote corner of his house before eventually throwing it away.

'It wouldn't play,' was Groucho's assessment of *Giraffes*, while MGM head Louis B. Mayer, to whom the Marx Brothers were contracted, dismissed it as 'too surreal' – a heroic understatement. One can only speculate what Dalí would have come up with, given the freedom and budget required. If he'd filmed even half the scenes he envisioned, the results would have been *Un Chien Andalou* meets Busby Berkeley. What they would not have been, however, is a good Marx Brothers movie. For all his gushing tributes, Dalí got it wrong. The brothers were, each in their own unique way, an anarchic challenge to societal norms: impudent and gleefully destructive. But their comedy works because it plays out against a background of rigid conformity. Place them in a world where everyone is crazy and they disappear. SB

GIRAFFES ON STAGE

In 1992, theatre troupe Elevator Repair Service staged *Marx Brothers on Horseback Salad* (above), a bid to capture the essence of Dalí's union with the brothers (including Harpo's barbed-wire harp), in New York. Remarkably, the piece was conceived four years before the script for *Giraffes on Horseback Salads* was rediscovered among Dalí's effects.

WILL IT EVER HAPPEN?

2/10 It's unlikely that anyone is ever going to fill Salvador Dalí's shoes – or, for that matter, those of the Marx Brothers. However the script, once thought lost but discovered among Dalí's papers in 1996, is there for anyone with the money, vision and sheer lunatic audacity to take it on. Perhaps if Damien Hirst teamed up with Cirque du Soleil. . .

¡QUÉ VIVA MÉXICO!

Director Sergei M. Eisenstein **Starring** Félix Balderas, Martín Hernández, Sara García
Year 1932 **Country** Mexico **Genre** Historical drama

SERGEI M. EISENSTEIN
¡Qué viva México!, the director wrote in
his memoirs, was 'the history of cultural
changes, but not presented vertically – in
years and centuries – but horizontally: as
utterly diverse stages of culture, coexisting
in the same geographical area, next to
each other'.

Despite the frosty political climate of the day, Russian auteur Sergei
M. Eisenstein found himself courted by Hollywood in April 1930.
However, his American Dream was shattered within months and,
when a contract with Paramount was terminated in October, it was expected
he would return to Russia. But having failed to make a single film, Eisenstein
wasn't ready to go home. He had become friendly with Charlie Chaplin, who
was hesitant to back any of the director's projects himself but recommended
him to socialist author Upton Sinclair. Carried away on a wave of mutual
respect, Sinclair arranged for Eisenstein, his collaborator Grigori Alexandrov and
cinematographer Eduard Tisse to travel to Mexico. Sinclair, his wife and other
investors, operating as the Mexican Film Trust, offered to finance an artistic
travelogue documentary. Sinclair's conservative business manager, Hunter S.
Kimbrough (also his brother-in-law), was appointed producer – on the proviso
that he stop his heavy drinking while in Mexico, lest he clash with the teetotal
Eisenstein. That, however, would prove the least of their worries.

SHOOTING THE FILM
The Sinclairs had negligible understanding of film-making, let alone of
Eisenstein's creative process, but still expected an apolitical, one-hour film
to be completed in three or four months. For his part, Eisenstein cared little
for financial realities and even less for contractual obligations.

In Mexico, the director began to conceive an anthology – to encompass a
thousand years of Mexican history – in six parts: a prologue, the Aztec and
Mayan empires, the Spanish Conquest, the Colonial period, the Revolution
and an epilogue. He also expected no restraints on his artistic integrity.

The venture got off to an ill-omened start on 20 December 1930, when
Eisenstein, Alexandrov and Tisse were arrested on their arrival in Mexico. It
was revealed later that Mexican authorities had received an anonymous tip-
off from Hollywood that Eisenstein was in the country to spread subversion.
However, there was nothing in Eisenstein's possessions to support the claim,
and he and his colleagues were released after several days with an official
apology and the promise of full cooperation with the project.

IVAN THE TERRIBLE
Eisenstein's cinematic woes didn't end with *¡Qué viva México!*. After 1944's triumphant first instalment of the *Ivan the Terrible* trilogy (which Eisenstein is shown shooting, above), Stalin disliked the second film and banned it. The aborted third was largely destroyed.

BARING THE CROSS
In Eisenstein's earlier pictures, religious imagery was obscured to conform to Soviet diktats on the depiction of beliefs that ran contrary to the political system of the day. His work in Mexico (below) allowed the director off the leash.

Once safely settled, Eisenstein spent time with painters Frida Kahlo and Diego Rivera – who inspired him to describe his films as 'moving frescoes' – and became increasingly enchanted with Mexican culture and politics. Shooting progressed in fits and starts as various problems arose: sickness, heavy rain and the accidental but fatal shooting of a young woman by her brother, an actor in the film, with a gun of Tisse's that he took from the set.

The negatives were sent to California to be developed, so Eisenstein never saw any of them. His plans became ever more grandiose, and the Sinclairs ran out of money while a sober (but probably wishing he wasn't) Kimbrough wrung his hands. By November 1931, Eisenstein was still shooting when Sinclair received an ominous telegram from Josef Stalin warning that the director was being accused of desertion from the fatherland. Dreading the fate that awaited him if he returned to Moscow with nothing to show for his foreign adventure, Eisenstein blamed Kimbrough for the delays, hoping Sinclair would intervene with the Soviets and the US State Department to enable him to stick around.

STALINIST INTERVENTION
Sinclair did reply to Stalin in Eisenstein's defence, but by that point he had had enough. He told Kimbrough to shut down production and return to the United States with the Russians and the undeveloped footage, estimated to total 170,000 to 250,000 feet (thirty to fifty hours' worth). Eisenstein hadn't even shot his account of the revolution – although he had persuaded the Mexican Army to provide 500 soldiers, 10,000 guns and fifty cannons for free.

The intention was for Eisenstein to edit the existing footage into something resembling a commercial, feature-length film. Sinclair considered sending a print suitable for projection to Russia for Eisenstein to work on there, although he was canny enough to retain the negatives. Then the situation descended into farce. Caricatures of Jesus, pornographic material and homoerotic sketches were discovered in a trunk of Eisenstein's that he had prankishly (or contemptuously) shipped to the straitlaced Sinclair and that was opened at customs in the recipient's horrified presence. Sinclair would never communicate with him again. Since their re-entry visas had expired,

Eisenstein, Alexandrov and Tisse were held at the US–Mexican border and languished in custody near Laredo, Texas, for weeks. They were then granted thirty days to leave for Moscow – a worrying destination for Eisenstein since the Stalinist purges of Communist Party members had begun.

BULLFIGHTING AND ROMANTIC TRAGEDY

Meanwhile, Kimbrough travelled to the United States with the film. Apart from a peek at rushes in New York before he was banished from the country, Eisenstein never saw it again. The Sinclairs enlisted distributor Sol Lesser (later a producer of low-budget Westerns and Tarzan movies) to help recover their investment by cobbling the miles of material into a short (1934's seventeen-minute *Death Day*) and two short features (1933's seventy-minute *Thunder over Mexico* and fifty-minute *Eisenstein in Mexico*).

Material actually shot included Mayan sequences in Yucatán for the prologue; a courtship and marriage in pre-conquest Tehuantepec for the feast day segment 'Sandunga'; bullfighting in the Spanish era for 'Fiesta'; a romantic

> *'Caricatures of Jesus, pornographic material and homoerotic sketches were discovered in a trunk of Eisenstein's that he had prankishly shipped. . .'*

tragedy and workers' uprising for 'Maguey' and twentieth-century Day of the Dead celebrations for the epilogue. The unfilmed 'Soldadera' segment was to focus on women soldiers in the revolution of 1910–20.

Reconstructed according, as far as possible, to his original intent, Eisenstein's documentary-like footage and startling imagery is a melancholy, feverish odyssey of Mexican mythology, folklore and socio-political/cultural evolution. It makes for fascinating viewing, but it's impossible to gauge the full dramatic impact of Eisenstein's vision, since he neither completed filming it nor had the chance to edit what he had shot. As he complained in a letter to a friend – actress-turned-screenwriter Salka Viertel – 'A film is not a sausage which tastes the same if you eat three quarters of it.'

Eisenstein publicly claimed to have lost all interest in his forgotten Mexican film, but privately it was a lasting source of regret and resentment – a work of genius undone by the grubby realities of money and politics, and by his own refusal to compromise. What had been a joyful period of discovery for Eisenstein became a nightmare that haunted him for the rest of his life. **AE**

WHAT HAPPENED NEXT. . .
Back in Russia, Eisenstein suffered from depression and returned to teaching, then made a comeback with *Bezhin lug* (1937). Stalin, having reversed his stance on the director, sanctioned his assignment to the 1938 biopic of Russian hero Alexander Nevsky (below). Eisenstein was awarded the Order of Lenin in 1939 and embarked on the ill-fated *Ivan the Terrible* trilogy (see opposite above). His health deteriorated rapidly and, aged fifty, he died of a heart attack in 1948.

WILL IT EVER HAPPEN?

0/10 Not as Eisenstein envisioned it. Biographer Marie Seton assembled footage according to Eisenstein's notes into 1940's *Time in the Sun* and, in 1969, several thousand feet of footage was sent to the USSR by New York's Museum of Modern Art. Re-edited by Grigori Alexandrov, it was released as *¡Qué viva México! – Da zdravstvuyet Meksika!* in 1979.

A PRINCESS OF MARS

OUT-OF-THIS-WORLD
TALES OF HEROISM
AND ROMANCE
ON THE RED PLANET!

FROM THE
ASTONISHING
STORIES BY
EDGAR RICE
BURROUGHS,
CREATOR OF
"TARZAN"!

A PRINCESS OF MARS

Director Bob Clampett **Year** 1936 **Country** US **Genre** Sci-fi **Studio** MGM

A *Princess of Mars* could have been the first feature-length animated film in cinema history – if, that is, MGM executives had followed their gut reactions to test footage made by an ambitious young would-be director. They didn't, and the distinction of first animated feature went instead to *Snow White and the Seven Dwarfs* (1937), a Hollywood milestone that set the tone and the style for both Disney's output over coming generations and for American animation itself. *A Princess of Mars*, on the other hand, languished in development hell from 1931 to 2012, when it finally hit screens in the form of big-budget live-action adaptation *John Carter*.

PLANETARY ROMANCES

Edgar Rice Burroughs is best known as the creator of Tarzan, who first appeared in print in 1912. Tarzan's jungle adventures occupy more than twenty novels and have inspired at least ninety films since his screen debut in 1918, played by Elmo Lincoln (there have also been countless radio, TV, stage, comic, video and computer-game manifestations). But Burroughs was also a prolific writer of sci-fi, fantasy, Westerns and romantic historical adventures. Among his vast sci-fi/fantasy output – which included the Pellucidar series, the Venus series and the Moon series – the dozen Mars-set 'planetary romances', known collectively as the Barsoom novels, enjoyed a storming success to rival Tarzan. They were also highly influential on other twentieth-century sci-fi writers, including Arthur C. Clarke, Ray Bradbury and Robert Heinlein.

Popular cosmologist Carl Sagan was also among the notable fans whose eyes Burroughs turned to the heavens, and from the time American Civil War veteran Captain John Carter first arrived on a dying Mars in 1912, readers were captivated. The books remained popular well into the 1950s, when they fell from favour in the face of changing trends and scientific discovery.

A Princess of Mars was first published as a serial, 'Under the Moons of Mars', in *The All-Story* magazine in February 1912, and then as a novel in 1917. It is set between 1866 and 1876, with narrator John Carter, a Confederate soldier-turned-prospector, relating how an encounter with hostile Indians led to his mysterious transportation from a sacred cave to Mars, which

BOB CLAMPETT

Born in California in 1913, Clampett began drawing at the age of five and making short films at twelve. After dropping out of high school, he made Mickey Mouse dolls of such quality that he got Walt Disney's okay to sell them.

Poster: Herita MacDonald

A Princess of Mars **25**

THE GENIUS OF BURROUGHS

Outdated though many of his ideas are, Burroughs's achievement with the Barsoom chronicles is a landmark in science fiction. For one thing, he is believed to have been the first writer to invent an extraterrestrial language. His Barsoom (the native name for Mars) is astonishingly rich in detail, from the geography, flora and fauna to the culture, architecture, government and technology of the planet's several sentient races. As a feat of imagination, his creation is arguably without equal.

the Martians call Barsoom. There, his honour, courage, superior strength, skill with weapons, commanding presence and, no doubt, his steely grey eyes land him the job of rescuing princess-in-peril Dejah Thoris from villain Tal Hajus. He restores the 'atmosphere plant' that boosts the planet's dwindling air supply and becomes embroiled in the violent struggle between the civilized Red Martians and the barbaric warrior hordes of six-limbed Green Martians.

LOONEY TUNES

In 1931, apprentice animator and Burroughs fan Bob Clampett – future director of classic Looney Tunes cartoons and creator of Tweety Pie and Porky Pig – approached the author with a view to making *A Princess of Mars* as an animated feature. Despite his tender teenage years (he had yet to graduate from high school), he received Burroughs's enthusiastic blessing.

Clampett – a protégé of Hugh Harman and Rudy Ising (founders of Warner Bros and MGM's animation departments) – worked on the film in his own time for five years, with input from friends at Warners and Burroughs's son John Coleman Burroughs. 'We were working in untested territory at that time,' he said. 'There was no animated film to look at to see how it was done.' In 1936, he showed test footage to a delighted Burroughs and to MGM executives, who offered to distribute the film, initially in serial form. Alas, test screenings for selected US exhibitors bombed. Puzzlingly, given the books' popularity, the film was deemed too sophisticated and scary for children, and too childish and fantastical for adults. MGM, keen to develop a Tarzan cartoon instead, pulled out. By then, Clampett's star was on the rise at Warner Bros, where he was an integral part of the Looney Tunes team and about to become a director. With these more pressing matters at hand, he put his work on *A Princess of Mars* aside and never returned to it. 'I just lost my enthusiasm,' he admitted.

Some of his test footage was rediscovered in the 1970s by Burroughs's grandson Danton in the Edgar Rice Burroughs Inc. archives, along with

'TH-TH-THAT'S ALL, FOLKS!'

'This is just the pencil drawings – which then, of course, we coloured in and put over scenic backgrounds,' explained Clampett of his sketches for *A Princess of Mars*. 'This is a fight with the Martian. . . At that time, it was quite a thing for us to try to animate figures.' While the animator's work on the film came to nothing, his place in animation history is assured. He worked on the first Merrie Melodies short (1931's *Lady, Play Your Mandolin!*) when he was only seventeen, assisted the legendary Friz Freleng, created Porky Pig and became part of the groundbreaking animation unit at Warner Bros alongside Tex Avery and Chuck Jones. He remained on the cutting edge of animation throughout his career, and in later years was applauded for his pioneering of television puppetry.

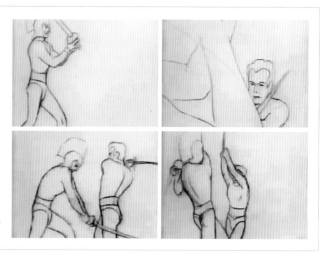

sculptures and designs created for the project by John Coleman Burroughs. Drawings, models and sample animation can be seen online.

CURIOUS INACTION

Despite the ongoing cinematic love affair with Tarzan, there was curious inaction on the John Carter front for decades. Reputedly, legendary visual effects wizard Ray Harryhausen became interested in adapting the Barsoom novels for the screen in the 1950s. It would have been a natural fit: some of Harryhausen's greatest successes of the decade – *The Beast from 20,000 Fathoms* (1953), *Earth vs. the Flying Saucers* (1956) and *The 7th Voyage of Sinbad* (1958) – pioneered a mix of live action and stop-motion animation that thrilled audiences hungry for monster movies and sci-fi. Sadly, that idea came to nothing, and the project slipped off the radar.

In the 1980s, Mario Kassar and Andrew G. Vajna – founders of Carolco and producers of the *Rambo* movies and the *Terminator* sequels – seized on the Burroughs saga with a view to attracting the Conan crowd, or even rivalling the *Star Wars* franchise, and obtained the rights for Disney. Writers were hired

> '*We were working in untested territory. . . There was no animated film to look at to see how it was done'*.
> Bob Clampett

and Tom Cruise was approached to star as John Carter. John McTiernan (later to make a name for himself with *Predator*, 1987 and *Die Hard*, 1988) was attached as director, but decided the available technology was not yet equal to the challenge. Disney chairman Jeffrey Katzenberg – who revitalized the studio's moribund animation department in the late 1980s – was in favour of reviving the project but when it continued to stall, the rights reverted to the Burroughs estate.

Another childhood fan of the novels entered the frame in the shape of *The Mummy/Scorpion King* franchise producer James Jacks. He persuaded Paramount to buy the rights and hired screenwriter Mark Protosevich (*The Cell*, 2000) to adapt *A Princess of Mars* into *John Carter of Mars*. In 2004, Robert Rodriguez was announced as director and started pre-production. He was later replaced, first by Kerry Conran (*Sky Captain and the World of Tomorrow*, 2004), then Jon Favreau (*Iron Man*, 2008). However, Paramount let the rights go when it opted to concentrate on rebooting *Star Trek*. Disney regained the rights in 2007 and recruited Pixar's Andrew Stanton to see the project home. **AE**

WHAT HAPPENED NEXT. . .
Starring Taylor Kitsch (below) in the title role and a host of credible thespians including Samantha Morton, Mark Strong, Ciarán Hinds, Dominic West, James Purefoy and Willem Dafoe, Andrew Stanton's *John Carter* (2012) opened to mixed reviews and was sunk by a lack of name recognition. 'John Carter' simply means nothing to contemporary audiences.

0/10 **WILL IT EVER HAPPEN?**
There are no plans to make an animated feature of *A Princess of Mars*. And that's not surprising: if you blinked, you missed *John Carter* (2012), Disney's budget-busting live-action adaptation. Despite it taking $210 million worldwide, Disney announced that it expected to lose $200 million on the film, making it one of the most expensive flops in history.

BRAZZAVILLE

Starring Humphrey Bogart, Geraldine Fitzgerald, Claude Rains **Year** 1943 **Country** US **Genre** Drama **Studio** Warner Bros

'HERE'S LOOKING AT YOU'
Happily, Warner Bros rejected Frederick Stephani's treatment ('The moment Rick becomes. . . an agent of the secret police, the interest in his position and character largely evaporates,' wrote Frederick Faust, who was hired to evaluate Stephani's proposal). Howard Koch – co-writer, with the Epsteins, of the original movie – wrote *Return to Casablanca* in the 1980s. This too was turned down by Warner, although late 2012 brought rumours of its revival.

The closing scene of 1942's *Casablanca* is *the* perfect movie ending – the glow of the runway lights; the airplanes coughing to life; Bogart tilting Ingrid Bergman's tear-streaked face to his; their final fleeting moment before he lets her go: 'Here's looking at you, kid.' But whatever your feelings about messing with perfection, when Bogart and Claude Rains saunter off contemplating 'the beginning of a beautiful friendship', a small part of you wants to know what happens next. You almost got a chance to find out.

LOOPY ABANDON
Emboldened by the film's success, Warner Bros set about devising a sequel, tentatively entitled *Brazzaville* – a reference to Rains's line to Bogart in that final scene: 'There's a free French garrison over at Brazzaville. I could be induced to arrange a passage.' Studio head Jack Warner offered the job to screenwriting twins Philip and Julius Epstein, chief architects of the *Casablanca* script. They declined. 'We were tired of it,' recalled Julius. 'We didn't like *Casablanca* much in the first place and thought we put all we had to offer in the original.'

Hollywood was crawling with novelists and playwrights – Raymond Chandler, William Faulkner, Clifford Odets – lured by easy money. So how the treatment came to be written by the director of the 1936 *Flash Gordon* serial is anyone's guess. That said, Frederick Stephani's synopsis starts out with some promise:

```
Pickup where Casablanca ended—at the airport. Rains has
just given orders to pickup the 'usual suspects' as he
and Bogart enter the car.

Arriving at Bogart's place, they find the German
delegation awaiting them. They demand that Rains either
arrest Bogart or turn him over to them for questioning.
Bogart prefers arrest. Rains smiles. . .
```

It then goes off the deep end with loopy abandon. We learn that Bogart's Rick Blaine is not a nightclub owner with a shady past but an undercover

After "Casablanca" there was only one destination

BRAZZAVILLE

HUMPHREY **BOGART** GERALDINE **FITZGERALD** CLAUDE **RAINS** SCREENPLAY BY FREDERICK STEPHANI PRODUCED BY JACK WARNER

agent preparing for the Allied invasion of North Africa. That's right: the whole cynical, drunken, brokenhearted thing was an act to fool the Nazis. And, it turns out, Rains's Captain Renault was secretly a good guy all along too! The very traits that made them immortals – their flaws – were a sham.

So what of Ilsa, Rick's lost love, and her freedom-fighting beau Victor (Paul Henreid)? In fact, Victor dies early on, freeing Ilsa (reportedly to be played by Geraldine Fitzgerald, owing to Bergman's unavailability) to follow Rick to Tangier. There, in the guise of a black marketeer, he is attempting to infiltrate a gang of Nazi saboteurs. But true love runs no smoother in Tangier than it did in Casablanca, as Rick's strategy relies upon bedding Maria, a Spanish Mata Hari in league with the Nazis. Rick loves Ilsa but can't tell her because that would blow his cover; Ilsa loves Rick but, in a feeble echo of the original, resolves to let him go for the greater good. Conveniently, Maria also loves Rick: in the final showdown with the chief Nazi, she takes a bullet for him and dies in his arms:

    DISSOLVE to an American ship, homeward bound. At the
    rail, watching the receding shores of Africa, [stand]
    our two lovers who have found happiness at last.

It's the classic Hollywood fade-out, but it's not Rick and Ilsa's. They were destined to be torn apart – that way they'll always have Paris. **SB**

WILL IT EVER HAPPEN?

2/10 Hopefully not – and a remake of *Casablanca* would surely make more commercial (albeit not artistic) sense. The original film did, however, finally generate a sequel: Michael Walsh's 1998 novel *As Time Goes By*. This shares a title with a self-referential novel published in 1997 by Bogart's son Stephen.

JESUS

Director Carl Theodor Dreyer **Year** 1949 **Budget** $3–5 million **Country** Israel **Genre** Historical drama

CARL THEODOR DREYER

'There hasn't been a day since [the German occupation of Denmark] when I haven't thought about my Jesus film,' Dreyer declared in a 1967 interview.

On 9 April 1940, Germany invaded Denmark. It was a swift affair – the Danes capitulated in hours – and its aftermath was not terribly oppressive. Nonetheless, it had a profound effect on Danish director Carl Theodor Dreyer: one that influenced his future films and the rest of his life. Dreyer had long considered a picture on the life of Christ, and experienced an epiphany of sorts as his country fell to the Nazis: Jesus, a Jew in Galilee, also lived under an occupying regime. From then on, such was Dreyer's fixation on a realistic portrait of Jesus that he visited the United States and the Holy Land to research and write the screenplay, and used his other films as experiments to prepare for what he thought of as his magnum opus. He even learned Hebrew.

A BAD TAILOR'S DUMMY

Dreyer's early pictures often concerned themselves with Christianity and the divine or supernatural. However, he later expressed unhappiness at the way he had sketched Jesus in *Blade af Satans bog* (1921), particularly his adherence to the orthodoxy of a fair-skinned Messiah, referring to it as 'a bad tailor's dummy of Christ'. However, the notion of Jesus being portrayed on film at all was offensive to some audiences, and Dreyer had not wanted to inflame the issue by straying from the accepted Christ of the Renaissance artists.

The subject of his new film would not be an abstract and unknowable Jesus. Dreyer was interested in the man, not in the Christ. Although determined to source his screenplay almost exclusively from the Gospels, he had two overriding aims. Firstly, to examine Jesus on a human level: the person who grew up in Galilee and came to a spiritual understanding of what it meant to be the Messiah as a man. Secondly, to present Jesus as Jewish (indeed, one of his drafts was entitled *The Story of the Jew Jesus*) and to stress that it was not his fellow Jews who killed him, but a Roman authority who saw him as a dangerous ally to revolutionaries threatening their rule in Judea.

Dreyer was a fierce opponent of anti-Semitism all of his life, particularly after he made *Die Gezeichneten* (1922), a drama about Russian Jews fleeing the pogroms after the 1905 revolution. He began drafting the *Jesus* screenplay in the early 1930s, but the idea was in its infancy and wouldn't take shape until

  Poster: Damian Jaques

JESUS

A FILM BY CARL THEODOR DREYER

after the war. Still, in 1933, he had talks with Société Générale des Films (which financed his 1928 classic *La passion de Jeanne d'Arc*) but rejected the company's offer to finance the project, as it wanted the picture shot in Europe. Even at that early stage, Dreyer was determined to shoot the film as authentically as possible, and that meant setting up production in the Holy Land.

The director continued working as a journalist and on new films during the occupation. However, in 1943, the Germans declared martial law and the situation deteriorated. After the release that year of his *Day of Wrath* (set during Denmark's Lutheran witch-hunts of the 1620s and seen as an allegory for Nazi persecution of Jews, although Dreyer denied it), he was persuaded to leave Denmark for neutral Sweden, where he spent the rest of the war working on his *Jesus* film. In 1945, in the immediate aftermath of the war, he visited New York (where his son Erik lived) to use the public libraries there for research. Then, during a second trip to New York, for the 1948 US premiere of *Day of Wrath*, he began attempting to secure US financing for the film.

In 1949, US theatre impresario Blevins Davis came to Copenhagen to produce *Hamlet* at Kronborg castle (Shakespeare's model for the play's Elsinore), where Dreyer was working on the documentary short *Shakespeare og Kronborg*. The two met and Davis offered to fund a research trip to Israel. Thus began an odd relationship between the men that would shape Dreyer's frustrated attempts to realize his passion project over the next twenty years.

POTENTIAL SAVIOURS

Davis returned to the United States, and Dreyer left for Israel. Mission completed, he travelled to Davis's farm in Missouri, where he wrote the screenplay. Davis was on the board of the American National Theater and Academy, and two years earlier had married a wealthy woman thirty years his senior who died shortly after their honeymoon. He was also a family friend of President Truman. Dreyer stayed on the farm for six months, completing the first proper draft of his film.

Davis, however, never came through with the money, having apparently lost interest in the picture. Puzzlingly, Dreyer was determined to remain loyal (no contract was ever signed between them) and insisted on trying to involve Davis whenever outside funding became a possibility. One potential source was British distributor (and devout Christian) J. Arthur Rank. Dreyer had almost taken advantage of the post-war boom in British cinema to make a film about Mary, Queen of Scots, but that idea had fallen through. In 1953 he received a grant from the Danish government to travel to London and study at the British Museum, whose Palestine collection Dreyer considered one of the world's best. Ultimately, however, nothing came of the discussions with Rank.

In 1955, after successfully running Copenhagen's Dagmar cinema, Dreyer raised enough money to fund another trip to Israel. He was determined to shoot there, with an authentic cast of Jewish and Italian actors. He filled boxes with research and photographs, and stored them in a warehouse in Jerusalem, so sure was he that he would return there for production. Dreyer also studied Hebrew with Bent Melchior (later Denmark's chief rabbi), and became so adept that he seriously considered filming the picture entirely in the language.

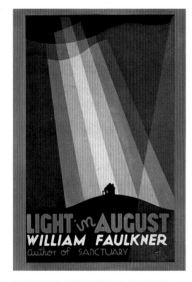

DREYER'S UNFINISHED DREAMS
Dreyer's post-war career was littered with unrealized projects. He worked on adaptations of William Faulkner's novels *Light in August* (above) and *As I Lay Dying* (which he saw as a bittersweet comedy), Henrik Ibsen's play *Brand*, Eugene O'Neill's play cycle *Mourning Becomes Electra*, August Strindberg's *Damascus* trilogy and *King Lear* – with an all-black cast.

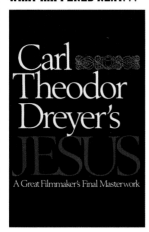

Having completed ten features before the war, Dreyer made only four full-length films in his last thirty-five years, all with one eye on his *Jesus* film. In 1972, his screenplay for it was published in English by Dial Press (left), providing the opportunity to examine his narrative. However, the loss is in not seeing how one of cinema's masters would have used colour. Dreyer is remembered as highly influential, with *La passion de Jeanne d'Arc* (right) cited by aficionados such as director Michael Mann as an all-time great. 'We directors have a very large responsibility,' Dreyer once wrote. 'We have it in our hands to lift the film from industry to art, and, therefore, we must go to our work with seriousness, we must want something, we must dare something and we must not jump over where the fence is lowest.'

Dreyer appeared to have found a saviour when, in 1959, Kay Harrison, the European president of Technicolor, expressed interest in financing an adaptation of the Euripides play *Medea*. This would have been a key stepping stone, as Dreyer had now decided to film *Jesus* in colour, and *Medea* offered the chance to experiment with the photography. Tantalizingly, Dreyer claimed to have found 'a special idea for the use of colour', but audiences never had the chance to see it. Inexplicably, he insisted on running Harrison's offer by Davis, who had become increasingly harder to contact since the mid 1950s. This insistence on including Davis is difficult to understand: the producer had offered little support since his initial burst of enthusiasm, and the director had made 1955's *Ordet* – another 'practice run', being a test of the audience's reaction to events such as miracles being filmed in a realist fashion – without any input from him.

Dreyer made one further feature, *Gertrud* (1964), but continued working on *Jesus* until his death in 1968. Indeed, it was at the very last that he came closest to securing funding. In 1967, the Danish government agreed to put up a guarantee of $350,000 against any losses suffered by potential investors and, just months before his death, the Italian corporation RAI came forward to finance it. It was too late though: Dreyer was in no condition to make a film. Weakened by illness in 1966, a fall in 1968 left him with a broken hip. He contracted pneumonia and passed away on 20 March 1968. **DN**

ALMIGHTY OPPORTUNITY

Dino De Laurentiis (above) offered Dreyer a segment in his 1966 epic *The Bible: In the Beginning* (see Robert Bresson's *La Genèse*, page 53). However, he refused, again citing his loyalty to producer Blevins Davis.

WILL IT EVER HAPPEN?

1/10 Despite the publication of Dreyer's screenplay, it would take an extraordinary act of chutzpah for another director to take on Dreyer's vision. Dramatic portrayals have been made of Jesus, from Nicholas Ray's *King of Kings* (1961) to Mel Gibson's *The Passion of the Christ* (2004), but none of them have attempted the human portrait in which Dreyer was interested.

H. G. WELLS'

WAR OF THE WORLDS

WAR OF THE WORLDS

Year 1949 **Country** US **Genre** Sci-fi

K ing Kong changed Ray Harryhausen's life. The thirteen-year-old saw Merian C. Cooper and Ernest B. Schoedsack's 1933 classic at a local movie theatre in Los Angeles, setting in train a remarkable career that, over the next seven decades, added immeasurably to the magic of movies. 'King Kong haunted me for years,' he said. 'I came out of the theater in another world. I'd never see anything like that before in my life. I didn't know how it was done and that was half the charm. I didn't just say, "Eureka, I've found what I want to do." That came over a period of time. But I'd done a few dioramas in clay of the La Brea tar pits [in LA] and I saw in King Kong how you could make them move. Luckily a friend of my father's worked at RKO and he knew all about stop-motion, so I started experimenting in my garage.'

AMBITION AND EVOLUTION

The effects in King Kong were created by the great Willis O'Brien, a pioneer of stop-motion animation. Harryhausen studied O'Brien avidly, even sending him a short stop-motion dinosaur film he had made. 'You know you're encouraging my competition, don't you?' O'Brien chided his wife when she brought it to his attention. Still, he encouraged Harryhausen himself, suggesting the young man take classes in graphic art and sculpture.

In the late 1930s, Harryhausen embarked on an ambitious project to make a stop-motion animated feature on the evolution of man. It proved an elusive dream, but footage salvaged from it acted as an excellent show reel. That the footage was of more dinosaurs suggests he didn't actually get very far with the evolutionary process, but it was enough to land him a job with producer George Pal, working as an animator on Pal's Puppetoons shorts for Paramount.

During the Second World War, Harryhausen made animated military training films and served as camera operator to Colonel Frank Capra in the Special Services Division. At the war's end, he purloined 1,000 feet of military film stock for a series of his own, Puppetoon-like fairy-tale shorts. These secured him work with Willis O'Brien on the latter's other giant gorilla flick, 1949's Mighty Joe Young. O'Brien received an Academy Award for the film's special effects, although it is accepted that Harryhausen did the lion's share of the

RAY HARRYHAUSEN
'I spent a great deal of time, spread over many years, trying to develop the project and interest people in making it into a feature film. . .' the pioneering stop-motion animator recalled. 'Sadly, all my hard work was to no avail.'

FAITHFUL DEPICTION

Opposite This charcoal and pencil drawing, notes *The Art of Ray Harryhausen*, 'depicts the scene soon after the Martian war machine emerges from the crater where the spaceship had crashed'. The tree-filled scene is faithful to H.G. Wells's original story, whereas Steven Spielberg relocated the initial action to urban New Jersey in his 2005 adaptation.

animation. But despite being overlooked by Oscar, Harryhausen saw his career take a quantum leap after *Mighty Joe Young*. Before long he had eclipsed even his mentor in the special effects world. However, that leap into the big time could have come half a decade earlier, had things panned out in Harryhausen's favour – and had he not been let down by the very man who gave him his start in Hollywood.

ELEGANT AND SPOOKY

In 1942, while still in the army, Harryhausen planned to make a big-screen version of H.G. Wells's 1898 sci-fi classic *The War of the Worlds*. It was hardly less ambitious than his *Evolution* project, yet he was confident enough to write an outline. Influenced by Orson Welles's legendary 1938 radio production – which had used an alarmingly authentic report of a Martian invasion – Harryhausen set the action in New York, recognizing the shock value in laying waste to such iconic landmarks as the Brooklyn Bridge and the Statue of Liberty.

He replaced Wells's anonymous narrator with a newspaper reporter named Randy Jordan, but intended to keep the striding Martian war machines, despite the enormous technical challenge this would present. These towering tripods feature in several of the fantastic sketches Harryhausen did for the film, but no footage of them was ever shot. Miraculously, though, a test sequence created by Harryhausen of one of the alien invaders has survived. The clip opens on the fuselage of a spaceship, wisps of smoke giving it life. Slowly a hatch begins to open, unscrewing from within until it falls free of the ship. A single tentacle emerges, then another, then another until eventually the Martian's head appears, a strange jowly creature with a bulbous, pitted cranium. The creature gazes around, then seems to fight for breath, choking on the alien air. Suffocating, it slumps forwards and slithers lifeless down the face of the ship. It's a simple sequence but the animation is wonderful, elegant and spooky – vintage Harryhausen. And the appearance of the Martian, an undulating

THEY'RE HERE!

Thoroughly enchanting, albeit frustratingly brief, 16mm test footage for Ray Harryhausen's adaptation of *War of the Worlds* shows one of the octopus-like Martians emerging from its spacecraft (and, rather comically, appearing to wipe sweat from its brow). 'Looking at it today,' the animator admitted in the 2005 book *The Art of Ray Harryhausen*, 'this creature is unimpressive and totally wrong – mainly because its two digits would never have allowed it to build the spacecraft let alone the war machines, but also because it would have been unacceptable as a terrifying alien invader, because it wasn't scary enough.' The sequence appears as an extra on Paramount's 2005 DVD Special Collector's Edition of Byron Haskin's otherwise unrelated live-action version of *The War of the Worlds*.

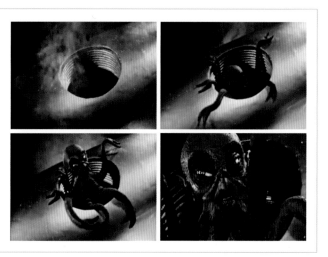

CHARCOAL, PENCIL AND CLAY

Above Harryhausen's drawing for the scene in which 'The Martians meet their end in New York.'

Right The Martian heads (featuring what the animator described as their 'fishlike jowls'). The one on the right was used in the test footage.

cephalopod, demonstrates his commitment to H.G. Wells's original vision, even though bringing it to the screen convincingly would have been a torturously time-consuming and meticulous process. 'Today, I think I might change the concept,' he admitted to *Cinefantastique* decades later, 'because the octopus-like creatures that come out of the tripods might get a laugh.'

With this sequence, plus the sketches, storyboards and outline, Harryhausen sought financing for the film. He received initial interest from Jesse L. Lasky, a founder of the US film industry. Lasky, who was then working as an independent producer, shopped the project to several studios but failed to rouse any interest, even from Paramount (in fact, especially from Paramount, as things turned out). Harryhausen contacted Orson Welles in the hope of getting his support but never received a reply. (Unabashed, Welles later used Harryhausen's animated flying saucers from 1956's *Earth vs. the Flying Saucers* to illustrate the *War of the Worlds* radio broadcast in his 1973 documentary *F for Fake*.)

Then, reports war-ofthe-worlds.co.uk, 'In October of 1950 he visited his friend Frank Capra, the renowned director of *It's a Wonderful Life* and, in a wide ranging discussion, the subject of George Pal's recent film *Destination*

> ## 'Today, I think I might change the concept, because the octopus-like creatures might get a laugh.'
>
> Ray Harryhausen

Moon arose. This prompted Harryhausen to realise that Pal might be the very person he needed. Pal was at Paramount, who owned the rights and had a solid science fiction background, so seemed ideal.'

Harryhausen met with Pal, who seemed enthusiastic. He intimated that both Fox and RKO were mulling over *War of the Worlds* projects but that, if Harryhausen left his material with him, he would attempt to get Paramount on board. What Pal neglected to mention was that he was already in negotiations with Paramount to produce a film of the book and had no intention of using Harryhausen. In 1951, Paramount signed a contract with H.G. Wells's heirs granting the studio exclusive rights to *War of the Worlds*. Like his be-tentacled Martian invader, Harryhausen's dream project had breathed its last. **SB**

WHAT HAPPENED NEXT. . .
George Pal's *The War of the Worlds* (1953), directed by Byron Haskins, took a radically different approach to that envisaged by Harryhausen or Wells. Its Martians were humanoid, using manta ray-shaped aircraft. Harryhausen's first film as solo animator was 1953's *The Beast from 20,000 Fathoms* (below), based on a story by his friend Ray Bradbury. His stop-motion effects on films like *Jason and the Argonauts* (1963) and *Clash of the Titans* (1981) have made him a legend.

WILL IT EVER HAPPEN?

0/10 There is more chance of a genuine Martian invasion than there is of seeing Ray Harryhausen's *War of the Worlds*. Harryhausen passed away in May 2013 at the age of ninety-two, although he hadn't worked as an animator since the short *The Tortoise and the Hare* (2000–01) and wasn't likely to be dusting off his miniature screwdriver and maquette moulding tools. Spielberg's 2005 version gave a nod to Wells with its tripod war machines, but its Martians were also disappointingly humanoid. The best we can hope for is a version that depicts the invaders as Wells described and Harryhausen envisioned: scary octopus things, not extras from *The X-Files*.

AUDREY
HEPBURN
LAURENCE
HARVEY

ALFRED HITCHCOCK'S

NO
BAIL
for the
JUDGE

Co-starring JOHN WILLIAMS Screenplay by SAMUEL TAYLOR From the novel by HENRY CECIL LEON Associate producer HERBERT COLEMAN

NO BAIL FOR THE JUDGE

Director Alfred Hitchcock **Starring** Audrey Hepburn, John Williams, Laurence Harvey
Year 1958–59 **Country** US **Genre** Thriller **Studio** Paramount

While filming *To Catch a Thief* in the south of France in 1954, Alfred Hitchcock happened on a novel by British author Henry Cecil called *No Bail for the Judge*. It's likely that the title was what first caught Hitch's eye but, perhaps weary of the glitz and glamour of the Riviera, his imagination was captured by the book's London setting. After working in the United States for fifteen years, he was keen to make a movie on his old manor. The plot, too, must have appealed to his penchant for gallows humour: the story of a High Court judge who finds his head in the noose when he's accused of murdering a prostitute had the makings of classic Hitchcock.

DARK HUMOUR

After enthusiastic feedback from John Michael Hayes, writer of *Rear Window* (1954) and *To Catch a Thief* (1955), Hitchcock planned to make *No Bail for the Judge* his next picture. But the Hayes Office, Hollywood's moral governor of the time, had other ideas. Its objections to the material persuaded Hitchcock to opt instead for a remake of his own 1934 film *The Man Who Knew Too Much*.

In 1958, after *The Wrong Man* (1956) had bombed and *Vertigo* (1958), his masterpiece, had failed to attract the ecstatic reaction he anticipated, Hitch turned his attention back to Henry Cecil's novel. This time, he called on the services of another writer, Ernest Lehman, whose brilliant script for *North by Northwest* he was in the process of shooting. But despite an exceptionally generous offer – $100,000 and five percent of the profits – Lehman turned the project down. Indignant, Hitchcock refused to speak to him for a week (even though they were in the middle of a picture together) and offered the job to *Vertigo* scribe Samuel Taylor. He was delighted to accept and, on 11 September 1958, turned up at Hitchcock's office on the Paramount lot, battered Smith Corona typewriter in hand, eager to start. But before he hit the first key, Hitchcock presented him with a pile of Cecil's novels to read.

Thanks, perhaps, to Hitchcock's insistence on rigorous research, Taylor's script captures not only the dark humour of Cecil's book but also its innate Britishness – which must have pleased his director. It also fleshes out the character of the judge's daughter, Elizabeth. In the book she is rather insipid;

ALFRED HITCHCOCK
The master in 1959, by which time he had notched up four Oscar nods for Best Director (for *Rebecca*, *Lifeboat*, *Spellbound* and *Rear Window*). A fifth would come for *Psycho* (1960), but he would again leave empty-handed.

THE HEPBURN CONNECTION
Despite his penchant for icy blondes, Hitch said, 'I'm quite prepared to try a cool brunette if I ever come across one.' Hepburn starred in the Hitchcockian *Charade* (1963) and *Wait Until Dark* (1967) but, sadly, would never fill that role in a movie by the master himself.

in the screenplay she's a wily, headstrong barrister who, despite her father's amnesia-induced doubts, is convinced of his innocence and teams up with a suave petty thief to prove it. Taylor also generates moments of vintage Hitchcock: for instance, Elizabeth meets her criminal accomplice when he shows up at the house to steal her father's stamp collection.

However, what is most intriguing – and tantalizing – about *No Bail for the Judge* is the proposed cast. Hitchcock wanted his favourite British actor John Williams for the judge, Laurence Harvey for the thief and, for Elizabeth, Audrey Hepburn. Given his fixation on icy blondes, the choice of Hepburn is fascinating; an exquisite, gamine brunette, could any actress have been further from the Hitchcock archetype? But it seems she had long been keen to work with the master. On 12 March 1955, Hitchcock's associate producer Herbert Coleman, who had worked with Hepburn on *Roman Holiday* (1953), wrote to the director: 'She wanted to know when you would be willing to do a picture with her. She is really most anxious to work for you.'

No Bail for the Judge seemed the perfect project to bring Hepburn and Hitchcock together. And given the sum of its parts – the archly comic source material; Taylor's marvellous script; London on the brink of a new era; the incendiary romantic pairing of Hepburn and Laurence Harvey (although some reports say Richard Burton or Cary Grant) – it could also have been one of Hitchcock's great films. Why it *didn't* happen is a source of some contention.

RAPE SCENE
One version has it that the project foundered when Hepburn refused to do a rape scene that had, allegedly, been added to the script after she had signed on for the role. It wouldn't have been out of character for Hitch to pull a stunt like that, but Taylor wrote only one draft of the script and one earlier treatment, both of which contained the scene in question – meaning Hepburn would certainly have seen it in the former if not the latter. And it's debatable whether

BACKSTORY
Henry Cecil – the author of *No Bail for the Judge* and himself a County Court judge – wrote twenty-six novels and three short story collections, most of them gently mordant comedies set in the back corridors of the British legal system. In 1957, his *Brothers in Law* was made into a film starring Richard Attenborough, Terry-Thomas (right), Ian Carmichael (far right) and Leslie Phillips. In 1962, it became a television show with Richard Briers. The same year, Cecil finally saw his name linked to Hitchcock when his story *I Saw the Whole Thing* became an episode in the first season of the series *The Alfred Hitchcock Hour*. Starring future *Dynasty* figurehead John Forsythe, this tale of a writer accused of causing a fatal car crash was the last time Hitchcock directed for television.

the scene is actually a rape at all. There is an encounter in London's Hyde Park between Elizabeth and the head of a prostitution racket that ends with her appearing, reluctantly, to succumb to him. It ends as follows:

```
And now he has her, and he has his arms around her.
And the CAMERA HAS MOVED IN to FILL THE SCREEN with
the two big heads. Elizabeth, summoning courage, tries
to smile. Edward brings his lips to hers and as he
kisses her, CAMERA CLOSES IN until his head obscures
her face altogether. The scene ENDS with the back of
Edward's head FILLING THE SCREEN and around his neck
the clenched hands of Elizabeth. Silence, but for the
band FAINTLY in the distance.
```

It's unpleasant, and jarring in the context of the film, but surely not grounds to derail an entire production, especially one with such promise. And there's no evidence that Hepburn did object to the scene – quite the opposite in fact. 'I adored the script Mr. Hitchcock sent over,' she told her biographer Diana Maychick in *Audrey Hepburn: An Intimate Portrait*. 'I'll never forget the story. I was to play a barrister in London. My father, a judge at the Old Bailey, is wrongly accused of murdering a prostitute and I was supposed to defend him. I hire a crook to help gather evidence, and the crook was to be played by Laurence Harvey. I was so excited, I told Mr. Hitchcock to send over the contracts.' No mention of a deal-breaking rape scene there.

Maychick attributes Hepburn's withdrawal to a miscarriage she suffered after requesting contracts. According to which report you believe, Hitchcock either pulled the plug and let Hepburn carry the can, or simply postponed the project for a year, perhaps in the hope that she would return. 'The delay actually might have worked out better for Hitchcock since he really wanted to film the Derby Day sequence which ends the treatment,' noted Hitch aficionado Steven DeRosa on alfredhitchcockgeek.com. 'The delays to start filming in 1959 caused him to miss filming the actual Derby so he and Sam Taylor devised a different ending for the script.'

At the same time, he was growing tired of lush, big-budget star vehicles – *No Bail for the Judge* was to be another widescreen, Technicolor affair – and had taken an interest in low-budget film-making. Why, Hitchcock mused, did so many shoddily made B-pictures make so much money – and what might a well-made B-picture do? A new era of 'classic' Hitchcock was on the way. SB

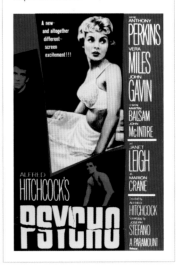

WILL IT EVER HAPPEN?

5/10   Henry Cecil's source novel might be showing its age, but it would make a splendid Hitchcockian period piece, with Emily Blunt as Elizabeth, Michael Fassbender as the thief, and Bill Nighy as the judge. Taylor's script has all the elements of a classic tale ripe for retelling: murder, amnesia, courtroom drama and the attempted theft of a valuable stamp collection.

A GEORGE CUKOR PRODUCTION

DEAN MARTIN
MARILYN MONROE

CYD CHARISSE AND PHIL SILVERS

SOMETHING'S GOT TO GIVE

ARNOLD SCHULMAN · NUNNALLY JOHNSON AND WALTER BERNSTEIN · JOHNNY MERCER

GENESIS
LA GENÈSE UN FILM DE ROBERT BRESSON

UN FILM D'HENRI-GEORGES CLOUZOT
"L'ENFER"

ROMY SCHNEIDER   SERGE REGGIANI   DANY CARREL

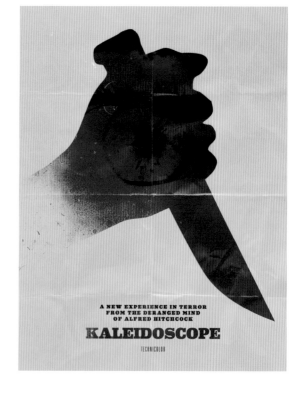

A NEW EXPERIENCE IN TERROR
FROM THE DERANGED MIND
OF ALFRED HITCHCOCK
KALEIDOSCOPE
TECHNICOLOR

FEDERICO FELLINI
IL VIAGGIO DI G. MASTORNA

KUBRICK
NAPOLEON

Chapter 2

The Sixties

A FILM BY
ORSON WELLES
DON QUIXOTE

A GEORGE CUKOR PRODUCTION
DEAN MARTIN
MARILYN MONROE
CYD CHARISSE AND PHIL SILVERS
SOMETHING'S GOT TO GIVE
SCREENPLAY BY
ARNOLD SCHULMAN, NUNNALLY JOHNSON AND WALTER BERNSTEIN
ORIGINAL MUSIC
JOHNNY MERCER

SOMETHING'S GOT TO GIVE

Director George Cukor **Starring** Dean Martin, Marilyn Monroe, Cyd Charisse
Year 1962 **Country** US **Genre** Romantic comedy **Studio** 20th Century Fox

Twentieth Century Fox was in trouble in 1962. Joseph L. Mankiewicz's epic *Cleopatra* – and its attendant Richard Burton/Elizabeth Taylor soap opera – was out of control, its budget ballooning to a record-breaking, unrecoupable $44 million. *Something's Got to Give*, by comparison, was supposed to be a safe, relatively low-budget money-spinner. This remake of the Oscar-nominated 1940 Cary Grant/Irene Dunne screwball hit *My Favorite Wife* – itself a comic reworking of Alfred Lord Tennyson's tragic poem *Enoch Arden* – was helmed by the veteran George Cukor. Its stars were Cyd Charisse, Dean Martin and the increasingly troubled Marilyn Monroe. Cukor had directed Monroe in 1960's *Let's Make Love* and presumably knew what he was getting into. Little did anyone anticipate that this would turn out to be a more dramatic soap than the one that was unfolding on those vast *Cleopatra* sets in Rome.

LEGALLY DEAD

Monroe was cast as Ellen Arden, a young mother of two declared legally dead after being lost at sea. Five years on, her husband Nick (Martin) remarries and is on honeymoon with his new spouse Bianca (Charisse) when Ellen is rescued from the island on which she has actually been stranded. She puts on a fake foreign accent and moves in with them as their housemaid, pretending her name is Ingrid Tic. But Nick is troubled by the knowledge that he has two wives, and even more perturbed when he learns that Ellen was marooned with another man, whom she dubbed Adam to her Eve. To counter his jealousy, Ellen hires a weedy shoe salesman (Wally Cox) to pose as 'Adam'.

Thanks to an old contract, Fox secured Monroe for a bargain $100,000. The deal seemed to suit everyone, as she would finally be free of her commitment to the studio upon the film's completion. But Fox was aware that her personal troubles were mounting. Her former husband, playwright Arthur Miller, had just remarried and his new wife – a photographer on the set of Miller and Monroe's *The Misfits* (1961) – was expecting a child. On 11 April, less than two weeks before production on the aptly entitled *Something's Got to Give* was due to commence, producer Henry Weinstein discovered Monroe unconscious from an overdose of barbiturates. He pleaded with Fox to delay the shoot. They refused.

GEORGE CUKOR
'She was, poor darling, quite mad. . .' the director said of Monroe in a 1981 BBC interview. 'She was a peculiar girl. Talented and charming, very charming, but her behaviour was very strange. And she did herself in, really.'

Anthony Summers's 1985 biography *Goddess: The Secret Lives of Marilyn Monroe* records the calculations behind Fox's decision to greenlight the project: 'There was a conference at 20th Century Fox. One executive (Weinstein) said the film should be called off, because Marilyn was clearly in no condition to work. "If she'd had a heart attack," he said, "we'd cancel. What's the difference if she's liable to kill herself any day with an overdose?" "Ah," a colleague replied, "if she'd had a heart attack we'd never get insurance for the production. We don't have that problem. Medically, she's perfectly fit."'

In truth, Monroe was anything but fit. Her variety of ailments included sinusitis and a crippling insecurity that Weinstein later described as a 'sheer dread of performing'. Last-minute script rewrites only compounded her anxiety.

In addition, she was increasingly paranoid. Pages of the script were sent to her with the suggestion that she put a cross next to any line she wasn't sure about and two crosses next to those she hated. In her booze and barbiturate-addled state, Monroe read this as a sign she was about to be double-crossed. She then got it into her head that Cyd Charisse was planning to upstage her by padding her bra and dying her hair blonde. Even an assurance that her leggy co-star would have light brown hair did nothing to placate Monroe. 'Her unconscious wants it blonde,' she insisted. Leaving nothing to chance, Fox even darkened the hair of the fortysomething actress cast in the role of housekeeper. Incoming scriptwriter Walter Bernstein also found himself instructed to remove any lines even hinting that Monroe's screen hubby Dean Martin could possibly be attracted to another woman.

BIZARRE INCIDENTS

The shoot commenced on Monday, 23 April 1962. Monroe promptly called in sick and remained absent for a week. Thereafter, she showed up only sporadically. On 7 May, Fox suspended the production. Three days later, Dr Ralph Greenson – the Hollywood psychiatrist on whom Monroe had become dependent – departed for Europe to be with his wife and mother-in-law.

One of the more bizarre incidents in Monroe's life is alleged to have taken place around this time. At a Hollywood Hills party attended by the likes of

THE BLONDE BOMBSHELL

Above For all her health woes, Marilyn Monroe seemed as luminous as ever on-screen. Her unclad *Something's Got to Give* swimming scene has become arguably the most famous sequence ever shot for an uncompleted movie.
Opposite Further on-set shots featuring (left) the actress with co-stars Dean Martin and Cyd Charisse on production designer Gene Allen's decorative set.

Dennis Hopper, she made a beeline for LSD guru Timothy Leary, then a
Harvard University researcher. She was eager to try the then-fashionable new
drug. According to Leary, she ended up palming Quaaludes off on him instead.
These sent the good doctor straight to sleep. The following day, they met again,
and Leary gave her 'a very small dose' of acid. One can only speculate on the
effect this had on the already disturbed and highly medicated star.

Production restarted on Monday, 14 May and Monroe worked until Thursday
lunchtime, when she departed for New York to prepare for her performance of
'Happy Birthday' at John F. Kennedy's Madison Square Garden birthday gala.
This was a commitment Weinstein had known about and agreed to before the
film went into production, but now he protested bitterly as his erratic star was
whisked away aboard Frank Sinatra's helicopter. It was to be Monroe's last
major public appearance.

> *'I don't know whether to feel sorry for her or not.*
> *I feel she should have been replaced.'*
>
> Lee Remick

Back on set the following Monday, the actress refused to work with Martin
because he had a cold. Wednesday, 23 May, was to prove the production's
most memorable day. On a Fox backlot, Monroe shot a midnight skinny-dipping
sequence. A flesh-coloured body-stocking, made to preserve her modesty,
looked unconvincing under the studio lights. She retained only a bikini bottom,
before shedding even that. At the canny star's own suggestion, photographers
clicked away as the world's biggest sex symbol frolicked before them. Monroe
duly achieved her aim of blasting Elizabeth Taylor off the front pages.

Work continued sporadically until Friday, 1 June – Monroe's 36th birthday.
The crew sang 'Happy Birthday' to her and she was presented with a cake
whose inscription read: 'Happy Birthday (Suit).' This was her last day on set.
She had showed up just twelve times during the thirty-five-day shoot. It was
later claimed that this yielded just seven-and-a-half minutes of usable footage.

Over the weekend, she suffered a major breakdown. In Anthony Summers's *Goddess*, Ralph Greenson's son Danny – who rushed to her Brentwood home after she made a desperate phone call – describes the scene that greeted him: 'She was in bed naked, with just a sheet over her, and she was wearing a black sleeping mask, like the Lone Ranger wore. It was the least erotic sight you could imagine. This woman was desperate. She couldn't sleep – it was the middle of the afternoon – and she said how terrible she felt about herself, how worthless she felt. She talked about being a waif, that she was ugly, that people were only nice to her for what they could get from her. She said she had no one, that nobody loved her. She mentioned not having children. It was a whole litany of depressive thoughts. She said it wasn't worth living anymore.'

The following week, Monroe's acting coach, Paula Strasberg, called Fox to say she was sick and would not be reporting for work. Dean Martin walked off the set and production was suspended once again. On viewing the rushes, Cukor and the producers were said to be appalled at Monroe's somnambulant performance. On Friday, 8 June, she was fired. Attempting to salvage something from the wreckage, Fox proposed replacing her with Lee Remick. 'I don't know whether to feel sorry for her or not,' Remick remarked. 'I feel she should have been replaced. The movie business is crumbling down around our ears because of that kind of behaviour. Actors shouldn't be allowed to get away with that kind of thing.' But Martin had a clause in his contract granting him final approval of his leading lady. And he didn't approve. In a press statement, he said: 'I have the greatest respect for Miss Lee Remick and her talent. . . but I signed to do the film with Marilyn Monroe and I will do it with no one else.'

On 11 June 1962, Fox threw in the towel and declared the production dead. A flurry of lawsuits ensued. The studio sued Monroe for $500,000 for breach of contract and Martin for refusing to accept another lead actress. The crew

---

TELLING TALES OF TENNYSON

If the plot of *Something's Got to Give* seems familiar, it's because Tennyson's poem had already been adapted for the screen numerous times. D.W. Griffith got in first with a two-part silent short, *Enoch Arden* (1911). Griffith wrote and had an uncredited cameo in another silent version of the same title (1915), while *The Bushwhackers* (1925) relocated the story to the Australian outback.

In 1940, Tennyson's tragedy was transformed into a screwball comedy. Even more bizarrely, two versions opened that year. Beating *My Favorite Wife* to the punch by two months was *My Two Husbands*, actually based on W. Somerset Maugham's *Enoch Arden*-inspired 1915 play *Home and Beauty*.

It's not hard to see why the theme struck such a chord in an era when so many men were marching off to war. But 1946's *Tomorrow Is Forever* – with Claudette Colbert (right, with the young Natalie Wood) and Orson Welles – was the last to present it as melodrama in a wartime setting. (This too fails to credit Tennyson, ascribing its origin to a novel of the same title by Gwen Bristow.)

Hollywood found a way to do it again with 2000's *Cast Away*. This isn't a remake or an update, but there are clear influences on the girlfriend, played by Helen Hunt, who marries another man while Tom Hanks is marooned.

placed a sarcastic announcement in *Variety* 'thanking' Monroe for putting them out of work. She subsequently apologized to each of them, insisting that their unemployment was not of her doing. Monroe then embarked on a round of interviews – notably with *Life* magazine, which had carried a selection of the less explicit skinny-dip photographs – reflecting on the fickle nature of fame.

UNHAPPY OR DEPRESSED

Attempts to revive the project without Monroe having failed, Fox attempted to lure back the star. The carrot was a massive increase in salary to $250,000 – more than double her original fee. Naturally, the lawsuit would be dropped too. They also agreed to her demand that Cukor be replaced by Jean Negulesco, who had directed her in *How to Marry a Millionaire* (1953) nearly a decade earlier. Rather ironically, the offer was made in person at Monroe's home on 25 July by Fox's executive vice-president Peter Levathes. When Monroe was fired, he had been widely quoted as saying: 'The star system has got way out of hand. We've let the inmates run the asylum and they've practically destroyed it.'

Quoted in Donald Spoto's 1993 biography *Marilyn Monroe*, Levathes recalled that their meeting was not only amicable but very positive. 'As so often with Marilyn's history at Fox, we simply decided to reinstate her. I was the one responsible for firing her, so I wanted to be the one to personally rehire her. No one wanted bad blood. She told me she didn't want her name tarnished, nor did she wish to ruin anyone. She did not seem unhappy or depressed at all. . . She was very happy and creative and glad to have a say in the revised script. She was in fine spirits and looking forward to getting back to work.'

Less than a fortnight later, on 5 August 1962, Marilyn Monroe was found dead in circumstances that remain controversial to this day. The official coroner's verdict was 'acute barbiturate poisoning'. Whether it was suicide, an accidental overdose or murder has been the subject of speculation ever since.

Contrary to Cukor's concerns about her performance, the footage surviving from *Something's Got to Give* offers no hint of trouble behind the scenes – suggesting that, had Monroe lived, the film might have been a success. She works well with Martin, a personal friend, and the charming scenes with their screen children have an added poignancy given her history of miscarriages. She was also in undeniably great shape, as evidenced by that playful skinny-dip sequence. *Playboy* magazine, which had acquired the rights to the saucier snaps, respectfully waited a whole year before publishing them. **RA**

WILL IT EVER HAPPEN?

3/10 A few scenes and test footage were unveiled in Fox's documentary *Marilyn* (1963). This was all anybody saw until 1990's *Marilyn: Something's Got To Give*, which illustrated the film's story with extensive clips. Another documentary, 2001's *Marilyn Monroe: The Final Days*, featured thirty-seven minutes of digitally restored film, culled from more than 500 hours of footage reportedly sitting in the Fox vault. And that's likely to be our lot – unless the digital clone-populated 'synthespian' revolution takes off.

GENESIS

LA GENÈSE UN FILM DE
ROBERT BRESSON

LA GENÈSE

Director Robert Bresson **Year** 1963 **Country** Italy **Genre** Biblical epic

Dino De Laurentiis, master showman of Italian cinema, is pleased with what he sees. His Dino Citta studio on the outskirts of Rome is alive with the arrival of great beasts in cages – lions, giraffes, hippos, tigers – from the city's zoo. It's 1963 and production is underway on his most ambitious project yet: a series of films portraying books from the Bible that will form a fifteen-hour spectacular. He has assembled some of the greatest directors in the world, including the Swedish Ingmar Bergman, American Orson Welles and fellow Italians Luchino Visconti and Federico Fellini. For the first film, French director Robert Bresson ('one of the cinema's greatest artists', in the view of Martin Scorsese) will tackle the Book of Genesis, from Creation to the Tower of Babel, taking in the Fall, Cain and Abel and the Flood. Bresson, among cinema's great minimalists, is thought to have embraced Dino's vision and the teeming menagerie is there for an epic scene of the loading of Noah's Ark. De Laurentiis applauds Bresson for the scope of his vision. 'One will see only their footprints in the sand,' Bresson tells him. To the irritation of the film's producer, his rushes reportedly turn out to feature just that: the tracks, with not a glimpse of the animals that, presumably at considerable expense, had been brought to the set. An hour later – according to Bernardo Bertolucci, who attends a dinner in the director's honour later that day – Bresson is fired.

IDIOTIC DISCUSSIONS

Whether the story is true or not, it's easy to believe that two men with such contrasting cinematic philosophies as De Laurentiis and Bresson would find working together impossible. Bresson himself said he left Rome to 'cut short idiotic discussions and desecrating obstruction'. Another legend has it that Bresson, reasoning that Eden had been located at the headwaters of the Tigris and Euphrates, insisted on casting a dark-skinned actress as Eve. Presented with a reel of potential candidates, De Laurentiis's publicity man, Lon Jones, outright refused, claiming the success of the film in Western markets rested on the characters being white. (When the production eventually went forward, in a much-altered form with John Huston at the helm, unknown Swedish student Ulla Bergryd was cast as Eve opposite US actor Michael Parks as Adam).

ROBERT BRESSON
Most of Bresson's films, as Alan Pavelin of sensesofcinema.com notes, 'had literary antecedents of one form or another', from Dostoevsky to newspaper reports. His adaptation of the Book of Genesis would surely have dwarfed all others.

Despite leaving the production, and witnessing its bowdlerized development in other hands, Bresson nurtured his vision of *La Genèse* – a script for which he had reportedly written in 1952, long before the De Laurentiis film – for the rest of his life. (Writer Philippe Arnaud likened this unrealized project to Carl Theodor Dreyer's on the life of Christ – see page 30.) It's not difficult to see why it was an idea he could not relinquish: the theme of innocence lost is the central theme of many of Bresson's films. 'The beauty of Genesis is God asking Adam to name things and animals,' he added. 'I find that magnificent.'

Bresson had already distilled such ideas into the narratives of his *Journal d'un curé de campagne* (Diary of a Country Priest, 1951) and *Procès de Jeanne d'Arc* (The Trial of Joan of Arc, 1962). (Another parallel with Dreyer, who chronicled the same trial in 1928's *La passion de Jeanne d'Arc*.) He recognized that his heroes often 'seem like shipwrecked men, leaving to

DID YOU KNOW?

De Laurentiis forged ahead without his array of brilliant directors, turning the picture into a single, sub-DeMille epic directed by John Huston. Despite its large budget, *The Bible: In the Beginning. . .* easily turned a profit for its producers, topping the US box office for months in 1966. On the casting of Adam and Eve, Huston noted, 'I stayed with the fifteenth-century painters in rendering [them] as fair.' Ulla Bergryd (above, with Michael Parks), who never had another starring role, was an anthropology student, spotted in Sweden by Huston's assistant director.

'I want to make people who see the film feel the presence of God in ordinary life.'

Robert Bresson

discover an unknown island – a story idea you can find as early as the creation of Adam.' Perhaps Bresson's greatest film, *Au hasard Balthazar* (By Chance Balthazar, 1966), was the project he worked on immediately after the De Laurentiis film fell through. It is tempting to view this complex examination of innocence and cruelty as a direct reaction to what happened in Rome.

CHALLENGES POSED

Even in the mid 1980s, after the release of his final film, 1983's *L'Argent* (Money), Bresson was still preparing to put the idea into production. 'At one point, it seemed that *La Genèse* would be made before *L'Argent*,' Bresson's assistant on the latter film, Jonathan Hourigan, told *Offscreen*'s Colin Burnett. 'It was also possible that *La Genèse* would be made in a language other than French. These circumstances meant that I had already been invited to return

SCHRADER ON BRESSON

'He taught me I could make films about unlikeable people,' Paul Schrader told the *Telegraph*. 'I could take an outcast, a lonely man, a guy who lives an interior life, and say, "Let's walk in his shoes." [Bresson's 1959 film] *Pickpocket* gave me the courage to write *Taxi Driver* [the Oscar-nominated 1976 classic starring Robert De Niro, right].' Schrader examined the work of Bresson and fellow directors Yasajirō Ozu and Carl Theodor Dreyer in his book *Transcendental Style in Film* (Da Capo, 1972). The French director's dry response: 'I have always been very surprised not to recognize myself in the image formed by those who are really interested in me.'

for *La Genèse*.' However, talking to fan Emmanuelle Cuau (later a writer and director in her own right), Bresson acknowledged the challenges posed by the project, including the necessity for Adam and Eve to be nude and – mindful of the difficulties he had encountered marshalling a single donkey in *Au hasard Balthazar* – the thought of a Garden of Eden full of livestock. (Bresson did not believe in giving his actors any leeway – happily explaining that their frequently downcast expressions were because they were following chalk marks on his sets – and was therefore apprehensive about performers he could not control.)

L'Argent received a mixed reaction at the Cannes Film Festival: Bresson shared the Best Director prize with Soviet film-maker Andrei Tarkovsky (the latter winning for *Nostalghia,* 1983) but was met with jeers from the audience when he accepted the award. In the aftermath, he was unable to secure the necessary funding for *La Genèse*. It was even suggested that he refused to clarify his birthdate (variously reported as 1901, the real date, and 1907) in the hope that his age would not put off potential investors. One source suggests that he received a pre-production grant in 1985, but this seems to have advanced the project no further. Bresson would write and direct no more films.

AN UNARTICULATED MANIFESTO

Despite never making the picture, the idea of *Genesis* was something that permeated all of the director's work, representing something of an unarticulated manifesto. 'A sort of matrix or Vauclusian spring that irrigates Bresson's entire work, this reflection on the origins of humanity is perhaps not destined to become reality,' wrote René Prédal in his *Robert Bresson: L'Aventure intérieure,* 'but it presents the dimension of the artist's work and defines its deeper nature.' Bresson once told writer-director and fan Paul Schrader (see opposite below) that 'the more life is what it is – ordinary, simple – without pronouncing the word God, the more I see the presence of God in that. . . I don't want to shoot something in which God would be too transparent. . . I want to make people who see the film feel the presence of God in ordinary life'. (Although the director described himself as a 'Christian atheist', he was a deeply devout Jansenist, a predestinarian offshoot of Catholicism. And, he told Charles Thomas Samuels in 1970, 'there are no real atheists'.)

Perhaps, then, De Laurentiis inadvertently protected Bresson's inspiration, his vision, by not allowing him to put his interpretation of **Genesis** on-screen. Perhaps some dreams are better left to the province of night. **DN**

WHAT HAPPENED NEXT. . .
Leaving Rome, Bresson wrote and directed *Au hasard Balthazar* (1966, below), a spiritual allegory detailing the cruel life and death of a donkey. It premiered to great acclaim at the Venice Film Festival in 1966, winning several awards, and is widely considered his masterpiece. Bresson continued to make lauded pictures in the 1960s and 1970s – and was, in François Truffaut's estimation, one of the few directors who could truly be called an auteur. He died in 1999, aged ninety-eight.

WILL IT EVER HAPPEN?

0/10   Certainly not in the form that Bresson envisaged. The 1999 film *La Genèse* shares little more than a title with his vision; although based on the Book of Genesis, it focuses instead on the power struggle between Jacob and his brother Esau. Starring singer Salif Keita, it was directed by the Mali-born Cheick Oumar Sissoko, who trained at French film school. Another film entitled *La Genèse* – an hour-long animation from 1975 – appears to share nothing with Bresson bar the nationality of its director, Pierre Alibert.

L'ENFER

Director Henri-Georges Clouzot **Starring** Serge Reggiani, Romy Schneider, Dany Carrel, Jean-Claude Bercq
Year 1964 **Country** France **Genre** Psychological drama **Studio** Columbia

HENRI-GEORGES CLOUZOT
The French director was notoriously hard on his actors. The cast of *Les Diaboliques* (1955) were made to feed on rotting fish, while Bernard Blier endured a real blood transfusion for *Quai des Orfèvres* (1947).

French cinema was undergoing a sea change in 1964. The classical directors of the 1940s and 1950s were being usurped by *La Nouvelle Vague*, the New Wave. Henri-Georges Clouzot, the acclaimed formalist behind *Les Diaboliques* (1955), hadn't made a picture since 1960's *La Vérité*, but had been the target of much criticism from the *Cahiers du Cinéma* crowd – criticism that made even him doubt the value of his previous work. It had been a time of turmoil for the director: his first wife, Véra, died shortly after the release of *La Vérité*, plunging him into a deep depression. Nonetheless, the announcement of his new film, *L'Enfer*, was greeted with keen anticipation – especially as he was receiving US backing, a rarity for a French film.

PARANOIA AND MADNESS

The insomniac Clouzot conceived *L'Enfer* as a bid to capture the anxieties that plagued his nights, and was interested in exploring the violent neuroses of jealousy. In it, Marcel (Serge Reggiani) and his wife Odette (Romy Schneider) – their names a nod to writer Marcel Proust and a character in his novel *À la recherche du temps perdu* – are hoteliers in a small town in France's Auvergne region. Much younger than her husband, Odette befriends locals her own age, socializing with Marylou (Dany Carrel), a carefree hairdresser, and Martineau (Jean-Claude Bercq), a handsome mechanic. The film tracks Marcel's growing jealousy, which turns first to paranoia and then to something like madness.

Perhaps in response to criticism of his films, Clouzot was eager to find a new way to express himself without abandoning the precision and craftsmanship that were his hallmarks. (The New Wave favoured improvisation over preparation – Clouzot's response: 'I improvise on paper.') He was fascinated by kinetic art (moving sculpture) and hired Jean-Pierre Yvaral, a key figure in the movement, to construct devices that could blend that aesthetic with cinema. He also entreated Gilbert Amy – a conductor who had written music under the direction of composer Pierre Boulez – to design a unique audioscape for the picture, in which sounds and music were integral to the protagonist's psychological state.

In March 1964, gathering together a small group of regular collaborators at the Studios de Boulogne, Clouzot began what was supposed to be a few weeks

UN FILM D'HENRI-GEORGES CLOUZOT
"L'ENFER"

ROMY SCHNEIDER   SERGE REGGIANI   DANY CARREL

A GLIMPSE INTO THE INFERNO

Top Romy Schneider had specified 'no nudity', but documentary maker Serge Bromberg found plenty of flesh on show among the film's reels. Was the director, mused Bromberg, 'basically making love with [her] through his camera?'

Middle For all the smiles, Schneider's character faced an ambiguous end: in the last shot, the husband was to stand by her sleeping body, a razor in hand.

Bottom Schneider struggled with drugs and alcohol but maintained an award-winning film career. However, after two failed marriages and the death of her son, she died in 1982, aged forty-three.

of testing new optical techniques (playing with the distorting effects of colour inversion, shadows, double exposure, etc.). Early on, studio executives from Columbia, the studio co-financing the picture, paid a visit to see the footage. Impressed, they gave Clouzot carte blanche in budget and creative direction. With this freedom and unlimited resources, Clouzot took the tests to another level, assembling huge crews for sessions lasting months rather than weeks.

Clouzot's plan was to shoot the everyday events of the film in black and white, but to film Marcel's paranoid delusions in shocking, psychedelic colour. Cinematographer Claude Renoir described Clouzot as a painter 'seeking to represent things and people on the screen by way of a totally recomposed, recreated colour, having no relation whatsoever with everyday reality'.

As with all of Clouzot's films, *L'Enfer* was meticulously planned: the entire script was thoroughly storyboarded, down to lens and focal depth details. But, to observers, there was a sense that Clouzot's quest for artistic expression was beginning to spiral out of control. These fears were reinforced in the early days

> *'. . . seeking to represent things and people [with] no relation whatsoever with everyday reality.'*
>
> Claude Renoir on Henri-Georges Clouzot

of principal photography. On 6 July 1964, Clouzot began shooting at a hotel near an artificial lake beneath the Garabit viaduct in southern France. The schedule was incredibly tight: they had only twenty days to film before the lake was to be emptied to supply power to a nearby hydroelectric dam. After that, they would return to the studio for four months of interior shoots. Clouzot had long known about the deadline, but saw the Garabit as the perfect location: the lake was key to the story and he wanted to use trains rumbling over the high iron bridge as a trigger for Marcel's fits of jealousy. Convinced that his customary fastidious planning would guarantee a swift and efficient shoot, Clouzot began production, knowing it would be impossible to return to the location for pick-ups. However, they quickly fell behind schedule.

DEADLINES AND PRESSURE

To cope with the small window they had for filming, Clouzot used three cameramen: Armand Thirard (cinematographer on *Les Diaboliques* and *La Vérité*), Claude Renoir and Andréas Winding. All were leaders in their field, and each was given a full crew of assistants, grips and electricians. In theory, this would enable Clouzot to get through more filming each day. He devised an intricate system whereby he would set up and shoot with one crew while the others prepared at another location. Scout units had shot a few seconds of each storyboarded scene at the relevant locations so Clouzot could sign off in advance on the angles and set-ups. Then he could rotate through the crews each day, not having to wait between shots for the preparatory work to be done. The reality was somewhat different. Clouzot began to stay with just one crew each day, insisting on countless takes and different set-ups as new

GRAND OBSESSION

A rich sexual vein runs through much of Clouzot's work, from the poison pen letters of *Le Corbeau* (1943, above) and *Quai des Orfèvres*'s (1947) whiff of lesbianism, to Véra Clouzot's submissive Linda in *Le Salaire de la Peur* (1953) and the deadly love triangle in *Les Diaboliques* (1955). Clouzot's last two projects – *L'Enfer* and *La Prisonnière* (1968), the latter a minor and exploitative work – were made at a time when film-makers were given more freedom to graphically represent sex on screen. It is perhaps no coincidence that when Clouzot no longer had to mask his obsessions, his craft greatly suffered.

ideas came to him. Despite working sixteen-hour days, they continued to fall behind, as the deadline crept ever closer. Clouzot complained that there was no shooting on Sundays, and would lurk in the hotel lobby on Sunday mornings to grab one of his cameramen and do location scouting on their day off. Claude Renoir took to climbing out of a downstairs bathroom window to escape.

Clouzot had a reputation for pressuring his performers to the point of torture (for *La Vérité*, he slipped Brigitte Bardot sleeping pills to create the appearance of drowsiness he desired. She later had her stomach pumped). On the set of *L'Enfer*, he was a terror. Plagued by insomnia, he would regularly wake up other cast and crew members in the small hours to discuss the next day's shooting. He caused blazing rows with Serge Reggiani and Romy Schneider, pushing them to their limits in pursuit of more intense performances. The latter reacted by simply yelling back at him. Reggiani, however, was quieter, preferring to avoid direct confrontation. But Clouzot regarded actors as a conduit for his own vision, and Reggiani had his own thoughts on interpreting the role of Marcel. A battle of wills ensued that would ultimately sink the film.

BLUE AND BLOOD RED

One scene featured Odette water-skiing with the mechanic Martineau as Marcel, consumed with jealousy, followed them at a run along the lakeside road. The footage of Schneider water-skiing was already in the can, much of it shot with colour inversion so the actors appeared blue and the water blood red (the actors had to be made up and wear grey/green costumes to achieve the effect). When it came to shooting Reggiani running alongside the lake, Clouzot took the opportunity to make a point. For several days, hours on end, he had Reggiani running along the twisting, steeply hilled roads until he was physically and emotionally exhausted. On 20 July, the crew arrived on location to discover the actor had left the production, citing illness. There was talk of Maltese fever, but many suspected Clouzot had pushed him over the edge.

Reggiani wasn't alone: a number of crew members also left, complaining that they couldn't work in such chaotic conditions. Clouzot had less than a

ON SET

Left Courtesy of Columbia, Clouzot could afford a plethora of equipment and shooting choices. 'My guess,' speculates Serge Bromberg, 'is that Clouzot would have finished the film if he'd had a more limited budget.' **Right** Clouzot (pictured in Chamonix) was 'certainly going somewhere,' notes Bromberg, 'but he was the only one to know where that was'.

After recovering from his heart attack, Clouzot made documentaries for French TV on conductor Herbert von Karajan. In 1967, he raised the money to make his final picture, *La Prisonnière*, about a repressed woman (Elisabeth Wiener, left) who becomes the model for a sado-masochistic gallery owner (Laurent Terzieff, far left). Its debt to Clouzot's work on *L'Enfer* is clear, although *La Prisonnière* is formally and thematically less ambitious. The filming was halted at one point, owing to Clouzot's ill health, and he deteriorated further throughout the 1970s. He worked on several scripts, including a long-gestating one about Indochina, but died in 1977, aged sixty-nine, without making another picture.

week until his main location was taken away from him, had no lead actor and was woefully behind schedule. Jean-Louis Trintignant (Bardot's partner in 1956's *Et Dieu. . . créa la femme*), called upon to replace Reggiani, left Garabit after two days, without filming a single scene. Clouzot kept the production rolling, spending his nights writing new material to shoot the following day with the actors he still had at his disposal, but it was becoming apparent that the film was a lost cause. Even if Clouzot could find someone to play Marcel, it would be impossible to reshoot all his scenes before the lake was emptied.

In the end, the decision was taken out of Clouzot's hands. While shooting a lesbian scene between Schneider and Dany Carrel on a boat, the director suffered a heart attack. He was rushed by ambulance to the nearby town of St-Flour, where it was determined that, although his life was not in danger, he was in no condition to continue filming. This, coupled with the situation regarding the lake, led to Columbia shutting down production.

Clouzot's previous films, shot with a precise and steely gaze, seemed to observe humanity objectively, almost as if he were making a psychological study of a different species. For *L'Enfer*, however, he turned his gaze inwards, on his own anxieties and obsessions, and in doing so lost all control. **DN**

WILL IT EVER HAPPEN?

0/10 Claude Chabrol – a founding father of *La Nouvelle Vague*, yet heavily influenced by Clouzot – directed *L'Enfer* (1994) with Emmanuelle Béart and François Cluzet. He made only slight changes to the original script, but this orthodox drama eschewed the experimentation of Clouzot's project. During the following decade, while stuck in an elevator with Clouzot's widow, producer Serge Bromberg learned that Clouzot had stashed away 185 cans of film from *his* version of *L'Enfer*. He consequently made the documentary *L'Enfer d'Henri-Georges Clouzot* (2009), featuring interviews with original crew members and fascinating footage shot during the tests and on location. This is, in all likelihood, the closest Clouzot's vision will get to a release.

IL VIAGGIO DI G. MASTORNA

Director Federico Fellini **Starring** Marcello Mastroianni, Ugo Tognazzi **Year** 1965 **Country** Italy **Genre** Fantasy

FELLINI, MASTROIANNI
In *A Director's Notebook* (1969, above), Fellini and Marcello Mastroianni parodied their prepping for *Il viaggio di G. Mastorna*. A cello-playing Mastroianni is fussed over by make-up artists and costume directors while the director frets that the real Mastorna is hiding. 'If you could believe that I am Mastorna,' replies the actor, 'I would automatically become Mastorna.'

Rising from the Laziali fields outside Rome is a replica of Cologne Cathedral, its Gothic openwork spires looming over a wide piazza. A closer look reveals not just the location to be odd – the buildings around the cathedral are fabrications, their five- and six-storey brickwork façades held up only by scaffolding. The fuselage of a jet airliner, shorn of its wings, stands in the centre of the piazza, also encased in scaffolding. Weeds have grown up through the paving; long grass sways between the derelict structures. A rusted taxicab awaits its driver up on bricks, wheels long since removed. A horse ambles through the piazza, grazing as it goes, the only sign of life. A voice-over in Italian: 'These strange, lonely shapes were built for a film I planned but I never made. . . More beautiful now, falling down and covered with weeds.'

INEFFABLE, MYSTICAL EXPERIENCE

In *A Director's Notebook* (1969), Fellini shows the husks of the giant sets built three years earlier for *Il viaggio di G. Mastorna* and reflects on the opus he never made. The story of a cellist who, after experiencing an emergency landing aboard an airliner, comes to realize he actually died in the incident, *Mastorna* was Fellini's attempt to illuminate the final words of his psychologist Dr Ernst Bernhard (who died just as work began on the screenplay): 'Suffer your death in full consciousness.' As Fellini put it, his ambition was to create 'an ineffable, mystical experience; convey the feeling of totality'.

The film would begin with the cellist Giuseppe Mastorna, a passenger on an airliner forced to land in the piazza of a strange town during a snowstorm. The passengers disembark and wander through quiet, dimly lit cobbled streets until they find a bus waiting to take them to an isolated hotel. There, the congregation gathers to watch the whole of Mastorna's life projected on a screen. He is unable to leave until he watches it and accepts the person he was. From there, Mastorna explores dreamlike locations, often guided by a beautiful air stewardess, his journey taking him through a construction of the afterlife seemingly in debt to the Swiss analytical psychologist Carl Jung.

Fellini struggled to find a satisfactory resolution to Mastorna's adventure, but its beginnings reached back to the director's final years as a teenager in

FEDERICO FELLINI

iL ViAGGiO
Di G. MASTORNA

his hometown of Rimini. Just before the outbreak of the Second World War, the Italian weekly magazine *Omnibus* (which was suppressed by Mussolini in 1939) serialized *Lo strano viaggio di Domenico Molo* (The Strange Journey of Domenico Molo) by Dino Buzzati (see below left). Fellini read the story as a high-school student and it haunted him for a quarter of a century. In 1965, he met Buzzati and proposed that they write a screenplay together. Fellini was contracted to make a film for Italian producer Dino De Laurentiis, and the pair had secured the rights to US novelist Fredric Brown's *What Mad Universe*, in which a journalist is propelled into a parallel universe, a bizarre reflection of the world he knows. Instead, the director wrote a treatment for *Mastorna* and convinced De Laurentiis to fund the project. Fellini worked on the *Mastorna* screenplay with Buzzati through the summer of 1966, while construction began on the film's sets at De Laurentiis's Dino Citta studio.

PATHOLOGICALLY SUPERSTITIOUS

The director, however, began to waver. Having awarded the lead role to Marcello Mastroianni – with whom he had worked on his two previous major pictures, *La Dolce Vita* (1960) and *8½* (1963) – Fellini told De Laurentiis not to finalize a contract with the actor. The reason for these doubts is unclear but, in September 1966, he wrote to De Laurentiis and told the producer he no longer wished to make the film. The fear of which Mastroianni speaks in

> '*You have no faith. . . If you could believe that I am Mastorna, I would automatically become Mastorna.*'
> Marcello Mastroianni

A Director's Notebook ('You have no faith. It's as if you are scared') plagued Fellini throughout his career. He was pathologically superstitious, and there are countless reports of him attending fortune-readings and séances during the pre-production of *Mastorna*. Legend has it that during one such event Fellini became convinced that bringing it to fruition would be the last thing he ever did. The wisdom of sages aside, it's not fanciful that Fellini should believe such predictions. His art was heavily influenced by his dreams, and for years he had been treated by the Jungian Dr Bernhard, who was responsible for the director compiling a dream diary as a way of interpreting his unconscious.

The real-world consequences were devastating. Having sunk hundreds of millions of lira into the production, De Laurentiis was furious and began legal action. The courts found in his favour, and he had valuables seized from Fellini's home and a lien put on outstanding payments due to the director for his work on *Giulietta degli spiriti* (Juliet of the Spirits, 1965). But however ruthless De Laurentiis the businessman was, he remained under the spell of cinema and still wanted to work with Fellini. Early in 1967 the two came to an accord and resurrected *Mastorna*. Fellini was now convinced that Mastroianni was right for the lead but he was unavailable. Instead he signed Italian star Ugo Tognazzi, later internationally known for *La Cage aux Folles* (1978).

THE OTHER *SATYRICON*
Mooted *G. Mastorna* co-star Ugo Tognazzi appeared in Gian Luigi Polidoro's *Satyricon* (1969) – a movie that would forever be eclipsed by Fellini's version of the story.

WHAT HAPPENED NEXT. . .

Federico Fellini continued to make acclaimed films. *Fellini Satyricon* (1969) and *Amarcord* (1973, left) both netted him Oscar nominations for Best Director, the latter winning Best Foreign Film. In his seventies, Fellini came as close as he ever would to realizing his unmade dream. Over the summer of 1992, the Italian magazine *Il Grifo* published a graphic adaptation of *Mastorna* by renowned Italian illustrator Milo Manara. At the same time, Fellini took a commission to make a series of three adverts for Banca di Roma. They premiered at the Venice Film Festival that year and, viewed together, tell the story of a man (played by Paolo Villaggio) who has dreams about his own death and of strange events from his childhood, all interpreted by a psychoanalyst (Fernando Rey). Once again, the ghost of *Mastorna* hung heavily over proceedings.

UNDEFINED AND THREATENING

Fellini, however, was not in a good place. What he later described as a 'thick fog with undefined and threatening parameters' descended upon him and, on 10 April, he was found unconscious. Rushed to hospital, he was diagnosed with acute pleurisy. After weeks in care, he went to Manziana, northwest of Rome, to convalesce. De Laurentiis still hoped that *Mastorna* would go ahead, and arranged for Paul Newman to visit Fellini, feeling the US star would be perfect for the lead role. After *The Bible: In the Beginning. . .* (1966), De Laurentiis was hungry for more US success. By the end of the summer, though, it was clear the film was doomed. Keen to avoid another bout in court, Fellini agreed to a multi-picture deal with De Laurentiis as compensation (the deal never bore fruit). But the director wasn't prepared to give up on *Mastorna*, and arranged for Alberto Grimaldi, who had produced the final two films in Sergio Leone's *Dollars* trilogy, to buy the rights from De Laurentiis.

Fellini and Grimaldi worked together on the anthology film *Histoires extraordinaires* (1968) and *Fellini Satyricon* (1969), but never got *Mastorna* into production. The director later commented that it haunted him, colouring all of his subsequent films. Traces of it are indeed recognizable in *I clowns* (1970), *Amarcord* (1973) and *Ginger e Fred* (1986), the last of which also starred Marcello Mastroianni. Over the next twenty-five years, Fellini periodically toyed with the idea of revisiting *Mastorna*, even securing the rights back from Grimaldi, but never got the film off the ground. **DN**

G. MASTORNA'S UNSUNG HERO

Italian writer Dino Buzzati's short story *Lo strano viaggio di Domenico Molo* – the antecedent of *G. Mastorna* – is the tale of a boy who, wracked with guilt after making a false confession, falls ill and dies, awaking in a purgatory where the dead find themselves on trial. Ultimately, he is allowed to return to the living world.

WILL IT EVER HAPPEN?

0/10

Fellini, De Laurentiis and Mastroianni have all passed away, and Grimaldi's only major credit since Fellini's *Ginger e Fred* was on Scorsese's *Gangs of New York* (2002). Fellini often 'conceptualized' his films, encouraging improvisation on set and dubbing dialogue in post-production, so it's doubtful whether a complete screenplay for *Mastorna* even exists.

A NEW EXPERIENCE IN TERROR
FROM THE DERANGED MIND
OF ALFRED HITCHCOCK

KALEIDOSCOPE

TECHNICOLOR

KALEIDOSCOPE

Director Alfred Hitchcock **Year** 1967 **Budget** Under $1 million **Country** US **Genre** Thriller **Studio** Universal/MCA

The late 1960s found an increasingly young audience rejecting Hollywood orthodoxy in favour of independent productions and European art movies that reflected modern views on race, gender and sexuality. In 1966, Antonioni's *Blow-Up* hammered a final nail in the coffin of the the industry's censorship guidelines. Denied MPAA approval, MGM released the film anyway to critical and commercial success. The film also impressed Alfred Hitchcock. 'These Italian directors are a century ahead of me in terms of technique,' he lamented. The master was, at the time, experiencing a lull. After the heights of the 1950s and early 1960s (*Vertigo, North by Northwest, Psycho, The Birds*), *Marnie* (1964) had been underappreciated. A new direction was needed.

SEDUCTION AND MURDER

For several years, Hitchcock had toyed with a prequel to his *Shadow of a Doubt* (1943), in which Joseph Cotten's character seduces and murders rich widows. He was interested in making a killer the central character to the film, telling the story from his point of view. The director registered an outline of the idea with the Writers Guild of America and tried to engage the services of Robert Bloch, who had written the book on which *Psycho* (1960) was based.

The plan was for Bloch to write a novel from the outline and for Hitchcock to purchase the film rights for $10,000. Bloch's agent, Gordon Molson, said the writer was amenable, but that the offer was too low. Hitchcock conceded that Bloch would be paid $20,000 if the film was made and $5,000 if it was not. However, by February 1965, the project had not got off the ground and Molson was hawking two other Bloch books, *The Firebug* and *The Scarf,* for adaption instead. With Hitchcock entering pre-production for 1966's *Torn Curtain* (to begin shooting in November), the idea was put on the back burner.

Everything changed in 1966. The production of *Torn Curtain* had not been smooth (Hitchcock was aggrieved that leads Paul Newman and Julie Andrews had been foisted upon him – MCA wanted bankable stars after *Marnie*'s failure) and the film received a lukewarm reception from critics when it was released that July. Returning to Los Angeles in late summer, Hitchcock sat down with his friend François Truffaut for conversations that led to the seminal

ALFRED HITCHCOCK
Hitch on the set of *Frenzy* in England in 1972. His usual lugubrious expression was, for once, perhaps warranted by the circumstances: the film emerged in the aftermath of the troubled *Kaleidoscope*.

INFLUENCED BY: *BLOW-UP*
Veruschka von Lehndorff and David Hemmings starred in Michelangelo Antonioni's intriguing period piece about a London photographer, which had an important impact on Hitchcock.

1967 book *Hitchcock*. Something in those talks with Truffaut – a leading light of the French New Wave who hailed Hitchcock as a major influence – led him to question both his own film-making and contemporary cinema as a whole.

It is not difficult to fathom Hitchcock's attraction to Antonioni's *Blow-Up* – he probably saw something of himself in it. *Blow-Up* bears narrative and thematic similarities to 1954's *Rear Window* (lonely, sexist photographers believe they witness a homicide during their voyeurism). Antonioni would have denied any influence. He once said, Hitchcock's films are completely false, especially the endings. However, *Blow-Up* follows the classical dramatic trajectory of the thrillers at which Hitchcock was so adept. The parallels between the two directors do not end there: when Antonioni said, 'Actors feel somewhat uncomfortable with me; they have the feeling that they've been excluded from my work,' he could have been channelling the master.

FLESHING OUT FRENZY

In early 1967, Hitchcock returned to his serial killer project, fleshing it out with Benn Levy, a collaborator from his days in England (Levy wrote the dialogue for 1929's *Blackmail* and Hitchcock produced Levy's directorial effort, 1932's *Lord Camber's Ladies*). The film was first entitled *Frenzy*, then *Kaleidoscope*, which had a more zeitgeist feel to it. They settled on Neville Heath – an English killer from the 1940s, notorious for charming his victims – as the basis for a character now named Willie Cooper, rather than Charlie Oakley from *Shadow of a Doubt*. Levy called the Heath theme 'a gift from heaven', and they imagined the picture, relocated to New York, as a grotesque love story.

Cooper was written as an attractive, charming bodybuilder, whose pathological reaction to water triggers his sexual psychopathy. Hitchcock wanted the narrative built around his relationships with three women, each ending in a 'crescendo'. First, he seduces a young United Nations employee, takes her for a picnic, and murders her at a waterfall. Victim two is an art-

TEST FOOTAGE

Hitchcock's test footage for *Kaleidoscope* made it clear how explicit the film would have been. The actresses are frequently in states of undress, notably the chase through the battleship (bottom left) and the murder at the waterfall (top left).

Of the film's recurring theme of water, stills photographer Arthur Schatz remarked: 'We went to upstate New York and we went to the maritime harbor where all the Liberty ships are berthed. . . Turns out that water figured very heavily in the story, and every time this young boy saw water and stuff, he got turned on and he had to commit a murder'.

There was brutal violence and, characteristically of Hitchcock, it was meticulously planned: one murder scene accounts for twelve pages of the script.

school student, whose death is the climax of a set piece: a chase through a mothballed warship in an abandoned shipyard. The final girl is a police officer who acts as bait and seduces Cooper, who falls in love with her. Hitchcock envisioned a finale between them, with the NYPD closing in, set amid the brightly coloured drums of an oil refinery (echoing Antonioni's *Red Desert,* 1964).

Levy supplied a treatment, first draft and revised script. However, a dissatisfied Hitchcock enlisted Hugh Wheeler (who had worked on *The Alfred Hitchcock Hour* television show) and Howard Fast (author of *Spartacus*) to write further drafts. Fast said the director gave him a free hand, as he was preoccupied with plotting camerawork: 'By the time the script was finished, he had specified over 450 camera positions – it was that technically detailed.'

NUDITY AND VIOLENCE

Embracing neorealist aspects of the New Wave and *cinéma-vérité*, Hitchcock opted to shoot the film on location with mobile cameras. He wanted to use natural light, even during interiors, and sent photographers and cameramen to shoot test footage to find the ideal exposures and film stock speeds. He even wrote a draft of the script himself – the first time he had taken the screenwriting reins since his uncredited work on 1947's *The Paradine Case.*

Hitchcock sent the script to Truffaut. 'There does rather seem to be an insistence on sex and nudity,' he noted, 'but it does not worry me too much – I know that you shoot such scenes with real dramatic power, and you never dwell on unnecessary detail.' (Hitchcock's wife and sounding board, Alma, presciently fretted, 'If we make it too horrific, we'll get too much criticism.') Hitchcock appeared on the verge of a renaissance – until the studio stepped in.

> *'There does rather seem to be an insistence on sex and nudity, but it does not worry me too much. . .'*
> François Truffaut

The director made a presentation to Lew Wasserman and the Universal/MCA board, explaining the project and his excitement about it. He planned to use a cast of unknowns and shoot the film for less than a million dollars. However, concerned at the damage such a controversial film could do to the Hitchcock 'brand', Wasserman turned it down. 'They had belittled Hitchcock's attempt to do precisely what they had been urging him to do,' noted Fast, 'to attempt something different, to catch up with the swiftly moving times.' **DN**

WILL IT EVER HAPPEN?

1/10 Ignoring the obstacle of Hitchcock's death in 1980, *Kaleidoscope* was a film of its time – a new direction for a celebrated film-maker in a new age of film-making. What would have been shocking in the 1960s would be routine to today's audiences, weaned on serial protagonists from Henry to Hannibal Lecter, and the torture porn of the *Saw* pictures.

WHAT HAPPENED NEXT. . .
Having shored up his stockholding in MCA – he was already one of the studio's three largest stockholders after trading the rights to *Psycho* and his TV show – Hitchcock resurrected ideas from *Kaleidoscope* and returned to Britain to shoot *Frenzy* in 1972. The tale of a serial killer in London, it was the one late Hitchcock picture that formally engaged with the New American cinema of its day. Unfortunately, it proved a mere shadow of what *Kaleidoscope* could have been.

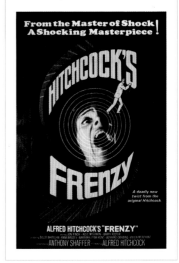

NAPOLEON

Director Stanley Kubrick **Starring** Oskar Werner, Audrey Hepburn **Year** 1967–71
Budget $6 million **Country** Various **Genre** Historical drama **Studio** MGM

STANLEY KUBRICK
'There was always going to be this
Napoleon film,' remarked Jonathan Cecil,
who starred in the director's *Barry Lyndon*
(1975). 'I always thought he [Kubrick,
above] could have played the part very
well himself.'

By Stanley Kubrick standards, pre-production on 1971's *A Clockwork
Orange* passed with almost unseemly haste. He even found time
for lunch with his star Malcolm McDowell. As they chewed over the
dystopian piece, a stunned McDowell watched the director alternate mouthfuls
of steak and dessert. 'This,' Kubrick explained, 'is the way Napoleon ate.' Prior
to *A Clockwork Orange*, Kubrick had spent four years immersing himself in
every conceivable aspect of his proposed biopic of the emperor. His passion
was fuelled, some thought, by the fact that Kubrick saw himself in Napoleon:
the implacable nature, the brilliant strategist, the natural commander. In their
own ways, both had an overpowering urge to conquer. In a rare rush of blood,
he announced that *Napoleon* was to be 'the best film ever made'.

TREASURE TROVE
A perusal of the pictures, production documents, treatments, letters, notes,
samples, swatches, doodles and the shooting script itself (all squirrelled away
in Kubrick's treasure trove of boxes, and since published) suggests this was no
idle boast to sway the tentative generals at MGM and United Artists, between
which studios the project shuttled. According to Alison Castle, who has served
as editor and 'archive excavator' for Kubrick's hoarded riches since his death
in 1999, the research surpasses that of any other film. Indeed, it has been
described as the largest repository of Napoleonic lore in the world. Kubrick read
over 500 books on Bonaparte. His treatment of *le petit caporal* (although, as
the director would have noted, 1.7 metres was hardly short for the time) – an
undertaking that began during post-production on *2001: A Space Odyssey* in
1967 – would have been a monument to Kubrick's formidable imagination.

Flushed with the critical and commercial success of *2001*, Kubrick was sure
that he could get any film off the ground, no matter how colossal the scope.
Rather than honing in on a strand of Napoleon's life – Sergei Bondarchuk's rival
production, *Waterloo* (1970), would focus on the hundred days leading up to
the Frenchman's defeat – Kubrick's vision, which he was keen to write himself,
would encompass everything from a Corsican infant squalling at his mother's
breast to a lonely death on the South Atlantic island Saint Helena. 'If you have

KUBRICK
NAPOLEON

a truly interesting film,' he said, 'it doesn't matter how long it is.' (He did, however, wisely admit it was unlikely to outstrip 1939's *Gone with the Wind*.)

UN-KUBRICKIAN FERVOUR

Beyond the grandeur and historical minutiae lay a markedly un-Kubrickian fervour to celebrate (and deconstruct) Napoleonic myth. For all the eighteenth-century realism, this was to be an 'epic poem of action'. Kubrick conceived scenes that sang with cinematic possibility. Picture Napoleon returning to France from exile, intent on regaining power, in 1815. Five thousand soldiers are sent to arrest him. Confronted by the army, Napoleon orders his own men to stand fast as he walks alone towards his would-be captors. Within range of their muskets, he exclaims, 'Do you recognize me?' They are transfixed. In a flourish that embodies the self-belief it takes to conquer half a continent, he bares his breast and cries, 'If there is any soldier among you who wishes to kill his emperor, he may do so. Here I am.' Naturally, instead of following their orders, the men swarm Napoleon with cries of '*Vive l'empereur*!'

With an IQ of 200, fed by an insatiable curiosity, Kubrick didn't research his subjects: he *consumed* them, applying the microscope of his intellect to every facet of his latest obsession. From this emerged breathtakingly meticulous work – to make a film exploring the possibilities of space travel, you spend months with NASA pursuing the limits of physics and what might lie beyond. First, he watched every film ever made about Bonaparte. For those under the

---

BLUE MOVIE c.1970

Shortly before Kubrick began work on *2001: A Space Odyssey* (1968), *Dr. Strangelove* (1964) screenwriter Terry Southern suggested – without, perhaps an entirely straight face – that he make a big budget porn film to subvert the genre.

Unlikely as it seems, some years later, Kubrick did toy briefly with the idea of a blue movie tentatively titled (with presumably intentional bluntness) *Blue Movie*. (Ironically, in a 1962 interview with Southern, the director had opined: 'The erotic viewpoint of a story is best used as a sort of energizing force of a scene, a motivational factor, rather than being, you know, explicitly portrayed.')

A scantily-clad plot involved a celebrated auteur who has such industry cachet that he manages to raise financing for a hardcore porno starring a pair of famous screen lovers – think Rock Hudson and Doris Day. It never happened, of course – but, when it was announced in the mid 1990s that Kubrick's next film would be *Eyes Wide Shut* (1999), inspired by Arthur Schnitzler's erotic novella *Traumnovelle*, rumours circulated that this would be a revised version of *Blue Movie*.

Regardless of Kubrick's attachment to the project, Southern was so enamoured of the idea that he badgered his friend for permission to write it as a novel. Also titled *Blue Movie*, the result was published in 1970 (right) and featured a famous director called Boris Adrien – loosely based on Kubrick – and his efforts to make a blockbuster skin flick with major movie stars. The author dedicated the book 'To the great Stanley K' and Kubrick's interest was sufficiently revived for him to ask Southern for a look at the publisher's galleys. 'Stanley,' scolded his wife Christiane when she saw them, 'if you do this, I'll never speak to you again.' Sensibly, Kubrick opted for marital harmony over career suicide.

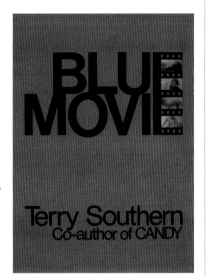

illusion that Abel Gance had already provided a definitive portrait of Napoleon with his five-hour 1927 epic, Kubrick provided a curt corrective. '[It] has built up a reputation among film buffs over the years,' he told critic Joseph Gelmis in 1968, '[but] I found it to be really terrible. Technically [Gance] was ahead of his time. . . but, as far as story and performance goes, it's a very crude picture.'

He also read every biography and historical testament in print. A mass of data about the film's characters was stored in an oak-wood card file, ordered by date and annotated with names. Thus Kubrick could determine where

> *'I wouldn't want to fake it with fewer troops, because Napoleonic battles were. . . a vast tableau.'*
> Stanley Kubrick

any of his principals were on any given date and what they might have been doing. A 15,000-strong gallery of images of eighteenth- and early-nineteenth-century society had its own cross-indexing. The idea was that anyone on the production could consult the file, and not pester the director with questions.

Kubrick put at the production's disposal prints of Bonaparte fourth cousins, dioramas of the Battle of Elchingen in which France defeated Austria, sketches, caricatures, paintings, miniatures, photographs of replica flags, candle-holders, coins, pistols, field dressings. . . all the paraphernalia of Napoleonic life. The chests of material even included an eighteenth-century horseshoe nail. And to enable him to shoot in dusky, naturalistic light, often illuminated by no more than candles, Kubrick co-opted friends at NASA and camera specialists Zeiss to invent ultra-fast 50mm lenses that could cope with low-light conditions.

SPECTACULAR AUTHENTICITY

Of all Kubrick's Napoleonic ambitions, most thrilling was his desire to replicate the battle scenes with spectacular authenticity. He would shoot on the very turf where Napoleon exercised his tactical genius, utilizing local soldiers and 40,000 infantrymen and 10,000 cavalrymen from the Romanian army to enact these 'lethal ballets'. 'I wouldn't want to fake it with fewer troops,' he explained to Gelmis, 'because Napoleonic battles were out in the open, a vast tableau where the formations moved in an almost choreographic fashion.' *Spartacus* (1960) and its chessboard formations of Roman legions would pale in comparison to the 'organizational beauty' of Napoleon's martial power viewed from afar, and bloody, steaming brutality up close. Insisting his extras undergo four months of historical military training – even instigating a rank system – Kubrick treated the production itself as a military operation.

But Kubrick had no taste for a runaway project like Mankiewicz's 1963 *Cleopatra*. Even as the budget swelled from three to six million dollars – huge for the time – he made artful economies. Instead of a cripplingly expensive sea battle, he would depict Napoleon's naval conflict with England using maps, concluding with a haunting shot of French ships at the bottom of the sea, a drowned admiral afloat in his cabin as papers, books and even a roast chicken

INFLUENCED BY. . .

Evidently impressed by Oxford scholar Felix Markham's *Napoleon* (above), published in 1966, Kubrick purchased the rights to the book, hired the author as historical adviser, and employed twenty of his graduate students to amass a 'master biographical file' on his proposed film's fifty primary characters.

IAN HOLM
Although the British actor didn't portray
Napoleon for Kubrick, he did play the
role three times. **From top:** with Sorcha
Cusack in the 1974 TV miniseries
Napoleon and Love; in Terry Gilliam's
Time Bandits (1981); in Alan Taylor's
The Emperor's New Clothes (2001).

drift by. Across the film's enormous historical canvas, maps and a sweeping
voice-over would provide context. Kubrick even found a New York company
who could manufacture uniforms out of a type of paper. Film tests proved that,
from only a few feet away, they were indistinguishable from real fabric.

Further compromises would be called for. The real battlegrounds, preserved
for posterity by local authorities, proved impractical. Undaunted, Kubrick
sought alternatives in Yugoslavia and Romania – locations within plausible
range of Napoleon's footsteps. They also offered attractive rates for rent of
their armies (five dollars per man per day in Romania). Such was Kubrick's
commitment to perfection, he took soil samples from Waterloo to ensure the
colour and consistency of the mud could be reproduced in his new locations.

OVER-PRICED MOVIE STARS
So long was the film's gestation, candidates for the lead role fell in and out of
contention as they fell in and out of fashion. In notes dated November 1968,
Kubrick drily listed the 'four principal categories of cost' that tend to burden the
budget of a military epic: 'Large numbers of extras. Large numbers of military
uniforms. Large numbers of expensive sets. Over-priced movie stars.'

He did his best to control the first three and resolved not to be held hostage
by the last. Rather than stars, he was going to use 'great actors and new
faces'. Early notes suggest his thoughts ran to Peter O'Toole, Alec Guinness,
Peter Ustinov and Jean-Paul Belmondo. In 1968, an offer was made to Oskar
Werner (famous for Truffaut's *Jules et Jim,* 1962 and *Fahrenheit 451,* 1966)
but, as the film stalled, Kubrick began to favour David Hemmings and Ian Holm
(see left). When development entered the early 1970s, the director considered
casting Jack Nicholson – who better to embody the unrestrained ego and
brilliance, human frailty, abuses of power, passion and terror? (It has been
suggested that whispers of Napoleon survive in *The Shining*'s Jack Torrance.)

Keen for psychoanalysis to play a part, Kubrick wanted to examine power,
privilege and misjudgement – what brought about Napoleon's downfall? How
did a cautious man 'bungle' his Russian campaign? It was also to be a tragic
love story. 'Napoleon's romantic involvement with Josephine. . .' the director
marvelled, was 'one of the great obsessional passions of all time'. Josephine is
both Napoleon's weakness and his strength, and their relationship, a battlefield
in itself, parallels his spiritual marriage to France, replete with infidelity. The
orgasmic conquering of nations would be cut with furious copulation in
mirrored chambers for 'maximum erotica'. (Although the prospective actresses
listed by Alison Castle – Audrey Hepburn, Vanessa Redgrave and Julie Andrews
– promised less unbridled sensuality than a decent pot of Earl Grey.)

ROAST IN THE INFERNO
As with all Kubrick movies, *Napoleon* continued to evolve as the months of
micro-managed pre-production rolled on. 'I have had new ideas,' he insisted
in 1971, having consumed yet more books and conducted more research.
Yet beyond costumes tests – including photos Kubrick took himself with his
daughters Katharina and Anya providing scale – not a frame was ever shot.

Irony can be cruel: like Napoleon, Kubrick was undone by politics. As he slowly fashioned his magnum opus, the ailing MGM was acquired by hotelier Kirk Kerkorian. He balked at *Napoleon*'s spiralling cost and yanked the development money. Even those in Kubrick's camp could do little to argue that the film was good box office. Three rival Napoleon movies, concluding with Bondarchuk's *Waterloo*, had made it to cinemas as Kubrick dawdled over petticoat hems and field gun placements, but all of them flopped. Kubrick won neither love nor money from a studio that was barely greenlighting anything, let alone a film as grand as his. A last-ditch attempt to pass the project to United Artists met the same response: too expensive, too risky, too old-fashioned.

A crestfallen Kubrick moved on to a three-picture deal with Warner Bros. As if cleansing his palate, he began production on *A Clockwork Orange*. But the more you delve into *Napoleon*'s sprawling remains, the more you feel the film's defeat. War and history have never been embraced on this scale, or with this seriousness, or with such wit and romance. It is fitting, then, to conclude with a glimpse at how Kubrick was to portray Napoleon's own great folly: his tragically miscalculated invasion of Russia in the grip of unconquerable winter.

```
As they beat their retreat across 1,000 miles of frozen
waste, this highly organized army have become "a
starving, feverish mob." Entering a village, soldiers
and officers barricade themselves into a tiny house
along with their horses. Those soldiers left outside
try to fight their way in. When a fire breaks out, both
soldiers and horses roast in the inferno while those
outside rush forward to warm themselves by the flames
and cook horsemeat on their swords.
```

Whatever the cost, *Napoleon* would have been extraordinary. **IN**

WILL IT EVER HAPPEN?

3/10 When Steven Spielberg delved into the Kubrick archive, it was thought he might resurrect *Napoleon*. Spielberg chose to make *A.I.* (2001) instead, but in 2013 he told French television station Canal Plus that he was adapting Kubrick's screenplay for *Napoleon* into a TV miniseries with the help of Kubrick's family. Before Spielberg's announcement, there had been rumours of Michael Mann and Martin Scorsese being tempted by the screenplay and in February 2011, historical film-maker Erik Nelson had proposed a documentary based on the director's extensive *Napoleon* archive itself.

WHAT HAPPENED NEXT. . .

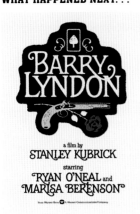

Kubrick was accepted with open arms at Warner Bros, which would fund whatever he chose to film, commencing with *A Clockwork Orange* (1971). He was never to face studio indifference again. And the exhaustive research didn't entirely go to waste: he siphoned much of his background material into a 1975 adaptation of William Thackeray's *Barry Lyndon*, which made impressive use of those Zeiss lenses. It is likely that *Barry Lyndon* was something of a surrogate for his pet project. And, as late as 1999's *Eyes Wide Shut*, scenes from his *Napoleon* script reappeared in new guises: Napoleon meeting a prostitute on a freezing winter night; an orgy sequence where couples cavort in plain view. In 1977, with *Roots* a hit on television, Kubrick claimed to critic Michel Ciment that he was toying with transforming *Napoleon* into a twenty-hour series starring Al Pacino. That turned out to be a passing whim – he had moved on and, tellingly, never formally offered Warner his *Napoleon* screenplay.

A FILM BY

ORSON WELLES

DON QUIXOTE

Francisco Reiguera | Akim Tamiroff | Oja Kodar | Beatrice Welles | Paola Mori

DON QUIXOTE

Director Orson Welles **Starring** Francisco Reiguera, Akim Tamiroff, Patty McCormack
Year 1969 **Country** Spain **Genre** Adventure

ORSON WELLES

'That's my own movie. . .' the director declared of his years-in-the-making *Don Quixote*. 'Is there such a thing as a home movie?. . . It's an experimental movie, a work that I love. . . When I'm finished with it, I'll release it.'

Orson Welles quit Hollywood in 1957. It was the second time he did so, but this time it was for good. Having announced his arrival with *Citizen Kane* (1941), barely recognizable as a Hollywood production, the director fought with the studios. His next three films – starting with *The Magnificent Ambersons* (1942) – were taken out of his hands and re-edited. Welles moved to Europe, where *Othello* (1952) took three years to make after his backers went bankrupt, and *Mr. Arkadin* (1955) was financed by old friend Louis Dolivet – who also wrested final cut from the director. Returning to Hollywood in 1956, Welles rebuilt his standing by appearing in *I Love Lucy* and directing TV pilots. When he landed *Touch of Evil* (1958), he was so keen to rejoin the system that he took wages only for acting in, rather than directing, the picture. He also brought it in on time and under budget. A multi-picture deal with Universal was mooted. History, however, was about to repeat itself.

DRIVEN MAD

When the director delivered a rough cut of *Touch of Evil*, Universal re-cut – and, in part, re-shot – the picture. Disgusted, Welles left for Mexico to start an independent adaptation of Miguel de Cervantes's *Don Quixote*, the tale of a medieval Spanish nobleman who, driven mad by romantic literature, takes to the road as a chivalric knight. The project was financed by Oscar Dancigers – a Mexican producer and collaborator of surrealist film-maker Luis Buñuel – who would be Welles's assistant director. (On viewing Universal's cut of *Touch of Evil*, Welles compiled a fifty-eight-page memo outlining all the changes that he considered crucial. The studio ignored him. The film-maker resumed work on *Don Quixote*, never to direct another picture in Hollywood.)

Quixote had been on his mind for several years. While filming *Mr. Arkadin* in Paris in 1955, Louis Dolivet had allowed him to shoot test footage in a park near the Seine. In scenes featuring the medieval characters transposed into a contemporary setting, *Arkadin* cast members Mischa Auer and Akim Tamiroff played the knight and his squire Sancho Panza respectively. Welles called the project *Don Quixote Passes By*, and hoped to sell it to CBS as part of a TV series on Spanish culture. Unimpressed studio executives squelched the idea.

AGED CHIVALRY
Stills from Jesús Franco's cut of Welles's film (see What Happened Next. . ., opposite) show Francisco Reiguera as Quixote and the iconic windmills that, in Cervantes's novel, the hero attacks, believing them to be giants. The scene, which gave rise to the phrase 'tilting at windmills', is alluded to but not featured in Welles's film.

Undeterred, Welles planned a feature contrasting the errant knight's idealistic chivalry with the modern world. 'I fell so completely in love with my subject,' he confessed, 'that I gradually made it longer and continued to shoot depending on how much money I had.' He recalled Tamiroff as Sancho Panza and replaced Auer with Francisco Reiguera, a political exile from Spain. Welles's friend Frank Sinatra invested $25,000 and the director hoped the singer would show at least some footage on his TV series *The Frank Sinatra Show*. Dancigers agreed to fund the rest of the eight-week shoot.

Filming in 16mm without either synch-sound or a completed script, Welles embraced the improvisational nature of early silent cinema. Using a technique he called 'pre-voicing', he recorded the dialogue himself before watching the footage. This established the kind of rhythm he wanted for the scene. He would then edit the image to that rhythm and redo the dialogue.

The only Cervantes-derived character – bar the knight and his squire – was Dulcinea, a farm girl who Quixote imagines to be his love. Now called Dulcie, she was played by twelve-year-old Patty McCormack (star of 1956's *The Bad Seed*). Welles was to play himself as a kind of narrator. When Dulcie finds him in a Mexican hotel reading Cervantes's novel, she asks if he is 'the famous Orson Welles' and enquires what he's reading. Welles takes her on his knee and begins to relate the duo's adventures. Dulcie later meets Quixote and Sancho and has her own adventures with them. One scene features the trio at the cinema. While Dulcie offers Sancho a lollipop, and shows him how to eat it, Quixote becomes enraged at the sword-and-sandal epic on-screen. Mistaking it for reality, he slashes the screen to jeers and cheers from the audience. As critic Jonathan Rosenbaum notes, the scene alludes to the iconic image of Quixote tilting at windmills and to a passage in the book in which he attacks a puppet show. Rosenbaum argues that the film should be considered a series of improvisations based on Cervantes's themes rather than a conventional adaptation.

PULLED THE PLUG
Inevitably, the shoot went over budget and Dancigers pulled the plug. Luis Buñuel remarked that the distraught director wept on the final day of filming, but the setback yielded an epiphany. Welles embraced *Quixote* as a project that he alone would control and vowed to fund the film from his own pocket. Over the next couple of years, he appeared as a performer in over a dozen for-hire jobs. Having returned to Europe in the early 1960s, he made a documentary series for Italian broadcasters RAI-TV. *Nella terra di Don Chisciotte* (In the Land of Don Quixote) was a straightforward travelogue that afforded Welles the chance to make money while he filmed scenes for his *Quixote* in Spain.

Production continued sporadically throughout the 1960s. Welles adapted Kafka's *The Trial* in 1962, taking a break from editing it in Paris to shoot in Málaga in Spain. McCormack, however, had grown up and could no longer play the young Dulcie. Welles toyed with the idea of a double, possibly using his own daughter, but eventually dropped the framing device altogether. (After Spanish dictator Francisco Franco's death in 1975, Welles altered the concept again, using the anachronistic characters of Quixote and Sancho to explore

Spain's new liberal democracy – which Welles did not view as necessarily a good thing. He had his own quixotic view of the country as some kind of Eden, in which any change was unwelcomed.) In 1964, he told *Cahiers du Cinéma* that audiences would hate *Don Quixote*, that it would be an 'execrated film', and, contrarily, that had *The Trial* been received more favourably by critics, he would have pushed ahead to finish *Quixote*.

ATOMIC APOCALYPSE

Principal photography was finished by 1969. Second unit work continued until 1972, when Tamiroff's death ended any chance of further shoots with the principals. That year, Welles joked to Rosenbaum that he might change the title to *When Will You Finish Don Quixote?*, and implied that other *Quixote* projects in development – Arthur Hiller's *Man of La Mancha* (1972) and Sergio Leone's unrealized adaptation – were delaying it. Rosenbaum, however, suspected the real stumbling block was the lack of a satisfactory conclusion. Cervantes's ending, in which Quixote renounces his delusions and dies, was too traumatic for Welles: a world where Quixote was no longer needed was not one in which he wished to live. He had planned an ending where Quixote and Sancho reached the Moon, but that was scuppered when the United States did just that. He even devised a finale in which the duo miraculously survive an atomic apocalypse. Sadly, neither that nor any other suitable ending was ever filmed.

In 1984, now living in LA, he returned to Europe to collect a workprint, and edited it in his garage until his death the following year. But no definitive cut could be assembled, even by Welles. Audrey Stainton, his secretary in the late 1950s, described *Quixote* to *Sight & Sound* as 'intensely private and personal – almost a secret psychoanalysis of Orson Welles'. The project had become more than a film: it was a living document, constantly in flux as his perception of the world changed. How could there be a single cut of that? **DN**

WILL IT EVER HAPPEN?

Film reels were scattered among (latterly warring) friends and collaborators in the United States and Europe, many mislabelled to prevent third parties knowing the correct sequence. Welles had also used coded slates during the shoot to ward off interference. Even if all of the footage could be brought together, the changes that he made to the concept over time and the fact that nobody could faithfully edit it in the way Welles would have wanted mean that the chances of realizing his vision are slim.

WHAT HAPPENED NEXT...

After Welles's death in 1985, archivists at the Cinémathèque Française worked with Greek director Costa-Gavras on a forty-five-minute cut of scenes and outtakes from *Quixote* that was shown at Cannes in 1986. Two years later, at a Welles convention hosted by New York University, Oja Kodar (Welles's mistress and collaborator for the last two decades of his life) presented a cut of similar length that Jonathan Rosenbaum claimed to be the most authentic representation of Welles's vision. Kodar then approached Spanish director Jesús Franco (Welles's second unit director on 1965's *Chimes at Midnight*, but better known for his softcore horror films) to make a feature-length cut. His version (left) – premiered at Cannes in 1992 and issued on video in Europe shortly afterwards – was a travesty of Welles's vision. Quite apart from the awful quality of the print he used, Franco arbitrarily included footage from Welles's Italian TV travelogue and butchered the original footage with optical zooms and shoddy mattes.

Chapter 3
The Seventies

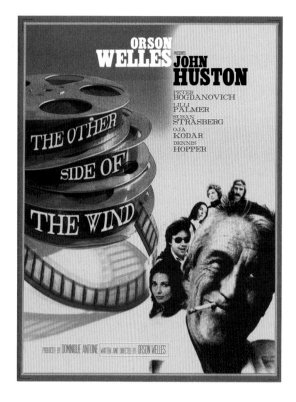

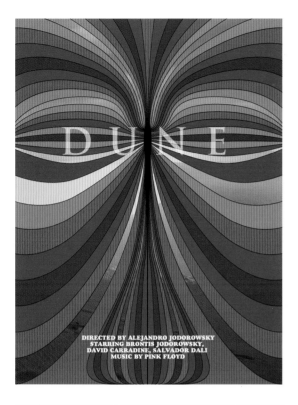

DIRECTED BY ALEJANDRO JODOROWSKY
STARRING BRONTIS JODOROWSKY,
DAVID CARRADINE, SALVADOR DALI
MUSIC BY PINK FLOYD

SEAN CONNERY is JAMES BOND

WARHEAD

What appears...   ...has first to disappear

BASED ON AN ORIGINAL STORY BY KEVIN McCLORY "WARHEAD" STARRING SEAN CONNERY
SCREENPLAY BY JACK WHITTINGHAM and SEAN CONNERY PRODUCED BY JACK SCHWARTZMAN DIRECTED BY KEVIN McCLORY

NEXT SUMMER
THE TREK CONTINUES

STAR TREK
PLANET OF THE TITANS

From the director of *Faster, Pussycat! Kill! Kill!* and *Beyond the Valley of the Dolls*

WHO KILLED BAMBI?

directed by
RUSS MEYER
written by
ROGER EBERT & RORY JOHNSTON
starring
THE SEX PISTOLS
with MARIANNE FAITHFULL
MALCOM MCLAREN and JAMES AUBREY

PIPPI LONGSTOCKING,
THE STRONGEST GIRL IN THE WORLD

Director Hayao Miyazaki **Year** 1971 **Country** Japan **Genre** Animated fantasy **Studio** A Pro

HAYAO MIYAZAKI
In addition to Pippi Longstocking's influence on the director's later work (see Will It Ever Happen?, opposite), the drawings Miyazaki made in Visby, on Sweden's Gotland, were recycled to form part of the town of Koriko in 1989's *Kiki's Delivery Service*.

Hayao Miyazaki is one of the world's greatest animators, whose work is characterized by feisty young heroines in magical settings. Swedish author Astrid Lindgren is the creator of one of *the* figures in children's literature: a fiery nine-year-old girl with superhuman strength. A perfect match, surely. But Miyazaki's dream of making an anime version of Lindgren's Pippi Longstocking came to nothing. And nobody seems to know why.

PIPPI, A PROPOSAL AND POSSESSION
Lindgren created freckly, pigtailed redhead Pippi when her daughter was sick in bed and demanded a story. The character first appeared in print in three books published between 1945 and 1948. These became a success around the world – Pippi's adventures have been translated into sixty-four languages. It's easy to see the appeal of a rebellious, bully-trouncing kid, prone to huge lies, who lives in an adult-free villa with her friends – a monkey and a horse.

Pippi quickly graduated to the big screen. A 1949 Swedish adaptation reportedly angered Lindgren by tinkering with the characters and having nine-year-old Pippi played by a twenty-six-year-old, which perhaps explains why the author became so possessive about her creation. Twenty years later, a more successful, authorized television series was made in Sweden. Cobbled together and dubbed, this became two feature films for US release. In 1971, Toei Animation graduate Miyazaki and collaborator Isao Takahata, with whom he would co-found Studio Ghibli, joined a studio called A Pro and began pre-production on their Pippi adaptation. So keen was Miyazaki that he took his first trip abroad, to Sweden. He made extensive location sketches in the port city of Visby on the island of Gotland, where the 1969 TV series had been filmed. Miyazaki and Takahata also met Lindgren to discuss their proposal, which was to be entitled *Pippi Longstocking, The Strongest Girl in the World*.

Subsequently, however, she denied permission and the project was shelved. The most likely explanation is that the fiercely protective author was worried about losing control of her best-loved character. It's worth noting that, in 1971,

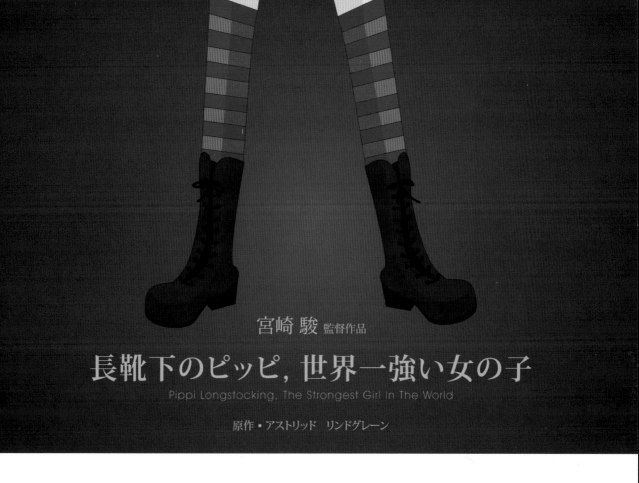

宮崎　駿 監督作品

長靴下のピッピ，世界一強い女の子

Pippi Longstocking, The Strongest Girl In The World

原作・アストリッド　リンドグレーン

Miyazaki was an unknown. His first feature, *The Castle of Cagliostro*, was eight years away; the Studio Ghibli glory days that began with 1986's *Castle in the Sky* were even further. But given how brilliantly he adapted Diana Wynne Jones's *Howl's Moving Castle* (2004) and Mary Norton's *The Borrowers* (as 2010's *Arrietty*), this must be one of the greatest missed opportunities in animation.

Lindgren apparently endorsed later adaptations, from a 1982 Soviet TV musical (*Peppi Dlinnyychulok*) to the 1988 US film *The New Adventures of Pippi Longstocking*. The latter bagged two Razzie nominations, including one for child model Tami Erin, who beat 8,000 applicants to bag the title role. An animated adaptation eventually appeared in 1997: a box-office flop by Canadian animators Nelvana that served as an HBO TV pilot. Lindgren died, aged ninety-four, in 2002 – a year before Miyazaki's *Spirited Away* (2001) became the first anime film to win an Oscar. A huge commercial success, it earned more at the Japanese box office than *Titanic* (1997). **RA**

WHAT HAPPENED NEXT. . .
The 1983 art book *Hayao Miyazaki Image Board* revealed typically beautiful watercolours that Miyazaki completed for the aborted Pippi Longstocking project. They also demonstrate Pippi's influence on Mimiko, the red-haired, freckled, pigtailed protagonist of 1972's short *Panda Kopanda* (Panda! Go Panda!), and the young Mei in 1988's *Tonari no Totoro* (My Neighbour Totoro).

WILL IT EVER HAPPEN?
1/10 As recently as 2008, the influence of Lindgren's creation on Miyazaki could be felt: what is the eponymous, wilful, red-haired fish-girl of *Ponyo*, if not an aquatic Pippi? Even if Miyazaki never gets to make the film he planned in 1971, one could argue that he's effectively been doing so ever since.

THE DAY THE CLOWN CRIED

DIRECTED BY AND STARRING
JERRY LEWIS

THE DAY THE CLOWN CRIED

Director Jerry Lewis **Starring** Jerry Lewis, Harriet Andersson, Pierre Etaix **Year** 1972 **Country** US **Genre** Comic drama

A comedian renowned for slapstick directs and stars in a concentration-camp comedy. He plays an adult who attempts to distract attention from the horrors of the Holocaust by pretending it's all just a game. The project attracts controversy, but its humour and pathos win over critics and audiences. The comedian earns an Oscar for Best Actor and makes a memorable appearance at the Academy Awards. . . But that's enough about Roberto Benigni's 1997 film *Life Is Beautiful*. Rewind twenty-five years and we find a remarkably similar project with a dramatically different outcome.

WRETCHEDLY UNFUNNY

Jerry Lewis had made his name in a duo with Dean Martin before becoming a comic star in his own right with such films as 1960's *The Bellboy* and 1963's *The Nutty Professor*. By the mid 1960s, however, Lewis was getting a little long in the tooth for juvenile antics. His slapstick style slipped out of fashion – except in France, where they retained a curious affection for him – and his film career was on the slide. In a bid to stop the rot, Lewis tapped into the rich comic potential of Nazis with 1970's *Which Way to the Front?*, which he directed and starred in, playing a rich US playboy who impersonates a wartime German general. 'You vill see *Which Way to the Front?* and you vill laugh!' screamed the poster. Critics begged to differ. 'One of Jerry's worst,' complained Leonard Maltin. 'Wretchedly unfunny. . . the cinematic equivalent of vanity publishing,' agreed Leslie Halliwell.

Undeterred, Lewis upped the ante with his next project. Done right, it could have blazed a trail for some of film's greatest comedies, from Monty Python's *Life of Brian* (1979) to Chris Morris's *Four Lions* (2010), produced by artists brave enough to push boundaries and break taboos. As far back as 1940, Charlie Chaplin realized that the most effective way to suck power from the iconography of fascism is to lampoon it. The result was his masterpiece, *The Great Dictator*. But to pull off such projects successfully, you need an intimate understanding of your target, a mastery of tone and a clear vision of what you hope to achieve. These were qualities conspicuously lacking in the jaw-dropping festival of wrongness that was Lewis's *The Day the Clown Cried*.

JERRY LEWIS
Nearly thirty years after touring the remains of Auschwitz and Dachau to prepare himself for the film, Lewis was asked at a 2001 press conference when it would be released. His answer: 'None of your goddamn business!'

Co-written by Joan O'Brien, who created the 1960s US TV sitcom *To Rome with Love*, and TV critic Charles Denton, the script had been knocking around for more than a decade. At various times, it had attracted the attention of Bobby Darin and Dick Van Dyke. In 1971, Lewis was offered the opportunity to direct and star by producer Nathan Wachsberger, who promised full financial backing. He found the script deeply moving, but fretted over whether it was a suitable vehicle for Lewis's familiar comic persona.

The actor recorded his response to Wachsberger in a 1982 autobiography, *Jerry Lewis: In Person*: "'Why don't you try to get Sir Laurence Olivier? I mean, he doesn't find it too difficult to choke to death playing Hamlet. My bag is

> ### 'My bag is comedy. . . and you're asking me if I'm prepared to deliver helpless kids into a gas chamber.'
> Jerry Lewis

comedy, Mr. Wachsberger, and you're asking me if I'm prepared to deliver helpless kids into a gas chamber. Ho-ho. Some laugh – how do I pull it off?" He shrugged and sat back. After a long moment of silence I picked up the script. "What a horror. . . It must be told"'.

We too can pick up the script, as versions are available online. They make interesting reading. Helmut Doork (or Dorque) is a washed-up German circus clown, arrested by the Gestapo for performing a drunken impersonation of Hitler in a bar. While his loving wife Ada searches for him, Helmut is taken to a prison camp, where he's taunted and bullied by other inmates. When Jewish prisoners start to arrive, Helmut rediscovers his love of performance by entertaining the children, even though they are segregated and separated by barbed wire. This earns the respect and admiration of the bullies. Then a new commandant arrives and orders that Helmut must be stopped. He defies the ruling and is savagely beaten and put into solitary confinement. But the commandant is persuaded that the clown could have his uses in keeping

BEHIND THE SCENES
Left At the Cirque d'Hiver in Paris in March 1972, Lewis jokes with co-star Pierre Etaix, director of Oscar-winning short *Heureux Anniversaire* (1962).
Right Lewis on set in April that year.

Jewish children distracted while they are loaded onto a boxcar to Auschwitz. Alas, a cruel twist of fate results in Helmut being trapped aboard the train with them. At the death camp, he pleads to be allowed to lead the kids, Pied Piper-style, into the gas chambers, to spare them the horror of their fate until the very end. As they giggle at his routine, the final credits roll.

There's nothing intrinsically wrong with the story – which could, in the right hands, have been transformed into a moving slice of awards bait. Lewis's hands, however, were not the right ones. Not that his commitment to his first serious role could be faulted: despite a reliance on painkillers, he shed forty pounds for the death-camp scenes and toured Auschwitz and Dachau in search of inspiration. To underline the project's sober intent, Ingmar Bergman favourite Harriet Andersson was hired to play Ada. But things started to go wrong the moment principal photography began in Sweden. Wachsberger ran out of cash, forcing Lewis to finance the film himself. The producer also neglected to pay O'Brien for the rights to the story. *The Day the Clown Cried* has, consequently, been tied up in litigation ever since and remains unreleased to this day.

HORRIBLY AWRY
But red tape is not the only reason so few people have seen the finished film. O'Brien, who died in 2004, complained that Lewis had altered the character of Helmut to make him more sympathetic. As written, he is arrogant and self-centred. Lewis was having none of that: he insisted the role have more pathos (read: mawkish sentimentality). This, she argued, fatally unbalanced the story.

In 1992, *Spy* magazine gathered together people who had actually seen *The Day the Clown Cried* to solicit their thoughts. Among them was Harry Shearer – star of *This Is Spinal Tap* (1984) and a voice artist on *The Simpsons* – who had been shown a rough cut in 1979. His verdict was damning: 'With most of these kinds of things, you find that the anticipation, or the concept, is better than the thing itself. But seeing this film was really awe-inspiring, in that you are rarely in the presence of a perfect object. This was a perfect object. This movie is so drastically wrong, its pathos and its comedy are so wildly misplaced, that you could not, in your fantasy of what it might be like, improve on what it really is. Oh My God! – that's all you can say.'

Thus did the horror that 'must be told' go horribly awry. Had it simply been well-meaning but misguided, and completed without incident, *The Day the Clown Cried* may have merely attracted poor reviews and been promptly forgotten. But the tantalizing accounts of Shearer and others cement its reputation as the most extraordinary cult classic we'll probably never see. **RA**

WHAT HAPPENED NEXT. . .
In 1977, Lewis was nominated for the Nobel Peace Prize for his tireless fundraising for the Muscular Dystrophy Association, but didn't make another film until 1980's aptly entitled *Hardly Working*. He did, however, make a memorable appearance in Martin Scorsese's prescient meditation on fame, *The King of Comedy*, in 1983 (below). Denton, O'Brien and Wachsberger are all deceased. Harriet Andersson returned to art movies, notably Lars von Trier's *Dogville* (2003).

WILL IT EVER HAPPEN?

5/10 It *has* happened. But whether we'll ever see it is another matter. Lewis reportedly owns a rough cut on VHS, which he screens for acquaintances. Legal red tape means that it's unlikely ever to receive wider distribution. Laurence Klavan's 2005 novel *The Shooting Script* centres on a fan's quest to track down a copy of the film. Maybe someone will option that.

ORSON WELLES
PRESENTS
JOHN HUSTON
PETER BOGDANOVICH
LILLI PALMER
SUSAN STRASBERG
OJA KODAR
DENNIS HOPPER
THE OTHER SIDE OF THE WIND
PRODUCED BY DOMINIQUE ANTOINE
WRITTEN AND DIRECTED BY ORSON WELLES

THE OTHER SIDE OF THE WIND

Director Orson Welles **Starring** John Huston, Peter Bogdanovich, Dennis Hopper **Year** *c*.1973 **Country** US **Genre** Drama

The Other Side of the Wind, an experimental picture about an ageing director's struggles to finish his final film is, along with *Don Quixote* (see page 77), a key unseen element of the Orson Welles catalogue. A satire charting the death rattle of the studio system and the rise of 'New Hollywood' (when young film-makers began to wrest control from the majors), the picture was born from two sources. In the late 1960s, Welles had worked on a script called *The Sacred Beasts*, about a macho film-maker – loosely based on 1922's *The Prisoner of Zenda*'s Irish director Rex Ingram and hard-living author Ernest Hemingway – who spends his twilight years following bullfights in Spain (the basis of Hemingway's final book, the posthumously published *The Dangerous Summer*). Welles wanted to make it with documentary film-makers Albert and David Maysles. However, dissatisfied with the script, he merged it with a story by Yugoslavian actress, and his future mistress, Oja Kodar. This concerned a charismatic director who suppresses his latent homosexual desires for his leading man by seeking to seduce his leading lady, the actor's lover – reasoning that, if he cannot physically possess the man, he can at least take his woman.

ORSON WELLES, JOHN HUSTON
'Orson is not a man who can bow down to idiots,' Huston (above right, with Welles) told *Rolling Stone*. 'And Hollywood is full of them. Orson has a big ego. But I've always found him to be completely logical. And he's a joy.'

OUT TO SEDUCE

Filmed on and off over almost seven years, beginning in 1970, *The Other Side of the Wind* is structured around a single evening – one 2 July, the anniversary of Hemingway's suicide. Ageing director Jake Hannaford (played by film-maker John Huston) is thrown a birthday party by wealthy friend Zarah Valeska (one-time stage and screen darling Lilli Palmer). He shows the guests footage from his new project: an Antonioni-esque art film completely at odds with his previous work. Actor Robert Random (who played Barnabas Rogers in the TV Western series *Iron Horse,* 1966–68) is the film-within-a-film's lead, with Kodar as his co-star, the woman Hannaford is out to seduce.

Welles's friend and benefactor Peter Bogdanovich plays a young director to whom Hannaford is passing the torch – a scenario redolent of Welles and Bogdanovich's real-life relationship. The former described the film as 'a dirty movie', adding – with reference to his friend's *The Last Picture Show* (1971) –

HOPPER, FORD AND HUSTON
Dennis Hopper and John Huston's association predated their starring in *The Other Side of the Wind*. In 1971, they visited John Ford (who directed one of Welles's favourite films, 1939's *Stagecoach*). 'I told Mr Ford that I had gotten permission from his wife to get him into his wheelchair so we could take a photograph together,' Hopper recalled. 'Mr Ford replied, "Kid, you know what your problem is? You've got no sense of drama: if you had a sense of drama you'd get in bed with me."'

'If you can make one, I can.' Bogdanovich later reported, 'Orson said to me, "If anything happens to me, you will make sure you finish it, won't you?"' Among others to be drawn into the movie was Dennis Hopper (see left).

The picture has two distinct aesthetics, alternating between the night of the party and Hannaford's own film. The scenes at the party were shot in faux-documentary style, as though captured by a news crew attending the event, and were to be cut in a fast-paced style, not dissimilar to the one Welles later employed in his and Kodar's *F for Fake* (1973). 'The word didn't exist at the time, but it's what we now call a "mockumentary,"' Bogdanovich (at whose home the party was filmed) told the *New York Sun*. In contrast, the scenes from Hannaford's film, called *The Other Side of the Wind*, were shot in colour

> *'Orson said to me, "If anything happens to me, you will make sure you finish it, won't you?"'*
>
> Peter Bogdanovich

in a languid, European style. Between the narratives, the tension between director and actor is teased out against a backdrop of hangers-on and sexual excess.

In common with most of Welles's pictures, completed or otherwise, the production was far from straightforward. Quite aside from the protracted shoot (Huston didn't join the film until 1973), behind-the-scenes jockeying for finance ultimately crippled the picture. Unable to fully fund it himself, Welles sought backing from other sources – something he was loath to do as he felt it always came with complications. His Palme d'Or-winning *Othello* (1952), for instance, had taken three years to make after his backers went bankrupt, and the plug was also pulled on his *Don Quixote*.

Through French producer Dominique Antoine, Welles struck a deal with Mehdi Bousheri, the Shah of Iran's brother-in-law. This relationship brought

TEST FOOTAGE
The inspiration for *The Other Side of the Wind*'s supercilious Juliet Rich (played by Susan Strasberg, top left) was Pauline Kael. The *New Yorker* critic had incurred Welles's wrath by suggesting that *Citizen Kane*'s co-screenwriter Herman J. Mankiewicz deserved equal credit for that classic; John Huston (top right) was a friend of Hemingway, on whom his character was based. The actor was unsurprised when the writer shot himself: 'It was exactly what I would have expected him to do. . . He was on his way out mentally'; Oja Kodar (bottom right), Welles's collaborator and sometime muse, was featured in scenes that the director admitted were 'almost. . . pornographic'; Strasberg with Peter Bogdanovich (bottom left), whose support of Welles extended long beyond the director's death.

several obstacles, not least Bousheri's insistence that he would only fund Welles though an intermediary, a Spanish producer who played both sides off against each other and ended up embezzling $250,000. Not believing Welles's claim that the money had never reached him, the Iranians lobbied for his removal, citing him as a liability. Of course, everybody working on the film was only doing so because of Welles, so firing him proved unrealistic.

When filming was complete, and amid legal action by the Iranians, Welles spent years editing the picture. His fast-cutting technique (decades away from being popularized by MTV and the likes of Michael Bay) proved hard to pull off, involving five editing machines running side by side. Matters were further complicated by 1979's Iranian Revolution. The country's new ruler, Ayatollah Khomeini, considered the film part of the deposed Shah's estate, and therefore the property of Iran, and ordered the negatives to be locked in a Parisian vault – although not before Welles smuggled out several prints to work on.

TOO MANY ARE DEAD

'I'm going to do it as an entirely different film,' he promised critic Bill Krohn in 1982. 'I'm going to stand outside of it and talk about it. . . Less as a narrator, and more as myself. . . The only way to make sense of it now – because too many of the actors are dead – is for me to show it to an audience somewhere, like at UCLA, and have me talking about it with them. But there's not much interest in the "essay movie". I had a great failure with *F for Fake*. . . but I'm hoping that the age of the cassette is going to change that, so I can go back to the business of talking directly with the audience, as I did in *F for Fake*.'

'So many of his things go unfinished,' John Huston observed to *Rolling Stone* in 1981. 'I don't know why. . . Even the one that we did together, *The Other Side of the Wind*. I haven't seen a foot of it myself, and I don't know why it hasn't been released. Now, there's always a reason. But it's happened too often with Orson for it to be entirely accidental.' Ultimately, the director edited only about forty-five minutes of the film. Cinematographer Gary Graver mourned the loss of what 'could be considered one of Welles's great films. . . Its release could make people re-evaluate Welles's legacy'. **DN**

WHAT HAPPENED NEXT. . .
Kodar, Bogdanovich (below) and Graver, the *New York Sun* reported, 'continued their attempts to finish the film. . . Lawrence French, [who] has written extensively on Welles and has read the screenplay, agreed that the film is a masterpiece. But he also cautioned that editing such a complex picture will present unique challenges to Mr Bogdanovich's team. "No one has ever managed to duplicate Orson's unique editing style," Mr French said. "It defies description. He does things you don't realize he's doing. Sometimes it isn't even logical."'

WILL IT EVER HAPPEN?

3/10 Given that Oja Kodar was the star and co-writer (and actually directed some sequences), it's possible she could finish it. However, legal disputes – first with the Iranians, then with Welles's estate (Kodar was bequeathed the rights to Welles's unfinished works in his will, but his daughter Beatrice has contested this numerous times) – have hindered efforts to bring the project to fruition. Kodar and Bogdanovich have hinted that a release could be forthcoming, the stumbling block being securing funding while keeping creative control – something Kodar, no doubt mindful of the 'restoration' of Welles's *Don Quixote* by Jesús Franco, won't compromise on. Although the film's formal experimentation will have lost its shock value over the years, the prospect of a new Welles, however remote, remains something to hope for.

THE TEMPEST

Director Michael Powell **Starring** James Mason, Mia Farrow, Michael York,
Topol, Vittorio De Sica, Malcolm McDowell **Year** 1975 **Genre** Drama

MICHAEL POWELL
'I had a way of doing the story that wasn't
just Shakespeare but a bit of Powell as
well,' the director told *Time Out*'s Trevor
Johnston in 1986. 'Everyone loved the
cast, but we couldn't get the money.'

Which came first: Michael Powell's disillusionment with cinema or the industry's rejection of him? The great formalist created masterpieces in the 1940s with his film-making partner Emeric Pressburger. But by the late 1950s they were enjoying less success as kitchen-sink realism – the antithesis of the duo's style – swept British cinema. After his partnership with Pressburger ended, one of the first films Powell directed was *Peeping Tom* (1960). It would also be one of the last. A disturbing portrait of a voyeuristic serial killer, it was met with vitriol by critics, who branded Powell a pornographer. He directed only three more big-screen features, two shot in Australia: a whimpering end to the career of one of Britain's greatest directors.

ALL-STAR PRODUCTION
Nonetheless, Powell pursued one project for the best part of a decade: his interpretation of *The Tempest*, Shakespeare's tale of a Milanese duke, Prospero, exiled to a deserted island with his daughter Miranda, and the storm he conjures to lure to the shore those who had betrayed him. It was an idea that came to Powell in the early 1950s. Envisioning a lavish, all-star production, he wanted John Gielgud for Prospero, knowing it was the actor's dream role (Gielgud had narrated Powell's 1941 short *An Airman's Letter to His Mother*), and Moira Shearer – who had starred in his *The Red Shoes* (1948) – for Ariel (an island spirit and Prospero's reluctant servant). Unfortunately, their schedules didn't fit with Powell's plans and the idea was abandoned.

By the close of the 1960s, Powell was an exile from the British film industry. Coming off shooting *Age of Consent* (1969), he roused his creative ambition and returned to *The Tempest*. Having established a close working relationship with actor James Mason on *Age of Consent*, he had found his Prospero. For Ariel, he envisaged Mia Farrow, a movie star in the wake of *Rosemary's Baby* (1968). But despite these big names, Powell found it difficult to raise funding. Over the next few years he wrote and rewrote the script and eventually secured backing from London-based Greek producer Frixos Constantine, with whom he formed Poseidon Films to make the picture. Michael York (who had graced screen adaptations of *The Taming of the Shrew* and *Romeo and Juliet*, in 1967

Poster: Damian Jaques

THE TEMPEST

A FILM BY MICHAEL POWELL

and 1968, respectively), Malcolm McDowell (star of 1968's *If. . .*), Topol (star of 1971's *Fiddler on the Roof*) and Vittorio De Sica all agreed to take parts (although De Sica, director of 1948's *Bicycle Thieves*, died in November 1974, before the screenplay was completed). There was also interest at various points from British comic actor Frankie Howerd and *Kojak* star Telly Savalas.

Powell saw Prospero as a Renaissance man, an heir of Leonardo da Vinci and Italian explorer Amerigo Vespucci, and wrote a new introductory scene in Elizabethan English that established Prospero as a contemporary of Galileo. When Powell read the scene aloud to James Mason, the actor interrupted to ask, 'Is that Shakespeare?' 'No,' the director replied dryly. 'No, it's Powell.' The scene also featured an orchestral overture by André Previn (at the time, Mia Farrow's husband). Cartoonist Gerald Scarfe – later to work on Pink Floyd's movie *The Wall* (1982) – was hired to design the sets, which Powell wanted to appear un-naturalistic, as if in a painting. He told Scarfe to take cues from Hieronymous Bosch's painting *The Garden of Earthly Delights*. Prospero's cell, from which he observes and controls the island, was to be carved into the side of a skull-shaped mountain, itself representing Prospero's mind (later it would be revealed to be hollow, containing only cogs and pulleys). The second half of the film, in which Prospero turns nature and his machines on those he has lured to shore, would have referenced another painting: Goya's *The Colossus*, which depicts people fleeing from a giant so tall that he breaks the clouds.

> 'We had very good actors, a great script. . . It was a tragedy for the film industry that it didn't take place.'
>
> Frixos Constantine

In a deviation from the text, the final scene featured Caliban (a monster, raised by Prospero, who Powell imagined as a Minotaur-like figure) dancing on the sandy shore, watching a royal fleet take Prospero and Miranda home, the island finally left under the control of Caliban and Ariel.

FINANCIAL DISASTER

The picture – now entitled *Trikimia*, a Greek translation of the original title – was scheduled to shoot on the Greek island of Rhodes in 1975. Powell had tapped Jack Cardiff as director of photography, having worked with him on many of his and Pressburger's greatest films. However, at the last moment, the project collapsed. Constantine had enough money to develop the picture and get it into production, but needed further financing to pay for the cast and post-production. He hoped to raise this with a distribution deal, but found no takers. 'We had very good actors, a great script and it was a tragedy for the film industry that it didn't take place,' the producer told the *Independent*. 'I still think it was one of my biggest failures.'

He and Powell suspected the Rank Organisation – specifically, its chairman, John Davis – of pressuring interested parties to drop out. Rank had produced and distributed most of Powell and Pressburger's masterpieces, including

WE CAN'T ALL BE LION-TAMERS
Unrealized projects by Powell (above right) and Emeric Pressburger (above left), listed on powell-pressburger.org, include *The Golden Years*, a biopic of Richard Strauss. Columbia nixed the idea, possibly owing to Strauss's links to the Nazis (the composer had been coerced into allowing his music to be used as propaganda). Instead, the studio offered them *Lawrence of Arabia*, produced by Alexander Korda, which they declined. This ultimately worked out quite well for director David Lean.

The Life and Death of Colonel Blimp (1943), *A Matter of Life and Death* (1946), *Black Narcissus* (1947) and *The Red Shoes* (1948). It was with the latter that the relationship soured. When Davis and company founder J. Arthur Rank saw the film, they walked out without a word, convinced it would be a financial disaster. In fact, it did modest business in the UK and opened in just one theatre in the United States, but ran continuously for over two years – convincing Universal to give it a wide release, ultimately making it highly profitable. Refusing to work with producers who did not appreciate their work, Powell and Pressburger left Rank for Alexander Korda (British directors David Lean and Carol Reed also left Rank for Korda, owing to creative differences).

FURTHER ACRIMONY

However, working with Korda didn't live up to the duo's expectations, so they accepted an olive branch from Rank. Davis was eager to sign them to a long-term seven-picture deal – but, wary of further acrimony, they committed only to a single film, 1957's *Ill Met by Moonlight*. Powell later conceded that not signing the deal Davis offered was a mistake. He and Pressburger never made another full-length feature together, and it became clear that the latter had long protected Powell from producers – and, arguably, from himself.

Peeping Tom led Powell to be ostracized by the UK film industry, but it particularly infuriated Davis and Rank. Without Pressburger to rein in his recklessness, Powell wrote the character Don Jarvis (no subtlety even in the spoonerism) as a merciless send-up of John Davis. Rank, then the major force in British cinema, washed their hands of him. Powell believed Davis had muscled the Children's Film Foundation into axing *The Magic Umbrella*, a planned sequel to his children's short *The Boy Who Turned Yellow* (1972). Whether Davis had a hand in it (and it's hard to believe Powell's exile wasn't to some extent self-imposed), the director never made another feature film. A couple of years after his death in 1990, his opening scene for *The Tempest* was filmed as a tribute to him by the BBC arts programme *The Late Show*, giving viewers the opportunity to wonder, 'Is that Shakespeare?' No. It's Powell. **DN**

WILL IT EVER HAPPEN?

1/10 Although the script and extensive production notes exist, it's unlikely that anyone will film Powell's unorthodox take on *The Tempest*. In 1979, avant-garde film-maker Derek Jarman released his own adaptation, admitting that he felt he had 'inherited' the project from Powell. It received another outlandish treatment courtesy of Peter Greenaway, whose *Prospero's Books* (1991) finally allowed John Gielgud to star amid a mostly naked cast.

WHAT HAPPENED NEXT...

MICHAEL
POWELL
A LIFE IN MOVIES

AN AUTOBIOGRAPHY

Powell returned to his Gloucestershire home and abandoned his cinematic career, occupying himself with two very entertaining volumes of autobiography (left). The only film work he did was *Return to the Edge of the World* (1978), a short, made-for-TV coda to *The Edge of the World* (1937), his first major picture as a director

(starring Belle Chrystall and Niall MacGinnis, right). Under John Davis, the glory days of Rank slowly faded away, the company distributing films from the *Carry On* series and horrible remakes of Hitchcock pictures. Eventually they abandoned film production entirely and consolidated themselves as a leisure holdings company.

DUNE

Director Alejandro Jodorowsky **Starring** Brontis Jodorowsky, David Carradine, Salvador Dalí
Year 1977 **Budget** $10 million **Country** France **Genre** Sci-fi

ALEJANDRO JODOROWSKY
In the singular style of the cowboy he played in the 1970 Western *El Topo* (The Mole, above), Jodorowsky approached *Dune* in maverick fashion. 'I did not want to respect the novel,' he wrote. 'I wanted to recreate it. For me, *Dune* did not belong to Herbert as *Don Quixote* did not belong to Cervantes.'

The rights to one of the world's most-thumbed paperbacks were in the hands of one of its strangest men in 1974. A former mime artist, one-time adviser to Marcel Marceau and avant-garde performance artist, Chilean-born Alejandro Jodorowsky was an underground phenomenon. Labelled a madman (often by his admirers), he embraced the term as a compliment. His plays, like 1965's four-hour *Melodrama Sacramental*, featured goose-killing, plate-smashing, self-flagellation and symbolic castration. His breakout 1970 film *El Topo* – a psychedelic Western about a black-clad cowboy – invented the cult midnight movie business. Jodorowsky's fans cherished his cosmic take on the world and his freaky idiosyncrasies, which often involved cryptic symbolism, violence and modish nudity. With money put up by John Lennon, Jodorowsky followed *El Topo* with *The Holy Mountain* (1973), an even more outlandish fusion of mysticism, eroticism, hallucinogenic drugs, a tiger, a hippo, real-life shaman and transvestites from a New York rock club. (It suffered a minor setback early in pre-production when Lennon's fellow ex-Beatle George Harrison dropped out, unnerved by a script that required him to show his anus.) But *Dune* was to be the big one: his transcendental epic – a film about a messiah (a prophet if not indeed a god) that would actually *be* messianic.

NATURAL HALLUCINATIONS

An interplanetary feudal saga, *Dune* originated in 1965 as the first in a series of novels by US sci-fi author Frank Herbert. It concerns a valuable, neo-narcotic substance called The Spice, over which two dynasties – the house of Atreides and the house of Harkonnen – wage internecine war. The drug angle was not incidental. Jodorowsky, forty-five when he began work on the movie, was graduating from an interest in surrealism to a more rarefied fascination with transcendental enlightenment. He wanted to induce natural hallucinations by, as he relates in the documentary *Jodorowsky's Dune* (2012), creating 'something sacred, free, with new perspectives [that would] open the mind'.

The director had never read the book, but claimed the impetus to make *Dune* came to him 'in a lucid dream' while he was staying in New York. He rose at 6 a.m., waited for the nearest bookstore to open, read the book in

Poster: Damian Jaques

one sitting, without pausing to eat or drink, and finished it at midnight. When he put it down, the first person he called was twenty-six-year-old Parisian film distributor Michel Seydoux, a millionaire cineaste who had distributed *The Holy Mountain* in France but had no feature film production experience whatsoever. Jodorowsky proposed that they buy the rights and make an international co-production for $10 million: thirteen times the budget of his last movie. Although he too had not read *Dune* – 'I think,' the director speculated, 'the prose of Herbert annoyed him' – Seydoux was in, and arranged to meet Jodorowsky in LA to make the deal. (A more prosaic version of this story has Seydoux, after his involvement in *The Holy Mountain*, mooting the idea of doing a film together. Jodorowsky – at the time broke and needing to support his family – suggests *Dune* and, when Seydoux agrees, is obliged to quickly read it.)

Hollywood wasn't interested, believing *Dune* to be unfilmable and regarding science fiction as a fading genre that had already peaked with Stanley Kubrick's *2001: A Space Odyssey* in 1968. Jodorowsky, however, wanted to go further than Kubrick. 'I was against *2001* realism,' he said later. 'I wanted operas,

THE JOY OF SCI-FI

Among Jodorowsky's key collaborators was *The Joy of Sex* illustrator Chris Foss (an example of whose art is below). Of his input, the director said: 'I was grateful for the existence of my friend. He brought the colours of the apocalypse to the sad machines of a future without imagination.'

spaceships. . . something baroque and organic.' In a grudging nod to Kubrick's achievement, the first person the director approached was *2001*'s photographic effects supervisor Douglas Trumbull, but Jodorowsky 'was unable to swallow his vanity, his airs of business leader, and his exorbitant prices'.

The director turned instead to Dan O'Bannon, the scriptwriter and effects guy on a low-budget movie that had caught his eye: John Carpenter's *Dark Star* (1974), a black comedy about four dysfunctional astronauts. Before O'Bannon was whisked to Paris, where production began in 1975, he told Jodorowsky that storyboards would be required to achieve the effects he envisaged. 'He wasn't familiar with storyboards,' O'Bannon said, 'so I explained it to him, and he got so interested in it that he had the entire film storyboarded – every shot.'

MACHINE ANIMALS AND SOUL MECHANISMS

Jodorowsky hired a cabal of cutting-edge artists. For the storyboards, he used French artist Moebius, aka Jean Giraud, who rose to popularity in the 1960s with his comic strips about a character called Blueberry. 'Giraud made 3,000 drawings, all marvellous,' Jodorowsky recalled. 'The script of *Dune*, thanks to his talent, is a masterpiece. One can see, living, the characters; one follows the movements of camera. One visualizes cutting, the decor, the costumes. . .'

Two other artists were integral to his vision. First was Britain's Chris Foss, whose work had graced books as diverse as the novels of Isaac Asimov and Alex Comfort's *The Joy of Sex*. Foss caught Jodorowsky's attention because his

UM, ER, GUMMA

By the time the *Dune* project collapsed, Pink Floyd were finishing their 1977 album *Animals*, having composed not a note for the film. But they may have already paid tribute with their 1968 album *Ummagumma* (above). Although they claimed the title was a euphemism for sex from their native Cambridge, the word 'umma' appears in Herbert's *Dune* books, meaning 'prophet'.

> *'I was against* 2001 *realism. I wanted operas, spaceships. . . something baroque and organic.'*
>
> Alejandro Jodorowsky

work was bold and imaginative, not rooted in modern technology, which the director called 'the very antithesis of art'. Foss reportedly did not read the work he illustrated, which perhaps struck a chord with a director who despaired of sci-fi's military-industrial spaceships and their practical gadgetry. Instead he wanted 'magical entities, vibrating vehicles, like fish that swim and have their being in the mythological deeps of the surrounding ocean. . . I wanted jewels, machine-animals, soul-mechanisms. Sublime as snow crystals, myriad-faceted fly eyes, butterfly pinions. Not giant refrigerators, transistorized and riveted hulks; bloated with imperialism, pillage, arrogance and eunuchoid science'.

The second artist was the Swiss-born H.R. Giger, who visited Paris in December 1975 and left a note for the director at his studio. 'Jodorowsky called me over and showed me the preliminary studies for *Dune*,' he recalled. 'Four science fiction artists were busy designing spaceships, satellites and whole planets. As a gesture to me, a couple of photocopies of vaguely suitable pictures from my [portfolio] had been left lying around. Jodorowsky said that he would like me to try some designs – I could create a whole planet, and I would have a completely free hand.' The effect, said O'Bannon, was extremely conducive to creativity. 'It was,' he said, 'like being in an art museum.'

SURREAL TO REEL

Artist Salvador Dalí, above, appeared in 1929's *Un chien andalou* (which he wrote with director Luis Buñuel), 1930's *L'âge d'or* (also with Buñuel), 1968's improvised curio *Fun and Games for Everyone* and the French film *Aussi loin que l'amour* (1971). He also penned *Giraffes on Horseback Salads* for the Marx Brothers (see page 17) and designed dream sequences for *Spellbound* (1945) and *Father of the Bride* (1950).

For the music, Jodorowsky's team were contacted by Virgin Records, which offered Mike Oldfield, one of rock's biggest new artists. Jodorowsky, however, had his sights set on something bigger and, he says, arranged to meet Pink Floyd. Then basking in the success of 1973's *Dark Side of the Moon*, the Floyd had collaborated with directors including Barbet Schroeder and Michelangelo Antonioni, while band leader Roger Waters had listed *El Topo* as his favourite movie in 1974. However, when Jodorowsky arrived at London's Abbey Road Studios, where the Floyd were finishing their *Wish You Were Here* album, he was dismayed to find them otherwise engaged, tucking into steak and chips. Filled with 'holy anger' on behalf of his film 'of such importance', the director stormed impatiently out into the street. Guitarist David Gilmour scampered after him to apologize. Suitably mollified, Jodorowsky agreed to screen *The Holy Mountain* for them to secure their involvement. 'They decided to take part. . . by producing an album, which was going to be called *Dune* [and] made up of two discs,' he said. 'They came to Paris to discuss the economic part and, after an intense discussion, we arrived at an agreement: Pink Floyd would make almost all the music.' The rest was to be performed by French rock band Magma.

('Never saw *The Holy Mountain*. . .' rebuts Floyd drummer Nick Mason. 'No recollection of any Abbey Road meeting and we rarely had steak and chips. . . I've never known David to run after anyone to apologize, and we wouldn't have treated someone we admired in such a cavalier fashion unless we had no idea who he was, and thought he was a lunatic off the street [Always possible].')

BUG-EYED SURREALIST

Jodorowsky was so intent on making *Dune* a sensory experience that casting it was almost an afterthought. Frank Herbert's son Brian wrote that the director 'intended to play Duke Leto Atreides himself, while Orson Welles would be Baron Vladimir Harkonnen. . . David Carradine would be Imperial ecologist Dr Kynes, and Charlotte Rampling would be Lady Jessica'. Paul Atreides – the messiah figure who seizes control of the planets – was to be played by Jodorowsky's teenage son, Brontis. In the event, Rampling refused, but Carradine made it to Paris, to replace the elder Jodorowsky as Leto. Neither Welles nor Mick Jagger – another name linked with the project – were involved.

The part that most obsessed Jodorowsky, however, was that of the emperor Shaddam Corrino IV, which he had tweaked from the novel. 'In my version. . .' he said, 'the emperor of the galaxy is mad. He lives on an artificial planet of gold, in a palace of gold constructed according to the non-laws of anti-logic. He lives in symbiosis with a robot identical to him. The resemblance is so perfect that the citizens never know if they are facing the man or the machine.'

The imperious, bug-eyed surrealist Salvador Dalí (above left) seemed perfect. By chance, Jodorowsky ran into the septuagenarian at the St Regis hotel in New York, later contacting him by phone. Dalí hadn't seen *El Topo* or *The Holy Mountain*, but his friends spoke highly of them. There was only one problem: money. When Jodorowsky told him he would be needed on set for seven days, Dalí countered that God had made the universe in seven days and that Dalí, 'not being less than God, must cost a fortune: $100,000 an hour'.

Jodorowsky consulted tarot cards, which advised him to walk away. Even Dalí's muse, singer-model-actress Amanda Lear (cast as the imperial consort Princess Irulan) thought the sum excessive, warning the director, 'Dalí is like a taxi: as time passes, the more expensive it is and. . . the less you want to pay'. Jodorowsky took evasive action: he cut the emperor's part to under two pages. After an initial burst of petulance, Dalí agreed to a reduced workload that would make him, by the director's estimation, 'the most expensive paid actor in the history of cinema. He will earn more than Greta Garbo'.

EQUALLY TERRIFYING

In October 1976, Frank Herbert and his wife flew to Paris to find out what was going on. The signs were not good. Jodorowsky had spent $2 million already, and what was contracted to be a 180-minute movie seemed unlikely to come in at under fourteen hours. The casting of Dalí also continued to be problematic. When the artist spoke out in support of Spain's dictator Francisco Franco, Jodorowsky – whose native Chile had been seized in 1973 by the equally terrifying General Pinochet – realized they could never work together.

The end came when the French financiers finally pulled the plug, scattering the film's artistic contributors. The heartbroken Jodorowsky blamed Hollywood. 'It had to be an international release, nothing less than 2,000 theatres in the U.S.,' he said. 'American managers refused because Hollywood did not want to see a French production on the same level as theirs.' Nevertheless, like many others involved in the adventure, he was philosophical about it, as was Moebius. As far as the artist was concerned, the *attempt* was every bit as relevant as the elusive finished product. '*Dune* was not a failure,' Moebius told documentary maker Louis Mouchet in 1994's *La constellation Jodorowsky*. 'The film was not made, that's all. What remains is the wonderful preparation. We were all euphoric. The film remains what it should be: a mirage. . .' **DW**

WILL IT EVER HAPPEN?

0/10 Jodorowsky is in his eighties and O'Bannon died in 2009, as did Moebius in 2012. A *Dune* mini-series in 2000 starred William Hurt as the head of the Atreides clan and Giancarlo Giannini in the role earmarked for Dalí. Peter Berg, director of *Hancock* (2008), once mooted an adaptation of *Dune* but chose to make *Battleship*, one of 2012's most critically derided films.

WHAT HAPPENED NEXT. . .

Dan O'Bannon returned to LA and, with screenwriter and producer Ron Shusett, conceived a sci-fi tale called *They Bite*, a version of which landed at 20th Century Fox. O'Bannon was keen to keep working with H.R. Giger, and the project evolved into Ridley Scott's *Alien* (1979). Meanwhile, Jodorowsky and Moebius conceived a comic book series called *The Incal*. Producer Dino De Laurentiis snapped up the option on the rights to *Dune*, hiring Ridley Scott, then David Lynch, as the director. The $40m result (1984, left) was, wrote critic Roger Ebert, 'an incomprehensible, ugly, unstructured, pointless excursion into the murkier realms of one of the most confusing screenplays of all time'. Such reviews thrilled Jodorowsky. 'I think David Lynch is a fantastic moviemaker,' he said. 'When I went to the theater to see it – always I tell this with great happiness, because I was so jealous – I was dying. I was grey. But then. . . I was so happy, because the picture was so bad! And then I could live again! Because if David Lynch had been able to make *Dune* as David Lynch, I think I would have died.'

WARHEAD

Producer Kevin McClory Starring Sean Connery Year 1977 Budget $22 million
Country UK, US Genre Action adventure Studio Paramount

IAN FLEMING
In 1959, the creator of James Bond advised financial backers that a film made under Kevin McClory's 'brilliant direction' was 'likely [to be a] success'. Within four years, he and the producer were pitted against each other in court.

W here there's a hit, there's a writ. So it follows that where there's a globe-straddling, hugely lucrative film franchise, there's a legal quagmire that drags on for decades, consuming litigants until they reach their deathbeds. *Fleming and others vs. Kevin McClory* makes *Jarndyce vs. Jarndyce* from *Bleak House* seem like a brisk trot through the small claims court. At its heart is the most bonkers James Bond film you will never see. It's got the Bermuda Triangle, a fabulous undersea lair and a robot shark carrying nuclear warheads into New York's sewers. It would have been called *Warhead*.

APPALLING BUSINESS
The origins of the bitter dispute between 007 author Ian Fleming and writer-director-producer Kevin McClory lie in the unimaginably distant past when nobody had heard of Commander Bond. Former naval intelligence officer Fleming created the character at his Jamaican home, Goldeneye, in 1952 as a distraction from the 'appalling business' of his impending marriage. To say Hollywood beat a path to his door would be an overstatement: Fleming sold the rights to *Casino Royale* to CBS for a princely $1,000. It wound up as a long-forgotten one-hour TV adaptation broadcast in 1954. Should you ever be asked in a quiz who was the first actor to play James Bond, the correct answer is Barry Nelson. (Grab yourself a smug bonus point for adding that he went on to play the hotel manager who interviews Jack Nicholson in *The Shining* in 1980.)

Fleming quickly tired of showbiz, remarking that 'the film and television world in America is a hell of a jungle'. So he must have warmed to rakish Irish playboy Kevin McClory when the two were introduced by mutual friend Ivar Bryce in 1958. McClory worked as an assistant to John Huston on such films as *The African Queen* (1951) and introduced Liz Taylor to one of her husbands.

Bryce gave McClory some of Fleming's novels to read. A series of meetings ensued, to consider the possibility of putting Bond on-screen. As Donald Zec, biographer of Cubby Broccoli, notes: 'Much of the discussion took place in McClory's home in London's Belgravia, where a black butler supervised the meals and the dubious hygiene of a pet monkey and a green macaw. This alone seemed guaranteed to make McClory Fleming's kind of man.'

SEAN CONNERY is JAMES BOND

WARHEAD

What appears...   ...has first to disappear

BASED ON AN ORIGINAL STORY BY KEVIN McCLORY "WARHEAD" STARRING SEAN CONNERY
SCREENPLAY BY JACK WHITTINGHAM AND SEAN CONNERY PRODUCED BY JACK SCHWARTZMAN DIRECTED BY KEVIN McCLORY

But as the months dragged on, the creative partnership soured. Scriptwriter Jack Whittingham was brought on board to help hone the screenplay for the proposed first Bond movie. Increasingly disenchanted, Fleming went off to work on a non-fiction travel book. On his return, he was told that Whittingham had completed the script, which was now called *Longitude 78 West*. Fleming reportedly approved, but changed the title to *Thunderball*. This was also to become the title of his ninth Bond novel, which is when the lawyers became involved. The novel was credited to Fleming alone, but McClory – who got his hands on an advance copy – claimed it was simply a novelization of the screenplay. And that was largely the work of himself and Whittingham. He also insisted that SPECTRE and the villain Blofeld were his own creations.

In 1961, McClory and Whittingham petitioned the High Court in London for an injunction to stop publication. This was rejected, but by November 1963, they were back to contest the alleged plagiarism case in earnest. When this was eventually settled out of court, Fleming agreed to pay damages and costs to McClory. Future editions of the novel were to be credited jointly to Kevin McClory, Jack Whittingham and Ian Fleming. Crucially, McClory also walked away with film rights to the screenplay. Fleming had been gravely ill with a heart condition throughout the long trial and succumbed to a fatal heart attack just nine months later, at the age of fifty-six.

CAT-STROKING NEMESIS

Meanwhile, Cubby Broccoli and Harry Saltzman's production company, Eon, turned Bond into a lucrative cinema franchise with *Dr. No* (1962), *From Russia with Love* (1963) and *Goldfinger* (1964). Each hauled in substantially more box-office loot than its predecessor. Eon had originally earmarked *Thunderball* as the first in the series, with Alfred Hitchcock directing and Richard Burton as 007 – an intriguing prospect thwarted by the ongoing litigation. To avoid a damaging rival Bond hitting the screen, they brought McClory on board and offered him a producer credit on *Thunderball* (1965). With Sean Connery making his fourth appearance as Bond, this proved the biggest hit yet. Indeed, when *The Economist* adjusted the figures for inflation in March 2012 – before *Skyfall* – it ranked as the most successful Bond movie to date.

McClory's agreement with Eon stipulated he could not make another film version of the *Thunderball* story for ten years. The franchise rolled on: Connery left, returned (for 1971's *Diamonds Are Forever*), and left again; George Lazenby fronted *On Her Majesty's Secret Service* (1969) and Roger Moore arrived (for 1973's *Live and Let Die*) to demonstrate the thespian exertion involved in raising a quizzical eyebrow. In the background, however, McClory was biding his time like a cat-stroking nemesis. His ten years were up in 1975 and he immediately dived into a new project. Bizarrely, Sean Connery was lured back – not as the star, but as a writer, alongside Len Deighton, creator of the Harry Palmer series (whose protagonist's dull name was deliberately chosen to distinguish him from fellow spy James Bond). McClory planned to go for broke with the craziest Bond film ever, entitled *Warhead*. Producer Jack Schwartzman eventually even persuaded Connery to play 007 once again.

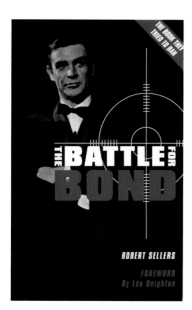

BATTLE ROYALE

When author Robert Sellers produced a definitive account of the *Thunderball/Never Say Never Again/Warhead* saga, he too fell foul of lawyers. Sellers had obtained *Thunderball* treatments by Fleming, scripts by Jack Whittingham and Fleming's private correspondence. Tomahawk Press published *The Battle for Bond* – and was promptly sued. The Ian Fleming Will Trust insisted it owned copyright on the letters. Sellers argued that he was free to use them because they had formed part of the 1963 trial. However, Tomahawk agreed to deliver unsold books to the Trust, presumably for destruction. The second edition of *The Battle for Bond* duly boasts: 'The book they tried to ban.'

WHAT HAPPENED NEXT. . .

Undaunted, McClory forged ahead. In 1996, after the Eon franchise had been revived by *Goldeneye*, he announced plans for yet another adaptation of *Thunderball*, this time called *Warhead 2000*. It was reported that Timothy Dalton (left) would return to star. Sony, the film's backers, acquired some of McClory's rights in a deal whose full details were not disclosed. Soon everyone was back in court for a smackdown between MGM/UA and Sony, the former describing the latter's plans as 'delusional'. An out-of-court settlement saw Sony ceding their right to make a Bond film. A separate legal action, launched by Sony, asserted that the screen Bond was distinct from the literary one, and that McClory as co-creator was entitled to a share of Eon's $3 billion profits from the films. This was thrown out in 2000. In 1999, McClory told *Variety* that he was discussing Bond movies – including one now titled *Warhead 2001* – with German and Australian backers. However, he died in 2006, aged eighty, *Warhead* still a dream.

Now ask yourself this: you have the choice of two Bonds. There's the lightly comic one in which suave Roger Moore makes with the puns. Or there's the nutty Sean Connery one in which the dastardly SPECTRE lure military vessels into the Bermuda Triangle, strip them of their nuclear warheads and take over the Statue of Liberty to launch a robotic shark-borne nuke assault on New York, making creative use of the city's sewers. Which one gets your admission fee?

Eon maintained that McClory was entitled only to make *Thunderball*, and that this film represented a breach of copyright. The producer argued that SPECTRE was his property: it doesn't feature in any of Fleming's original books, was created solely for *Thunderball*, and yet was used in every Connery-era Bond movie. As the project became mired in litigation, Connery started to get cold feet and backers Paramount pulled out. *Warhead* had been disarmed.

Like any good Bond villain – or, according to perspective, Bond himself – McClory didn't simply vanish. The legal obstacles were overcome and a final blocking move by Fleming's estate was thrown out by the High Court. But the film McClory got to make was the far less outlandish *Never Say Never Again* (1983). Connery's return to Bond after twelve years enjoyed reasonably good reviews and succeeded in making money. But in 1983's much-hyped Battle of the Bonds, the public voted with their feet. . . for Eon's *Octopussy*. **RA**

WILL IT EVER HAPPEN?

0/10   Never say never again again. But Jack Schwartzman sold the rights to *Never Say Never Again* to MGM in 1997. *Casino Royale* (1967) was the only Bond property not owned by MGM until the *Warhead 2000* case (see What Happened Next. . ., above). As part of Sony's settlement, the company gave up the rights it held. In a final twist, in 2004, a consortium headed by Sony gobbled up MGM and now has control over all things Bond on the big screen.

STAR TREK:
PLANET OF THE TITANS

Director Philip Kaufman **Starring** William Shatner, Leonard Nimoy
Year 1977 **Country** US, UK **Genre** Sci-fi **Studio** Paramount

PHILIP KAUFMAN

'My idea was to make it less "cult-ish" and more of an adult movie,' said the director of his plans for *Star Trek*'s first foray onto the big screen, 'dealing with sexuality and wonders rather than oddness.'

It's strange now to think of a time when *Star Trek* was deemed to have no future. The franchise grew to an unprecedented size during the 1980s and 1990s, across multiple TV series and films. But during the 1970s it was on the ropes: familiar through reruns but rarely considered a going concern. Its revival in a live-action form was by no means assured. The original five-year mission of the USS *Enterprise* and its crew (Captain James T. Kirk, Mr Spock, Lieutenant Uhura, Dr 'Bones' McCoy et al) stalled in 1969 after three seasons: NBC slashed the final season's budget, buried it in a graveyard slot on Friday nights, then cancelled the show completely. However, *Star Trek* found a colossal new fan base in syndication – unusually, as there were only seventy-nine episodes and the customary minimum for syndication is one hundred – playing to younger audiences in earlier time-slots across the US and in more than sixty territories worldwide. *Trek*'s increasing cult following inevitably led to rumblings of a revival within its producers, Paramount, and, in May 1975, creator Gene Roddenberry was given $3 million to develop a script for a film.

THE GOD THING

Roddenberry's first favoured screenplay was his own. Entitled *The God Thing*, it involved Kirk reassembling his old crew on a newly refitted *Enterprise* to clash with a malfunctioning spaceship that had come to believe it was God. This was rejected by studio executives, as was a second Roddenberry idea based around time travelling. In the following months, ideas were fielded from established sci-fi authors like Ray Bradbury, Theodore Sturgeon, Robert Silverberg and Harlan Ellison. Ellison's treatment also featured a time-travel narrative in which lizard aliens travel back to Earth's past to manipulate evolution. Kirk and his crew's dilemma was therefore based on *Star Trek*'s 'Prime Directive' of non-interference: should they allow events to unfold, thereby dooming the human race or commit genocide in order to save it? We'll never know the exact outcome, since Ellison walked away from the project early on, exasperated by a studio suit who insisted he somehow fit the Mayan civilization into the story.

Paramount's prevailing opinion was that nothing it was hearing was 'big' enough: even a script about a black hole about to destroy the entire universe

Poster: Jay Shaw

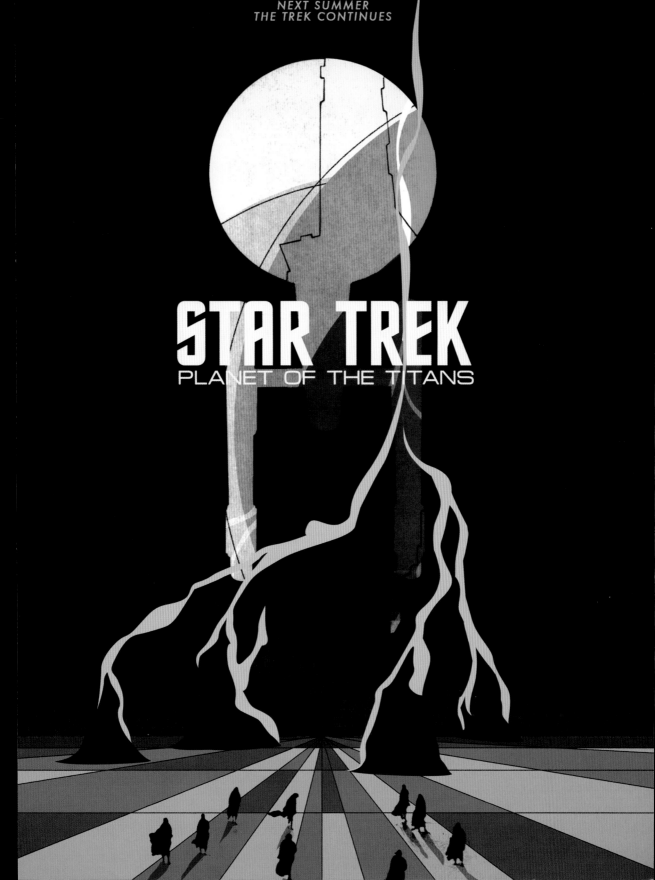

POD MOVIE

Philip Kaufman directed a remake of *Invasion of the Body Snatchers* in 1978 and, proving that his time on *Planet of the Titans* hadn't been entirely wasted, exploited his new connections by casting Leonard Nimoy as psychiatrist David Kibner (above). The actor, a victim of the body snatchers, plays blank emotions that would not have been alien to Spock.

POCKET-SIZED SPOCK

Star Trek creator Gene Roddenberry had toyed with casting the 1.19 metre-tall Michael Dunn (above, with Elizabeth Hartman in Francis Ford Coppola's 1966 comedy *You're a Big Boy Now*) as Spock in the original TV series.

was deemed not sufficiently grand of scale. In October 1976, however, Chris Bryant and Allan Scott – writers of the *Don't Look Now* (1973) screenplay – submitted a treatment called *Planet of the Titans*, which seemed to fit the bill.

IMMORTAL GIANTS OVERTHROWN

Details of Bryant and Scott's story are sketchy, lost to time and faltering memories. The thrust was the crew of the *Enterprise* finding themselves on the home planet of the mythical, long-dead Titans, the immortal giants overthrown by the Olympians (recast here as Cygnans), as recounted in Ancient Greek poet Hesiod's *Theogeny*. Travelling a million years into Earth's past, Kirk and his cohorts accidentally teach primitive man how to make fire – and realize that they are the Titans. There's some thought that the mystical concept of the extra-perceptive 'third eye' was woven into the story too.

The search for a director – possibly more a wish list than a collection of realistic prospects – took in Francis Ford Coppola, Steven Spielberg, George Lucas and Robert Wise. Philip Kaufman, however, was first to accept the job.

Kaufman had a track record across a variety of genres, and had enjoyed success with 1972's heist-gone-wrong Western *The Great Northfield Minnesota Raid* and 1974's Arctic adventure *The White Dawn*. He had not tackled science fiction before, but was a fan of British philosopher and sci-fi author Olaf

'I'm sure the fans would have been upset, but I felt it could really open up a new type of science fiction.'

Philip Kaufman

Stapledon, hence Veronica Cartwright's character in Kaufman's later remake of *Invasion of the Body Snatchers* (above left) namechecking him – ideas from the writer's *First and Last Men* and *Star Maker* novels are echoed in the premise of *Planet of the Titans*. Given a crash course in key episodes of the TV series by Roddenberry himself, Kaufman found that – having expected 'juvenile science fiction' – he appreciated the show's surprisingly mature themes.

STAR WARS VISIONARY

Locations in the UK were scouted, James Bond/*Dr. Strangelove* designer Ken Adam began work on the sets, and artists including *Star Wars* visionary Ralph McQuarrie were brought in to start sketching designs (Kaufman was a friend of George Lucas, who had begun work with McQuarrie on *Star Wars* in 1975). But despite the director's enthusiasm and momentum building on the production side, the script was a problem. Six months after submitting their initial treatment, Bryant and Scott hadn't come up with a final draft that met with Paramount's approval. Finding it impossible to please a committee of executives that knew what it didn't want but was less clear about what it did, the writers asked to be let go. Their wish was granted in April 1977.

Kaufman was left to rework the screenplay, which apparently soon ceased to be *Planet of the Titans*. Bryant and Scott recalled Kaufman, feeling constrained

Paramount threw its energy into *Star Trek: Phase II*, a TV series helmed by Roddenberry. Many of the originals were to return, bar a reluctant Nimoy, but production ceased when the Paramount Television Service channel, on which it was to be shown, was abandoned. (One *Phase II* script resurfaced as 'The Child', an episode of the first of the franchise's four live-action TV spin-offs, *Star Trek: The Next Generation*.) The show did, however, yield themes and new characters (notably Lieutenant Ilia, played by model Persis Khambatta) for 1979's *Star Trek: The Motion Picture* (left). Dubbed 'The Slow-Motion Picture', the film aimed for the portentousness of *2001* rather than the space opera of *Star Wars*. Only with 1982's *Star Trek II: The Wrath of Khan* (right) did big-screen *Trek* deliver a properly ripping yarn.

by the cast of 'TV actors' from the original series. The director himself confirmed that he was frustrated by Roddenberry being 'anchored in a ten-year-old TV show which would not translate for a feature audience'. Following the writers' departure, his response was to sideline all the crew bar Spock, who would find himself in a personal battle of wills with a Klingon nemesis.

Popular legend has it that Toshiro Mifune – the Japanese actor known for his collaborations with Akira Kurosawa – was lined up to play the Klingon. It's certainly a fascinating thought, but it's doubtful Mifune ever heard about the project, let alone entertained an offer to play a leading role. More likely is that he was simply the actor Kaufman had in mind for the part as he was thrashing out his ideas: Nimoy vs. Mifune suggests that Kaufman's concept was a kind of *Trek* version of *Hell in the Pacific*, the 1968 drama that pitched the Japanese star against Lee Marvin. Kaufman envisaged 'a big science fiction movie, filled with all kinds of questions, particularly about the nature of Spock's [duality] – exploring his humanity and what humanness was. To have Spock and Mifune's character tripping out in outer space. I'm sure the fans would have been upset, but I felt it could really open up a new type of science fiction'.

The film was officially abandoned in May 1977. Paramount had decided that *Star Trek*'s home was television, and that a big-screen version simply wouldn't fly. With exquisite timing, *Star Wars* opened later the same month. **OW**

WILL IT EVER HAPPEN?

1/10 Extremely unlikely, especially since Bryant and Scott's screenplay was never finished and the film essentially became a different project when Kaufman took over the writing. *Star Trek Into Darkness*, the sequel to a triumphant 2009 reboot, confirmed the brand's box office power in 2013, so the franchise's foreseeable future seems to rest with director J.J. Abrams.

From the director of *Faster, Pussycat! Kill! Kill!* and *Beyond the Valley of the Dolls*

WHO KILLED BAMBI?

directed by
RUSS MEYER
written by
ROGER EBERT & RORY JOHNSTON

starring
THE SEX PISTOLS

with MARIANNE FAITHFULL
MALCOM MCLAREN and JAMES AUBREY

WHO KILLED BAMBI?

Director Russ Meyer **Starring** Johnny Rotten, Sid Vicious, Steve Jones, Paul Cook
Year 1978 **Country** US **Genre** Musical comedy **Studio** 20th Century Fox

B efore he passed away, Roger Ebert was arguably the greatest living film critic in the United States; perhaps even in the English-speaking world. For decades, his witty, humane, brilliantly pithy film reviews found a home in the pages of the *Chicago-Sun Times*. On any given day, Ebert could be found 'awake in the dark', as one of his book titles puts it, trawling through preview screenings of upcoming releases. Even a brutal and disfiguring battle with thyroid cancer barely slowed his impressive work rate. It's intriguing, then, to note that – were it not for a few developmental mishaps on a movie project thirty-five years ago – Ebert could have gone down in history for writing the most offensive and controversial musical of all time: *Who Killed Bambi?*

SEXUALLY DERANGED PSYCHEDELIC FREAK-OUT

When Russ Meyer got in touch with him in 1977, Ebert had never heard of the Sex Pistols. 'They're a rock band from England,' he recalled the director telling him. 'Now they have some money and want me to direct their movie.'

A living legend in the world of exploitation cinema, Meyer was renowned for his comically violent, gloriously trashy productions, starring Amazonian females with large chests and slender acting capabilities. But, like his contemporary Roger Corman, Meyer recognized good, cheap talent when he found it, and Ebert proved one of his finest discoveries. In the late 1960s, Meyer enlisted the fledgling writer to hammer out the screenplay for *Beyond the Valley of the Dolls* (1970). It was intended as nothing more than a tacky cash-in on Jacqueline Susann's best-selling 1966 novel *Valley of the Dolls* (subsequently a hugely successful movie), but the movie exceeded all artistic and commercial expectations. A sexually deranged psychedelic freak-out, it blasted out of the drive-in ghetto and landed in that magically elusive place where the counterculture straddled the mass market. Ebert claimed that it was one of Fox's most profitable movies and probably helped save the ailing studio.

So despite his aura of benevolence and erudite respectability, Roger Ebert had already been there, done that and written the screenplay when it came to the more shocking fringes of popular culture. Meyer knew he was the man for the job when it came to the Sex Pistols movie and wasted no time filling him in

RUSS MEYER

The director blamed the failure of *Who Killed Bambi?* on one person alone: Sex Pistols manager Malcolm McLaren. 'An asshole. Plain and simple,' he told *Total Film*'s M.J. Simpson. 'He didn't have the balls, the courage, to do it.'

REIGN OF THE TUDOR
The song 'Who Killed Bambi' graced the soundtrack of the Sex Pistols' 1980 movie *The Great Rock 'n' Roll Swindle* and the B-side of their 'Silly Thing' single. It was performed by Edward Tudor-Pole, who co-wrote the song with Malcom McLaren's partner, designer Vivienne Westwood.

on everything there was to know about this bizarre new English band – who, in many onlookers' eyes, made the Manson Family look like the Partridge Family.

Meyer had himself been approached to make the film by the Pistols' outlandish manager. Malcolm McLaren was a roguish dilettante whose career had encompassed art school (where he had been influenced by the late 1960s antics of the Situationists), a succession of clothes shops and the thankless role of manager for glam rockers the New York Dolls. Until his death in 2010, McLaren was a man who never allowed his somewhat sketchy musical knowledge to stand in the way of his latest scheme for mobilizing – or, as his detractors would have it, exploiting – radical new forms of youth culture.

CLOCKWORK ORANGE MEETS CALIGULA

Punk, the movement the Sex Pistols spearheaded, had such a seismic impact in the UK that a kind of Year Zero mindset took hold of musicians, the media and fans alike after 1976. For non-rock outsiders like Meyer and Ebert, however, it was an opportunity to 'go up the mountain' once more – Meyer's phrase for hitting the heights of success, fame and controversy that they had enjoyed with *Beyond the Valley of the Dolls*. That film was a favourite in the Pistols camp, making Meyer and what McLaren described as 'his fully cantilevered ladies' a natural choice for collaboration.

> *'Rotten disliked Americans very much, so I spoke
> frankly to him about how I felt about him.'*
>
> Russ Meyer

The director duly visited the nascent icons. '[Singer Johnny] Rotten disliked Americans very much,' he told TV presenter Jonathan Ross (on UK Channel 4's *The Incredibly Strange Film Show*), 'so I spoke frankly to him about my feelings as to how *I* felt about *him*. All we had to do was make a good movie. [Bass player Sid] Vicious was almost impossible to fathom. [Guitarist Steve] Jones and [drummer Paul] Cook were great. They wanted to own Cadillacs.' (Cook remembered it rather differently: '*Who Killed Bambi?* was Malcolm's idea. We were musicians. We didn't want to make a film. Malcolm was very good at spending other people's money. There was a load being put into the film from the band's royalties, which we didn't know about.' 'It was just trash,' concurred Rotten, 'rubbishing the whole point and purpose [of punk].')

Vicious, McLaren recalled to Jonathan Ross, 'was a guy that [Meyer] always wanted creeping out of drains – coming up through the drains in Wapping. We used to drive round London and he loved the names, like Wapping, Battersea, Bayswater – names that conjured up sort of sexual connotations; that somehow submitted to his fantastic imagination'.

Dutchman Rene Daalder, director of the proto-*Heathers* drama *Massacre at Central High* (1976), was the first to take a pass at the script. Meyer, for whom Daalder had worked as a cameraman, promptly binned the result, entitled *Anarchy in the U.K.*, although Ebert kept its opening scenes of punk sprouting against a backdrop of dole queues and social unrest in England. (Daalder has also been credited for the idea of Sid Vicious singing Frank Sinatra's 'My Way.')

Holed up at LA's Sunset Marquis Hotel for a long weekend, Ebert set to work hammering out script pages by the fistful. Each evening he would meet with Meyer to discuss the next day's work. 'We rarely knew more than a day ahead what would happen next,' the writer said. However, recalled the Pistols' US representative Rory Johnston (credited as co-writer), 'The stuff we'd come up with with Roger Ebert in LA would have been a fucking great film.' Indeed, the script that emerged – still, in July 1977, tilted *Anarchy in the U.K.* – was so sharp, tight and professional that any hack director could have delivered what the director, according to McLaren, described as 'a soft, soapy, sexy' update of The Beatles's *A Hard Day's Night*.

That was a misleading logline for what could have been a masterpiece of exploitation cinema: a genre-smashing milestone in the vein of *A Clockwork Orange* (1971) meets *Caligula* (1975) – or, at the very least, a punked-up sibling to *The Rocky Horror Picture Show* (1979). This may be deduced because Ebert posted the entire script on his blog in 2010 – jaw-dropping reading.

HORRIFIED FASCINATION

The Sex Pistols themselves are portrayed as disaffected, borderline-feral youth, sharp as needles and hard as nails. Ebert took great care to allocate worthwhile scenes and dialogue to all four members of the band, despite his awareness that the notoriety of singer Johnny Rotten and bassist Sid Vicious far outstripped that of guitarist Steve Jones and drummer Paul Cook. McLaren becomes Proby, 'dressed in a jacket and pants with big, loud checks, as if he were Zero Mostel just come from the opening night of [*The Producers*'] "Springtime for Hitler"'. In among the sex, drugs and rock 'n' roll there are recurring comic themes. Rotten fights off groupies with disdain, but Jones avails himself with gusto, often while simultaneously enjoying a burger:

TEST FOOTAGE

Just one day of shooting was completed, on 11 October 1977. The resulting footage, of actor James Aubrey apparently killing a deer with a crossbow, made it into the trailer, albeit not the final cut, of *The Great Rock 'n' Roll Swindle*, the Julian Temple film salvaged from the ashes of *Who Killed Bambi?* In the latter, Aubrey's character M.J. – a key character in Ebert's script – was demoted to the fleetingly glimpsed B.J. (innuendo fully intended). Aubrey's associations with rock 'n' roll didn't end there: he also appeared in Tony Scott's 1983 movie *The Hunger*, starring David Bowie. Arguably, however, the picture that provided the greatest thematic link to Aubrey's work with the Pistols was his big-screen debut: Peter Brook's 1963 adaptation of William Golding's classic novel *Lord of the Flies*.

INT. MUSIC STORE—SHAFTSBURY
Johnny Rotten creates a disturbance. Standing in front
of a huge juke box, he grabs a nearby microphone stand
and violently mimes the song behind played ("Pretty
Vacant"), supplying terrific amounts of kinetic energy.
Sue Catwoman moves off into the background.

CUT TO: INT. A SOHO BROTHEL, AS BEFORE
Steve Jones, rummaging under the bed, finds what
he's looking for. As the Hooker continues her oral
ministrations, he comes up with a big sack from
Wimpy's, takes out a hamburger and begins to eat it,
looking dreamily at the ceiling, all his needs met.

CUT TO: INT. THE CONCERT HALL
Paul Cook moves very quietly down into the auditorium
and up to the stage, where roadies are supposed to
be guarding the instruments of a rock band. The only
Roadie in view is stoned and asleep. Paul lifts a piece
of amplifying equipment and steals away.

CUT TO: INT. THE MUSIC STORE
As the store's staff move in on Johnny Rotten, we see
Sue Catwoman, quick as her namesake, lift the guitar
and melt out onto Shaftsbury Avenue with it. Johnny
Rotten looks quite properly angered at the interruption
of his performance.

COOK GETS STUNG
A sequence in which drummer Paul Cook (top) is attacked by musician and aspiring movie star Sting (far right) was cut from *Who Killed Bambi?*'s successor *The Great Rock 'n' Roll Swindle* (opposite above), but appears in Julian Temple's *The Filth and the Fury* documentary (2000).

The band are depicted as gradually winning over a grassroots audience as music business sharks circle and older stars and fans look on in horrified fascination. But the title *Who Killed Bambi?* – a stroke of genius by Ebert – ends with a question mark. This wasn't nihilistic trash – it was asking questions (albeit, in retrospect, rather naive ones) of the society that produced the Pistols.

The titular deer is shot by M.J. (presumed to be an acronymic reference to Mick Jagger), a youthful though redundant rock star of an earlier generation. In the film's closing scene he is killed by a vengeful little girl – just before he gets the chance to leech out the energy of the Pistols and their new punk scene.

The script closes with Rotten looking straight into the lens and starkly asking, 'Ever get the feeling you're being watched?' – a line that proved prescient. In January 1978, the singer, staring straight into the audience, ended the band's final concert with the oft-quoted, 'Ever get the feeling you've been cheated?'

Ebert recalled being fed ideas by McLaren, who specifically requested a scene in which Sid Vicious shoots heroin while in bed with his mother. Ebert amped this up into a full-on incest-and-opiates scenario. Upon reading the script, Sid opined that his mum wouldn't like the bit about heroin. Singer and actress Marianne Faithfull – no stranger, at that point, to heroin, and the

WHAT HAPPENED NEXT. . .

A few elements of *Who Killed Bambi?* were recycled into Julian Temple's *The Great Rock 'n' Roll Swindle* (1980) – a semi-fictionalized account of the Pistols' career, completed after Rotten had quit in disgust and Vicious had died. It cast Steve Jones as a detective on the trail of Malcolm McLaren, who – playing a Fagin-esque version of himself – claimed sole credit for creating both the band and the controversy that engulfed and destroyed them. Among others to appear in it were 'The Great Train Robber' Ronnie Biggs, porn star Mary Millington and veteran British character actress Irene Handl.

former partner of the original M.J., Mick Jagger – signed up to play Sid's mother. 'I would have liked to have worked with [Meyer] but, when he wasn't going to direct, I didn't wanna do it, Sid or no Sid,' she said in 1979. 'It was pretty horrible actually. I'm kind of glad I didn't do it now. . . My mother would have hated it.'

Who Killed Bambi? didn't happen, although no one can agree why. McLaren claimed 20th Century Fox axed it after reading the script, but Ebert considered this unlikely. Meyer told Ebert that McLaren had no money to pay the crew in England and he had been forced to walk away. 'We had a chance to make a pretty good film,' the director grumbled, 'and he muffed it.' Meyer also accused McLaren of not wishing to share money from the movie. The most outlandish theory is that the film was nixed by Princess Grace of Monaco – a member of 20th Century Fox's board – owing to her personal distaste for Meyer.

Apart from being the exalted potentate of boobie movies, Meyer should be remembered as the only person to extract serious money from McLaren, the great rock 'n' roll swindler himself. 'I delivered wads of cash to his rented apartment,' recalls Sue Steward, who worked in McLaren's office and who remembers the director as 'elegant as a Fifties movie star with camel coat and Clark Gable moustache.' Sadly, it was to no avail: *Bambi* was dead. **PR**

WILL IT EVER HAPPEN?

1/10 Sid Vicious died in 1979, as did Russ Meyer in 2004 and Malcolm McLaren in 2010. Given the decidedly mixed reception to Alex Cox's *Sid and Nancy* (1986), starring Gary Oldman, it is unlikely that anyone would again attempt a fictionalized account of the Sex Pistols' story. Nor is it plausible that anyone would attempt to capitalize on the availability of Ebert's now very dated script. As the writer himself remarked, 'I can't discuss what I wrote, why I wrote it, or what I should or shouldn't have written. Frankly, I have no idea.'

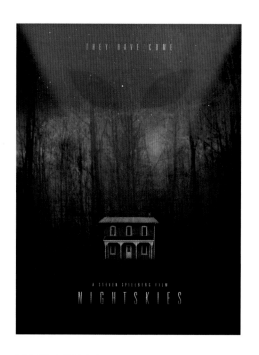

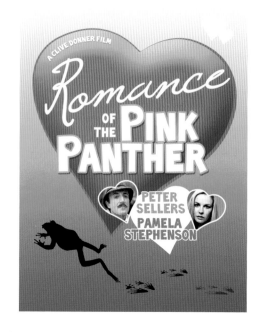

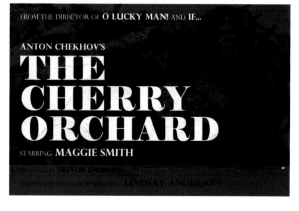

Chapter 4

ORSON WELLES a film...
RUPERT EVERETT
AMY IRVING

THE CRADLE will ROCK

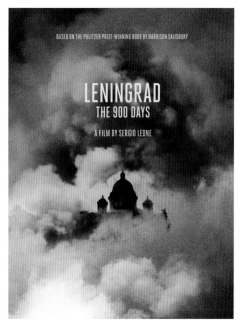

THE WHITE HOTEL

BASED ON THE BOOK BY
D.M. THOMAS

COMING SOON

BASED ON THE PULITZER PRIZE-WINNING BOOK BY HARRISON SALISBURY

LENINGRAD
THE 900 DAYS

A FILM BY SERGIO LEONE

The Eighties

NIGHT SKIES

Director Steven Spielberg **Year** 1980 **Budget** $10 million **Country** US **Genre** Sci-fi **Studio** Columbia

STEVEN SPIELBERG

'Everyone has a hobby and mine is aliens,' the director admitted to *Total Film*. 'Some people go to the wood shop and make bowling-pin lamps, stuff like that. I tell stories about aliens.'

By 1980, Steven Spielberg found himself in a new, strange place. His last film of the old decade, *1941* (1979) – a would-be Second World War comedy about post-Pearl Harbor paranoia – had gone massively over schedule and over budget. This was nothing new: both *Jaws* (1975) and *Close Encounters of the Third Kind* (1977) had run out of control timewise and financially. The situation that Spielberg *hadn't* faced in several years was a failure to connect with either critics ('A hectic, smug, self-destructive farce,' said the *Washington Post*, summing up the consensus on *1941*) or, more importantly, with audiences. Had Hollywood's golden boy lost his Midas touch?

DARK HEADSPACE

All was not rosy in Spielberg's personal life either. In December 1979, after a three-month engagement, his four-year relationship with actress Amy Irving broke down. 'Life has caught up with me,' he said at the time. 'I've spent so many years hiding from pain and fear behind a camera. I avoided all the growing pains by being too busy making movies. So right now, in my early thirties, I'm experiencing delayed adolescence. I suffer like I'm sixteen. It's a miracle I haven't sprouted acne again. The point is, I didn't escape suffering, I only delayed it.' It was this dark headspace that allowed the normally upbeat Spielberg to consider *Night Skies* as a potential project.

The seeds were planted in an incident that the director unearthed during his research into Ufology for *Close Encounters*. In the fall of 1955, members of the Sutton family of Christian County, Kentucky, alleged that they had seen unidentifiable creatures and lights in the sky above their rural farmhouse. Their story was corroborated by local policemen and state troopers, who gave the tale enough credence for it to be investigated by the US Air Force.

Eyewitness reports offered further detail. The 'Hopkinsville goblins' – so-called because the event occurred near the small city of Hopkinsville – were described as around 90cm tall, with pointed ears, atrophic limbs and spindly arms topped with metallic talons. Silvery-grey in colour and around twelve to fifteen in number, they appeared to float above the ground and could suddenly appear in high places. The aliens showed no signs of hostility – despite which,

Poster: Heath Killen

THEY HAVE COME

A STEVEN SPIELBERG FILM

NIGHTSKIES

in true Hollywood fashion, farmers Elmer 'Lucky' Sutton and Billy Ray Taylor began blasting at them with shotguns. In terrifically spooky detail, witnesses recalled one of the aliens being shot point-blank and the sound resembling bullets hitting a metal bucket.

Spielberg remembered the story when Columbia mooted the idea of a sequel to *Close Encounters*. Perhaps stung by Universal tarnishing the *Jaws* legacy with Jeannot Szwarc's 1978 sequel, Spielberg calculated that an alien-based sci-fi project, albeit one with a horror angle, would sate the studio suits yet preserve the purity of his 1977 classic. His original treatment was entitled *Watch the Skies* – an iconic line from *The Thing from Another World* (1951) and the working title of *Close Encounters* – and shared DNA with a two-and-a-half hour 8mm film called *Firelight* about hostile aliens abducting earthlings to create a human zoo. Made by Spielberg when he was sixteen, *Firelight* was, he says, 'one of the five worst films ever made'.

Spielberg wanted Lawrence Kasdan to pen the screenplay, as he had done for their forthcoming *Raiders of the Lost Ark* (1981). However, Kasdan was embroiled in fleshing out *The Empire Strikes Back* (1980) for their friend

THE HOOPER LOOP

'Spielberg gave me a call asking me to come over and discuss something,' the director of *The Texas Chain Saw Massacre* (1974), Tobe Hooper (above left, with Spielberg) told writer Philip Nutman about his invitation to direct *Night Skies*. 'What I really wanted to do was a ghost story – I was a big fan of Robert Wise's *The Haunting* (1963) and, it turned out, so was he – so he got rather excited and said, "Okay, let's make a ghost story."' The result was the hit *Poltergeist* (1982), directed by Hooper and written and produced by Spielberg.

> *'My reaction was to think of a tender relationship between an extraterrestrial and an eleven-year-old.'*
>
> Steven Spielberg

George Lucas, so Spielberg turned to John Sayles. There was an element of irony to this: Sayles had made his name writing *Piranha* (1978), a smart but blatant *Jaws* cash-in for exploitation mogul Roger Corman.

From the get-go, Sayles had little truck with Spielberg's benign worldview. 'There's no reason why the aliens had to be wonderful creatures,' he said. Spinning off from the 'Hopkinsville goblins' myth, Sayles fashioned a story about a band of extraterrestrials – leader Skar, henchmen Hoodoo and Klud, comic relief Squirt, loner Buddee – who touch down on Earth near an isolated cattle ranch. Unable to decide whether chickens, cows or humans are the dominant life-form, the aliens begin to experiment on anything that moves, terrifying a hick family in the process. 'You were never quite sure of the aliens' intent – whether they were confused or downright nasty,' recalled effects co-ordinator Mitch Suskin, who worked on *Night Skies* in its infancy.

UNEQUIVOCALLY NASTY

One character in Sayles's script was unequivocally nasty: Skar, described as having a beaklike mouth and eyes like a grasshopper, and named after the Comanche baddie in John Ford's *The Searchers* (1956). This was not the only Ford Western to influence *Night Skies*: Sayles also drew inspiration from *Drums Along the Mohawk*, a 1939 picture that featured Henry Fonda and his family defending their upstate New York farm against marauding Indians. *The White Dawn* (1974) – Philip Kaufman's culture-clash drama about whalers stranded in an Eskimo tribe – also became a touchstone.

Initially, neither Spielberg nor Sayles intended to direct the film. Instead, Ron Cobb – a cartoonist who had broken into film as a concept artist designing John Carpenter's no-budget *Dark Star* (1974), the Cantina denizens of *Star Wars* (1977) and the spaceship in *Alien* (1979) – was in the frame. Cobb had worked with Spielberg to realize interiors of the Mothership for the Special Edition of *Close Encounters*, but his commitment as production designer on John Milius's *Conan the Barbarian* (1982) nixed his involvement. Despite a budget of $10 million put up by Columbia, *Night Skies* was without a director.

It might have lacked a guiding hand but the film at least had an up-and-running special effects shop. Sayles's script featured five fully functioning extraterrestrials, and his imagination had given them technically challenging tasks in the pre-CGI era. In one scene, they leaped onto tables. In another, they rode cows like bucking broncos and drove tractors. And, in a grisly double whammy, they dissect a cow, then decide to dissect a human too. For these effects, Spielberg turned, at the suggestion of director John Landis, to Rick Baker, the prosthetic effects maestro who was developing the astonishing transformation sequences for Landis's *An American Werewolf in London* (1981). Baker quoted an effects budget of $3 million. Spielberg agreed, then left for London to begin prepping *Raiders of the Lost Ark* (1981). Pre-production on *Night Skies* began in April 1980. Baker and a seven-strong crew spent five months building a $70,000 prototype Skar that worked through 'anatomation', a process in which an operator's movements are duplicated by a puppet.

MURKY WATERS

It's here that the waters begin to get murky. While Spielberg and producer Kathleen Kennedy marvelled at a videotape of Baker's prototype in London, executives at Columbia began to balk at the cost of the project. Given Spielberg's track record, the studio's reticence was understandable, especially in the days before the blockbusting *Poltergeist* (1982), *Back to the Future*

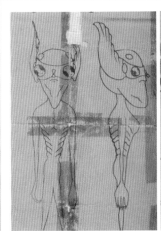
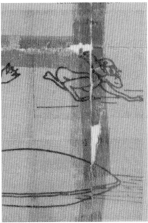

LOVING THE ALIEN

'One of the girls in the Kentucky family [an eyewitness to the "Hopkinsville goblins"] drew a picture of what the alien looked like,' (left) make-up effects wizard Rick Baker told *Cinefantastique* magazine. 'It had a triangular head and body and weird, hard angles. I didn't want to build it.' Instead Baker moved forward with his own design, which won approval all round. Yet despite the quality of the work, Spielberg felt it was too expensive and hired his *Close Encounters* collaborator Carlo Rambaldi to work on his next venture: *E.T.* (1982). The decision caused a rift, Baker claiming similarities between the aliens in *Night Skies* and E.T.. The dispute was subsequently smoothed over and Baker created the creatures for the Spielberg-sponsored *Men in Black* franchise.

(1985) and *The Goonies* (1985). Spielberg was a safe bet as a director but not as a producer: *I Wanna Hold Your Hand* (1978) had sunk without a trace, as would *Used Cars* (1980) and *Continental Divide* (1981). After Tobe Hooper declined an offer to take the helm ('We met and he pitched this idea about some kids meeting an extraterrestrial,' recalled *The Texas Chain Saw Massacre*'s director. 'I told him that didn't really appeal to me'), Spielberg began to consider directing *Night Skies* himself. Although neither he nor the studio could have known it, that proved a momentous decision.

'Steven had realized how painfully ambitious the *Night Skies* aliens were,' said Mitch Suskin. 'It's hard enough to build one completely articulate alien and control system from scratch, let alone five completely different creatures and systems. So Steven decided to drop the number of aliens down to one and change the script.' However, the change in direction was not due solely to budget and technical limitations – it was also down to Spielberg's desire to return to core values. Homesick and lonely shooting *Raiders* in the deserts of Tunisia, he began to feel at odds with the sci-fi movie's dark content and tone.

'I might have taken leave of my senses,' he later reflected to *Film Comment*. 'Throughout *Raiders* I was in between killing Nazis and blowing up flying

INTERSTELLAR

If *Night Skies* stemmed from a tradition of sci-fi/horror hybrids, then *Interstellar* was firmly rooted in science fact. The project was the brainchild of California Institute of Technology physicist Kip Thorne (born 1940, right), who based the idea on his controversial theory that wormholes not only exist but can be used as portals for time travel. Thorne developed a 'scriptment' – somewhere between a detailed outline and a finished screenplay – that pitched a group of explorers through a wormhole into another dimension.

The project boasted both the potential for thought-provoking spectacle and personal resonance for Spielberg: in 1991, he was an uncredited executive producer on Errol Morris's documentary based on Stephen Hawking's *A Brief History of Time*, and his father was an engineer and amateur astrophysicist.

First reported in connection with Spielberg in 2006, *Interstellar* was produced by Lynda Obst, whose track record was mostly in romantic comedies such as *Sleepless in Seattle* (1993) and *How to Lose a Guy in 10 Days* (2003). She worked with Thorne on developing the project. In March 2007, Jonathan Nolan – who, with his brother Christopher, co-wrote *Memento* in 2000 (another film interested in twisty-turny time structures) and *The Dark Knight* (2008) – was hired as a screenwriter. Spielberg began talking it up in interviews: 'I don't want to categorize it yet 'cause I'm at the beginning of the process. I don't see it as *2001*.'

However, the wormhole seems to have closed. Spielberg became busy with adventure (*Indiana Jones*, 2008; *The Adventures of Tintin*, 2011), historical drama (*War Horse*, 2011; *Lincoln*, 2012) and a different sci-fi epic (*Robopocalypse*, scheduled for 2014). But this does not necessarily spell the end of *Interstellar*. Spielberg projects have notoriously long gestation periods – twelve years in the case of *Lincoln*. And his fondness for sci-fi remains undimmed. 'I'm always coming back to science fiction,' he says. 'I began my career with science fiction. I absolutely love it. I have so many more stories that are beyond fiction.'

wings. . . I was sitting in Tunisia, scratching my head, thinking I've got to get back to the tranquillity or at least the spirituality of *Close Encounters*. My reaction was to immediately think of a very touching and tender relationship between an extraterrestrial and an eleven-year-old who takes him in.'

Happily, Spielberg had someone to share his daydreams with. Screenwriter Melissa Mathison – best known at that point for children's fable *The Black Stallion* (1979) – was Harrison Ford's girlfriend and a fixture on the *Raiders* set. Between sandstorms and bothersome turista, she and Spielberg would spitball ideas. The story that emerged was first called *A Boy's Life*, then *E.T. and Me*, and finally *E.T.: The Extra-Terrestrial*. The rest is movie history.

DRASTIC CHANGES

Despite drastic changes in tone, from horror to beguiling wonder, trace elements of *Night Skies* remain in *E.T.*. Sayles's script opens with Skar killing farm animals by touching them with a long bony finger that emits an eerie light – the inverse of E.T.'s healing digit. The most likable alien of the bunch, Buddee, forms a bond with autistic child Jaybird via finger-painting and checkers, and performs cute shtick – hiding in a clothes hamper – that feels very E.T.. There is also a slapstick element – the clownish Squirt being chased around a kitchen by a grandma while eating a pie – that informs the later film's middle section. And it ends with Buddee left injured on Earth following a showdown with Skar, cowering in the shadow of an encroaching hawk.

Before hiring Mathison, Spielberg politely gave John Sayles first refusal on writing *E.T.*, but he was busy with other projects. 'I felt my script was more of a jumping off point than something that was raided for material,' he recalled after reading Mathison's take. 'I thought she had done a great job and didn't feel I had anything to kick about.'

Ironically, once *Night Skies* had gained heart, Columbia lost the heart to make it. In February 1981, the studio sold *Night Skies/E.T.* to MCA, claiming it didn't want to make a 'Disney-type picture'. MCA struck a deal to repay Columbia the $1 million development costs and cede it five percent of *E.T.*'s net profits. After the latter became the biggest hit of all time, John Veitch, then president of Columbia's worldwide productions, reflected, 'I think we made more on that picture than we did on any of *our* films that year.' **IF**

WHAT HAPPENED NEXT. . .

E.T.: The Extra-Terrestrial (1982) won four Oscars and spent eleven years as the highest grossing film of all time, granting Spielberg superstar status and unparalleled creative freedom. He and Irving reunited and, in 1985, married – for three years. Ron Cobb contributed conceptual designs to *Back to the Future* (1985), *Aliens* (1986) and *Total Recall* (1990), and finally made his directorial debut with the comedy *Garbo* (1992). John Sayles forged a respected career in independent cinema. His 1984 film *The Brother from Another Planet* featured an alien stranded on Earth.

WILL IT EVER HAPPEN?

2/10 Probably not, but elements of *Night Skies* have played out in Spielberg's work in various guises. Having stripped the horror aspects from *E.T.*, Spielberg ploughed them into the same year's *Poltergeist*, in which spectres emerge from a television to scare the bejesus out of a suburban family. The Spielberg-produced *Gremlins* (1984) channelled the Buddee–Skar dynamic into Gizmo and Stripe, and *Night Skies* can be seen on a movie theatre hoarding alongside *A Boy's Life*. As a director, Spielberg finally turned to malevolent aliens with 2005's *War of the Worlds*, a 9/11-influenced retelling of the H.G. Wells story, starring Tom Cruise.

A CLIVE DONNER FILM

Romance
OF THE **PINK**
PANTHER

PETER
SELLERS
PAMELA
STEPHENSON

ROMANCE OF THE PINK PANTHER

Director Clive Donner **Starring** Peter Sellers, Pamela Stephenson **Year** 1980
Country UK, US **Genre** Comedy **Studio** United Artists

Despite the name, the Pink Panther movie series is really the Inspector Clouseau series. The beginning came with director Blake Edwards's *The Pink Panther* (1963), focusing largely on David Niven's dashing thief, The Phantom, seeking the legendary Pink Panther diamond. It was a vehicle for Niven, with Peter Sellers in very much a supporting role as Clouseau. The film is more a romp than a broad comedy and Sellers played the part relatively straight, with a passable French accent compared with the farcical manglings of later instalments ('It's in the top left-hand druewer.'). The film was a hit, bringing Sellers to the attention of US audiences and prompting a sequel to be rushed out only three months after the original. *A Shot in the Dark* (1964), the pinnacle of the series, created the format for the ten films that followed: Cato, Clouseau's faithful manservant and sparring partner, was introduced, as were Herbert Lom's exasperated Chief Inspector Dreyfus and Clouseau's bumbling manner and bizarre accent. *A Shot in the Dark* was a critical and commercial hit and an iconic character was born.

REVENGE OF THE CASH COW

Hollywood rarely likes to let a cash cow go unmilked and, for the best part of the next thirty years, a steady trickle of Pink Panther films emerged of varying degrees of quality. Bar the Alan Arkin-starring *Inspector Clouseau* in 1968, either Sellers or Edwards were at the heart of each instalment. To say that they had a volatile relationship is putting it mildly and the fact that they churned out five Panther films together (as well as 1968's *The Party*) is a minor miracle.

For Sellers's final appearances as Clouseau (*The Pink Panther Strikes Again* in 1976, outtakes from which were used in 1982's *Trail of the Pink Panther*, and *Revenge of the Pink Panther* in 1978), the strain of the actor's hedonistic lifestyle was beginning to show. He suffered two serious heart attacks and a stunt double was used for various action sequences. The working relationship between the director and star was also at a low ebb. 'If you went to an asylum and you described the first inmate you saw, that's what Peter had become,' said Edwards, during the making of *Strikes Again*. 'He was certifiable.' For his part, Sellers felt he was not receiving due credit for his contributions, causing

CLIVE DONNER

The proposed director of *Romance of the Pink Panther* made his name with 'Swinging Sixties' pictures like *What's New Pussycat?* (1965), starring Peter Sellers, and *Here We Go Round the Mulberry Bush* (1967), based on Hunter Davies's novel from 1965.

BACK STORY

Peter Ustinov was originally in line to play Clouseau in *The Pink Panther* (1963), but exited the project shortly before shooting commenced. Ustinov would eventually get a shot at a famous European detective and his own amusing accent when he took on the role of Agatha Christie's Hercule Poirot in *Death on the Nile* (1978, above).

WHO COULD ASK FOR MOORE?

Sellers's mooted successor Dudley Moore (above left) met Blake Edwards (above right) at group therapy. 'I said to him,' the actor recalled, '"You're a director I admire, you did all those Peter Sellers films, and I just want to stop there because this is not meant to be an audition."'

Revenge to be credited as a joint Sellers–Edwards production. After that, the duo swore never to work together again. But with United Artists eager to continue the series with its star, and happy to give him a reported $3 million upfront, plus ten percent of the gross, Sellers began to develop a new Panther film independent of Edwards in 1978. This was *Romance of the Pink Panther*.

To help write the script, Sellers brought in Jim Moloney, with whom he would also work on *The Fiendish Plot of Dr. Fu Manchu* (1980). Meanwhile, the studio declined his wish to direct the film himself. Sidney Poitier – yes, *that* Sidney Poitier – was attached as director and duly waited for a script and start date. And waited. By 1979, when a script had still not been delivered, Poitier exited the film. At the time, Sellers's mental and physical health were deteriorating and he was passionately preoccupied with another project, 1979's *Being There* – a gentle, melancholy comedy that, in contrast to the Panther films, shows the actor at his most understated and versatile.

Post-Poitier, Sellers enlisted his *What's New Pussycat?* (1965) director Clive Donner and the film continued to gestate. (Sellers, Noël Coward, Richard Burton and Elizabeth Taylor had helped finance Donner's 1963 adaptation of Harold Pinter's *The Caretaker*. Starring Alan Bates, Robert Shaw and Donald Pleasance, the film won a Silver Bear at the Berlin International Film Festival.)

FRENCH CAT BURGLAR

Two rough drafts of the script exist, both centring on Clouseau's pursuit of a female French thief named, with marked disregard for political correctness, the Frog. With echoes of *The Pink Panther Strikes Again*, Clouseau and the Frog fall in love, despite living on opposite sides of the law. The film would have seen the series return to its cat-and-mouse roots, and featured familiar characters: Herbert Lom as Dreyfus, Burt Kwouk as Cato, Graham Stark as Hercule Lajoy and André Maranne as Sergeant François Chevalier – conveniently ignoring their fates in previous outings. For the seductive Frog, Sellers had in mind the New Zealand-born comedienne Pamela Stephenson, famous at the time for the British TV series *Not the Nine O'Clock News*.

The movie, Sellers told Hollywood columnist Marilyn Beck, would be 'absolutely the end of that series of films' – a claim, Beck observed, that he had made about its predecessors – 'and, as such, it's got to be absolutely the best: absolutely superduper, so we can go out with a bang'.

Two different endings were proposed. In one, Clouseau is promoted to the rank of commissioner; in the other, he runs off with the Frog to enjoy a life of crime. It would, Sellers told Beck, 'expose a side of [Clouseau] no one has seen. He's going to be involved with a woman who's deeply in love with him and we'll see his reaction to that'. This romantic theme is intriguing, not least for its subversion of the well-meaning but inept Clouseau that audiences loved.

Intriguing or not, the elements failed to add up to a cohesive whole. The script Sellers delivered was a mess, and the studio threatened to pull the plug. But Sellers's wife, Lynne Frederick, stepped in as executive producer and pre-production commenced. Further rewrites were planned, concept art was created and filming was scheduled to start at the Studio de Boulogne in Paris.

Then, on 24 July 1980, just days after handing in the second draft of the script, Sellers died of a heart attack. Not missing a beat, the studio offered the Clouseau role to Dudley Moore – coincidentally, or not, fresh from Blake Edwards's zeitgeist-capturing *10* (1979). Moore insisted he would only take it on with Edwards at the helm (and, fully aware of the shadow Sellers would cast over his performance, was reluctant to commit to the studio's request for a multi-picture deal). Edwards, however, refused to either recast Clouseau or to work with Sellers's script. The result was 1982's patchy and compromised *Trail of the Pink Panther*, featuring unused footage of Sellers, David Niven, Herbert Lom and Bert Kwouk from previous Panther films.

DISMAL NADIR

Following that, and depending on your point of view, the series reached its dismal nadir or bizarre apogee in 1983 with Roger Moore's cameo as Clouseau in *Curse of the Pink Panther*. The film was a feeble attempt to shift focus to a new character and star: Ted Wass as Sgt Clifton Sleigh, a klutzy NYPD version of Clouseau. But critics and audiences were no longer interested and the film

> *'It's got to be absolutely the best: absolutely superduper, so we can go out with a bang.'*
>
> Peter Sellers

flopped. Subsequently, all concerned wisely retreated from the series – before unwisely returning to it a decade later with 1993's *Son of the Pink Panther*, starring Roberto Benigni as Clouseau's illegitimate offspring. Note how bastardized the title had become: the Pink Panther, after all, is a diamond, not a trenchcoat-wearing French detective. Blake Edwards moved on to pastures new, the series was relegated to the history books and Sellers's script for *Romance of the Pink Panther* continued to gather dust.

Although the Panther films were hit-and-miss, they contain classic moments that stand comparison with anything in the back catalogues of Sellers or Edwards. One can only imagine what sparks of scripted or unscripted genius *Romance of the Pink Panther* might have yielded. Sellers was only fifty-four when he died and his performance in *Being There* – for which he earned his third Academy Award nomination – showed he was still capable of greatness. He remains a much-loved comedy legend and it is bittersweet to think that he was denied a final outing as his most famous creation on his own terms. **SW**

WILL IT EVER HAPPEN?

1/10 Peter Sellers's death and Blake Edwards's unfavourable opinion of the script effectively killed its chances, and the 2006 Steve Martin reboot would further confuse matters for audiences not familiar with Sellers's originals. That said, there is still peripheral interest in the unmade film and it was referenced in the 2004 biopic *The Life and Death of Peter Sellers*.

THE TEXANS

Director Sam Peckinpah Year 1981 Country US Genre Western

SAM PECKINPAH
The legend of *The Texans* is affected not at all by the movie never coming even close to production. It is a testament to the madness that characterized the final years of a once-great director.

Bloody Sam must have known he was done after 1978's *Convoy*. It did better business than any of his other films, yet all anyone could talk about was the mayhem of the production: the fights; the drinking; the drugs; the out-of-control shoot going over schedule and over budget; the rotten reviews it received. Peckinpah was wearing out what friendships he had left, and the studios had seen enough. 'My personality seems to be not exactly what Hollywood has in mind. . .' he said. 'I've made a lot of money but I've made a lot of problems.' He retreated to a remote cabin in Montana with booze, cocaine and guns, got married and divorced, had a heart attack, went a little crazy and wrote a 250-page opus called *The Texans*.

DRINK AND DRUGS

The cabin probably seemed a good idea at the time. But as that time was a three-day drinking marathon during the *Convoy* shoot with actor Warren Oates (who wasn't even in the film), it's hard to say how much thought went into it. On paper, it was the perfect place to hide. Two months late and $3 million over budget (which was only about $3 million to begin with), *Convoy* was wrested from Peckinpah's control at the editing stage. It wasn't the first time this had happened. In 1965, Columbia re-edited *Major Dundee* into an incoherent mess. After that, it took Peckinpah nearly four years to make another film. But then he hit a hot streak, making seven of his most acclaimed pictures in just five years, beginning with *The Wild Bunch* (1969). That was all in the past though. He was a drunk now, and the only thing that tempered his drinking was cocaine. He soon found cabin life didn't suit him. There was no electricity, no indoor bathroom and the nearest liquor store was miles away.

Increasingly, he lived in a nearby town, Livingston, in hotels and motels. His love of cocaine grew to such an extent that he planned to film Robert Sabbag's 1976 book *Snowblind*, about smuggling cocaine from Colombia to New York. He roped in actor Seymour Cassel, an old drinking buddy who had worked on *Convoy*, and headed to Bogotá for research. Peckinpah's idea of research landed them both in jail. The director later fled with Cassel's passport, leaving him stranded in Colombia until his wife arrived with new documentation.

Poster: Lawrence Zeegen

THE TEXANs

A SAM PECKINPAH MOVIE

PECKINPAH GOES POP

The Osterman Weekend (1983) was his final feature, but Bloody Sam's last gasp as a film-maker was directing videos for John Lennon's pop star son Julian (above). Hired by producer Martin Lewis, Peckinpah shot videos for the hits 'Valotte' and 'Too Late for Goodbye.' They landed Lennon a nomination as Best New Artist at the 1985 MTV awards. Sadly, Sam was not there to share the glory – he died of heart failure on 28 December 1984.

When Peckinpah's daughter visited Montana in early 1979, she found her father in the cabin, paranoid and delusional, sleeping with a shotgun in his bed and ranting about the government spying on him. She convinced him to return to Livingston and stay with her. There, just months later, Peckinpah suffered a heart attack. The doctors weren't optimistic about his chances, but stabilized him and fitted a pacemaker. (According to Peckinpah biographer Marshall Fine, the director saw his heart monitor flatline when the pacemaker's wires became tangled, and yelled at his doctor, 'I'm dying, you son of a bitch! Here I go!')

He moved into a hotel to recuperate and wed a woman he had met during *Convoy*. The marriage lasted a month. Meanwhile, Michael Cimino, filming *Heaven's Gate* (1980) nearby, invited his fellow director to visit and even offered him some second unit work. However, Peckinpah believed Cimino was recklessly spending millions of studio dollars that could have funded other films.

Then producer Albert Ruddy tapped him to write *The Texans*. Ruddy had a two-picture deal with Hong Kong production company Golden Harvest. *The Cannonball Run* (1981) was the first, and – having bought the script years earlier from John Milius, who wrote it as a contemporary take on the 1948 Howard Hawks classic *Red River* – he wanted *The Texans* to be the other. Unimpressed by Milius's screenplay, Peckinpah insisted he would direct only if he could rewrite it. Ruddy agreed, giving Peckinpah a summer 1980 deadline.

'My personality seems to be not what Hollywood has in mind. . . I've made a lot of problems.'

Sam Peckinpah

The deadline came and went. All Ruddy received was a ream of expenses, including multiple Xerox machines, Cuban cigars and trips to South America. (Peckinpah often preferred to take a smaller fee and rack up massive expenses as he wasn't taxed on the remuneration.) With the screenplay three months overdue, the producer visited the hotel. What he found didn't inspire confidence. Peckinpah had taken over an entire floor and spent most days in his pyjamas and robe. His paranoia had risen to the point that he imagined his pacemaker was a CIA bomb that could be remotely detonated at any time. He also suspected that Begoña Palacios (an actress he met filming the 1965 movie *Major Dundee*, and who – in a bumpy ride of divorce and reconciliation – became his second, third and fourth wife) was a sorceress placing curses on him. Peckinpah handed Ruddy 120 pages and told him that was only half of it. When he delivered the finished article in November 1980, it was 250 pages long. Ruddy estimated the film would run to almost five hours.

ABSURDLY OVERWRITTEN

The Texans recounts the story of Jace Tranton, the ageing chairman of an oil company, who harbours a dream of driving cattle up the Chisholm Trail from Texas to Kansas like his great-grandfather, Case Tranton, a cattle baron who both fought and befriended the Comanche across whose land he drove his herd. Ruddy conceded that the screenplay included some of the best scenes Peckinpah had ever written, but he was outraged about its length.

The absurdly overwritten screenplay opens with a meta-narrative overture depicting the film's own premiere at Grauman's Chinese Theatre. Peckinpah makes his feelings about Hollywood clear, describing the audience as 'tuxedoed ex-studio heads, the last of the beat generation who have forgotten Kerouac. . . and the other variations [of] animal and insect life'. In a barb clearly aimed at Cimino, one member of the audience yells, 'So they drop eighty million and don't even wonder what pocket it came from!'

The film transitions through the on-screen projection to a scene concerning Case Tranton and a Comanche chief. It features quintessential Peckinpah touches: a snake fight with rattlers as weapons, a knife fight, severed ears and a further transition to Jace Tranton in the present day by way of a passing helicopter. This exhilarating opening, however, is followed by sixty pages of meandering conversation between oil executives aboard said helicopter.

Ruddy could not make Peckinpah see the problem with a script of such length, and the latter refused to make any changes. Having laid out $16,000 in expenses, Ruddy in turn refused to pay Peckinpah's fee. The dispute went for arbitration to the Writers Guild of America, which ruled that Peckinpah had breached his contract by failing to meet the agreed deadline. Ruddy sacked him and hired Hal Needham – in vogue after *Smokey and the Bandit* (1977) and *The Cannonball Run* (1981) – to take over. However, the screenplay required so much work that Ruddy instead decided to use Needham to fulfill his Golden Harvest deal by making the big-budget flop *MegaForce* (1982).

Tinged equally with brilliance and madness, fuelled by booze and cocaine, a thorn in the side of his producers and ultimately rejected by the industry – *The Texans* was Sam Peckinpah's career in microcosm. **DN**

WILL IT EVER HAPPEN?

3/10 Any attempt to film the screenplay would be very different to the one Peckinpah intended. Unable to get *The Texans* made in the years after Peckinpah's death, Ruddy eventually shelved it. Recently, however, he rediscovered the script and hired television writer Jim Byrnes to rewrite it, paring it down to 150 pages in the hope of attracting financing and a director.

WHAT HAPPENED NEXT. . .

His health deteriorating, Peckinpah directed just one more film – *The Osterman Weekend* in 1983 – before his death in 1984. His final years were littered with unmade projects, such as adaptations of Elmore Leonard's *City Primeval* (called *Hang Tough*) and Edward Abbey's *The Monkey Wrench Gang* (about eco-guerrillas). He also planned to direct an original Stephen King script, *The Shotgunners* (which King developed into the novel *The Regulators*). After his death, several films that suffered from his battles with studios have been restored into something resembling his original vision, notably 1965's *Major Dundee* starring Richard Harris (left, with Peckinpah), and 1973's *Pat Garrett and Billy the Kid*.

MOON OVER MIAMI

Director Louis Malle **Starring** Dan Aykroyd, John Belushi **Year** 1982 **Country** US **Genre** Political satire

LOUIS MALLE

Wired, Bob Woodward's controversial biography of the doomed John Belushi, quotes Malle as saying, of *Moon over Miami*, 'If we had been faster with the script, we might have saved his life. [His death] probably wouldn't have happened if he had been working.'

The late 1970s and early 1980s saw the Abscam scandal rock US politics. The operation involved FBI operatives setting up a fake company called Abdul Enterprises: a front to record nefarious transactions between the fictional Sheik Kraim Abdul Rahman and US government officials. At meetings on a yacht in Florida, at a house in Washington DC and in a Pennsylvania hotel, Rahman offered cash for political favours, including asylum in the US and help with getting his money out of whichever Middle Eastern country he claimed to be from. Abscam (a diminutive for 'Abdul scam') was the first wide-scale attempt to uncover corruption in the upper echelons of government, and was masterminded by convicted con man Melvin Weinberg. It led to the conviction of a number of high-ranking government officials, a state senator, five congressmen and members of the Philadelphia City Council. Not long after the affair was done and dusted in court, acclaimed French director Louis Malle saw the subject's potential for a dry dig at the US establishment.

SUICIDE, INCEST AND NAZIS

The scandal surrounding Abscam, even if it was likely to be heavily laden with sardonic wit, may have seemed a sensitive choice for a director of Malle's calibre. However, coming from a wealthy and privileged background, Malle always approached his career with a somewhat devil-may-care attitude and public opinion was unlikely to have concerned him greatly (his previous films had tackled suicide, incest and Nazis). As critic David Quinlan wrote: 'Malle made a gloriously wide variety of films, underlining his own attempts to escape categorization.' These ranged from romance to tragedy; from the cutting edge of US cinema to the outer reaches of the French New Wave. A subject with boundless potential for drama, comedy and suspense clearly appealed.

Alongside playwright John Guare – with whom he created 1980's hit *Atlantic City*, a crime drama featuring Burt Lancaster and Susan Sarandon – Malle developed a wry satire based on Abscam. Looking for actors who could inject a degree of irreverent humour into the leading roles, Malle and Guare tailored the screenplay to suit John Belushi and Dan Aykroyd, who had hit the big screen in 1980's *The Blues Brothers* and 1981's *Neighbors*. (*Saturday Night*

MOON OVER MIAMI

A Film By Louis Malle

WILLIAM RUSTOND PRESENTS "MOON OVER MIAMI" STARRING DAN AYKROYD, JOHN BELUSHI, JULIE ADAMS, PERSIFF WILLIAMSON, NED BRANDIS CO-STARRING ADAM BISSEK, RAY CAMERON AND REESE ALDON • ASSOCIATE PRODUCER RAYMOND DELTON WRITTEN BY GREYSON ANGEL • PRODUCED BY ASTOR BROOMFELD DIRECTED BY LOUIS MALLE • IN COLOR

Live, the TV sketch show that made Belushi and Aykroyd famous, had sent up the scandal in a skit called The Bel-Airabs, based on *The Beverly Hillbillies*. Abscam was later referenced in shows such as *Simon & Simon* and *Seinfeld*.)

Moon Over Miami – named after a 1935 jazz standard, and unrelated to Walter Lang's 1941 musical comedy of the same title – was to feature Belushi as a minor league crook (presumably based on Weinberg) uniting with a straitlaced FBI agent, played by Aykroyd, in an Abscam-like con. The film could have been a hit, had everything gone to plan. Instead, on 5 March 1982, Belushi was found dead from a cocaine and heroin overdose in his bungalow at the Chateau Marmont on Sunset Boulevard. The project promptly sank.

Malle went on to make several more successful films and documentaries before his death in 1995, notably the acclaimed *Au revoir les enfants* (1987), for which he was nominated for an Oscar and won a BAFTA and three Césars. *Moon Over Miami* would certainly have stirred up controversy, but whether it would have enjoyed similar success is a question that will remain unanswered.

WHAT HAPPENED NEXT. . .
There was still plenty of life in Abscam: playwright John Guare himself produced a successful stage version of *Moon Over Miami* at the Williamstown Theatre Festival in Massachusetts in the late 1980s. In a curious twist of fate, this production starred John Belushi's younger brother Jim. **CP**

WILL IT EVER HAPPEN?

1/10 Chances are slim to none. But in 2012 the Hollywood rumour mill began cranking out claims that Christian Bale would work again with David O. Russell – who directed him to an Oscar in the 2010 film *The Fighter* – on *American Bullshit*, a drama based on the Abscam scandal, scheduled for 2013.

THE CHERRY ORCHARD

Director Lindsay Anderson Starring Maggie Smith Year 1983 Country UK Genre Historical satire

A nton Chekhov's final play, which debuted just six months before his death, is a work with which directors have long struggled. Its story tells of a once-wealthy family, who return to their historical estate – including the orchard of the title, a place of nostalgic significance to family matriarch Madame Ranevskaya – on the eve of it being sold to pay their debts. For its premiere at the Moscow Art Theatre in 1904, *The Cherry Orchard* was played as a tragedy rather than the comedy Chekhov intended, and balancing its serious subtext and farcical elements has posed problems ever since.

CRITICAL DERISION
Chekhov had little sympathy for the demise of Russia's aristocracy, whom he portrayed as unable to save themselves in a rapidly changing world. That a leftist director like Lindsay Anderson would be attracted to *The Cherry Orchard* is, therefore, no surprise. A documentary maker and theatre director, Anderson first staged a production of the piece in 1966 at Britain's Chichester Festival Theatre, its cast including a young Tom Courtenay and, making his professional debut, Ben Kingsley. A radical interpretation, true to the roots of the play, it was well received by British audiences, many suffering their own economic woes.

In 1983, Anderson toured another production around Britain before taking it to London's Theatre Royal Haymarket. After this second production, he began to contemplate a feature film of the play. It had been adapted numerous times for television on both sides of the Atlantic, but a feature for theatrical release had never been made. (Director Alexander Korda came close in 1947 but the project stalled when Greta Garbo, then retired, turned down the role of Madame Ranevskaya. Anderson later commented that Garbo would have been good, but Bette Davis would have been better and Mary Astor the best of all.)

Anderson worked on a screenplay, but struggled to find backing – his clout was at a nadir after the critical derision aimed at 1982's *Britannia Hospital*, the final part of his Mick Travis trilogy. Then he encountered producer/director Menahem Golan, best known for 1981's *Enter the Ninja* (and, later, steroidal B-movies like *The Delta Force*, 1986). Golan contracted Anderson to write and direct, and Maggie Smith took a lead role. Unsurprisingly, Anderson and

LINDSAY ANDERSON
The Cherry Orchard was not the Indian-born, British-raised director's first Chekhov adaptation. He had staged the Russian dramatist's *The Seagull* at London's Haymarket Theatre in 1975.

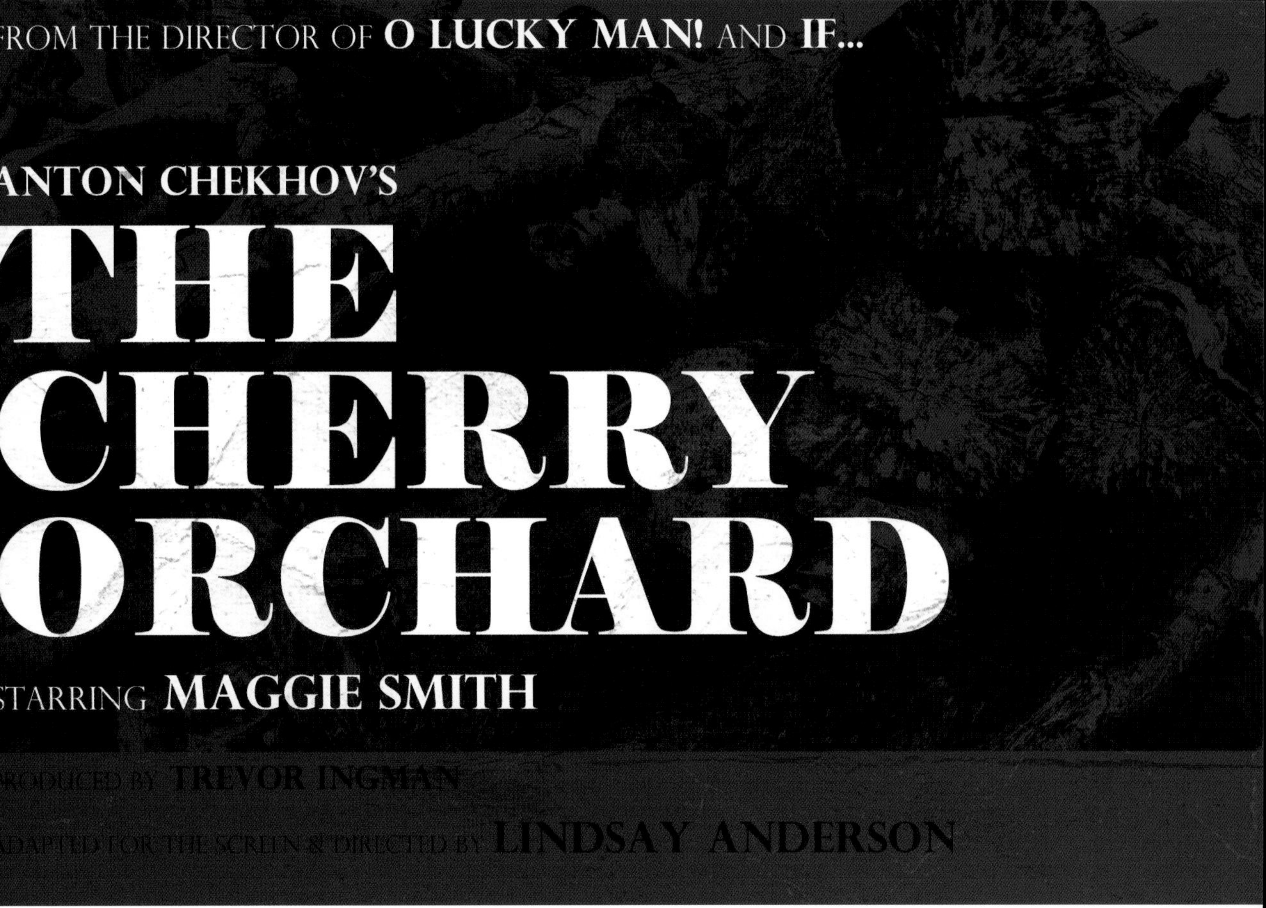

ANTON CHEKHOV'S

THE
CHERRY
ORCHARD

STARRING **MAGGIE SMITH**

PRODUCED BY **TREVOR INGMAN**

ADAPTED FOR THE SCREEN & DIRECTED BY **LINDSAY ANDERSON**

Golan failed to see eye to eye, the latter concerned about the script (not enough kickboxing, presumably) and the former unenthusiastic about the producer's plans to shoot the entire film in Russia. Anderson eventually withdrew.

With Maggie Smith still attached, Anderson teamed up with producer Trevor Ingman and Yaffle Films in 1992. They planned to shoot in Prague and had a tentative agreement with Dustin Hoffman to take a lead role, but he pulled out when the financing fell through and the project stalled again. Anderson and Ingman approached the BBC, but that production never got off the ground either – perhaps because the corporation had already filmed the play three times in the previous thirty years, as both stage and television productions.

Anderson tried fruitlessly to secure backing from other production companies and broadcasters (interestingly, his archives at Scotland's Stirling University contain a 1976 correspondence with former Ealing Studios writer and producer Monja Danischewsky, who sent Anderson a screenplay for *The Cherry Orchard*. The director praised the script but suggested it was better suited to television than cinema). One response he received, from Britain's largest satellite broadcaster, spoke volumes about both Anderson's standing at the time and the producers' cultural awareness. The rejection letter began, 'Dear Mr. Chekhov'.

WHAT HAPPENED NEXT. . .
Anderson died in 1994, at seventy-one, the project an unrealized dream. **DN**

WILL IT EVER HAPPEN?
1/10 Five years after Anderson's death, Cypriot director Mihalis Kakogiannis released a film of *The Cherry Orchard*, with Charlotte Rampling as Madame Ranevskaya. The director's final film, it remains the only major cinematic adaption of the play. A revival of Anderson's screenplay seems unlikely.

THE CRADLE WILL ROCK

Director Orson Welles **Starring** Rupert Everett, Amy Irving **Year** 1984 **Country** Italy, US **Genre** Autobiography

ORSON WELLES

'I've wasted the greater part of my life looking for money. . .' the director once admitted. 'I've spent too much energy on things that have nothing to do with a movie. It's about two percent moviemaking and ninety-eight percent hustling. It's no way to spend a life.'

When asked in 1964, 'What films do you really want to do?' Orson Welles replied, 'Mine. I have drawers full of scenarios written by me.' Two decades later, that still held true. While unrealized works like *Don Quixote* (see page 77) were never far from his mind, he endeavoured to seize the reins of a project for which he was originally the subject, rather than the director. In the early 1980s, producer Michael Fitzgerald (*Wise Blood*, 1979; *Under the Volcano*, 1984) commissioned Ring Lardner Jr. – one of the so-called Hollywood Ten, jailed for refusing to answer questions before the House Un-American Activities Committee in 1947 – to write a script about the staging of the political musical *The Cradle Will Rock*, a production directed by the twenty-two-year-old Orson Welles. In June 1984, Fitzgerald brought the script – at that point entitled *Rock the Cradle* – to Welles. Intending to simply get his approval, the producer ended up asking him to direct. Welles agreed, on the proviso that he could rewrite the script, shifting the focus to his life as a young man working in radio and on Broadway in the 1930s. Fitzgerald was amenable so, almost by accident, Welles began readying a screen autobiography.

CONTROVERSIAL, POSSIBLY SUBVERSIVE

The Cradle Will Rock was originally part of the Federal Theatre Project by the Works Progress Administration (WPA). The WPA was the largest of the New Deal agencies, responsible – in the aftermath of the Great Depression – for putting millions of Americans to work building public projects like roads and bridges. Large artistic ventures also fell within its scope, hence this musical, written by Marc Blitzstein as a Brechtian exposé of corporate greed. Set in Steeltown, United States of America, it details everyman hero Larry Foreman's attempts to unionize the local labour force and stand up to Mr Mister, whose ownership of a factory and newspaper makes him the most powerful man in town.

The show was due to premiere on 16 June 1937, at the Maxine Elliott Theatre on Broadway. However, just days beforehand, the WPA shut it down, citing budget cuts. Welles, Blitzstein and producer John Houseman – with whom Welles had begun a long association in 1935 – suspected that the agency was attempting to censor what it saw as a controversial, possibly

  Poster: Simon Halfon

An ORSON WELLES Film
RUPERT EVERETT
AMY IRVING
The CRADLE Will ROCK
RUPERT EVERETT, AMY IRVING 'THE CRADLE WILL ROCK' PRODUCED BY MICHAEL FITZGERALD. WRITTEN AND DIRECTED BY ORSON WELLES

subversive, work (Blitzstein had admitted to being a member of the Communist Party in the 1940s). WPA security padlocked the theatre and surrounded the building, preventing access to the costumes and sets.

Undeterred, Welles, Blitzstein and Houseman hired another venue, the much larger Venice (later New Century) Theatre. There was no time to announce the change of plan – so, when 600 people turned up to see the sold-out first night at the Maxine Elliot, Welles was waiting outside to direct them twenty blocks uptown to the New Century, filling the extra seats by offering

'I have drawers full of scenarios written by me.'
Orson Welles

free admission to passers-by. Ironically, the production was plagued by union problems: the orchestra wasn't permitted to play by its union unless full payment was guaranteed, and the actors' union wouldn't let them perform from the stage. So Blitzstein set up a piano on a bare stage and played the numbers himself (a feat replicated by his friend Leonard Bernstein when he helped revive the piece off-Broadway in 1964). The cast sang their pieces from seats in the audience.

APOCALYPSE THEN – ORSON WELLES'S HEART OF DARKNESS

A year after *The Cradle Will Rock*'s first incarnation on stage, the infamous *War of the Worlds* radio broadcast in 1938 made Orson Welles a hot property in Hollywood before he had even stood behind one of its cameras. In 1939, RKO president George Schaefer offered Welles a carte blanche two-picture deal, unprecedented for a rookie director. The only restrictions were that his budgets must not exceed $500,000 and his films could neither be overtly political nor court controversy. But Welles was no respecter of studio rules.

His first choice, an adaptation of Joseph Conrad's (right) anti-colonial novella *Heart of Darkness*, was daring in form and politics. Welles relocated the story to the present day, creating parallels with the threat of Nazism and the potential role of the US in the coming war. What Schaefer thought of the film politically is open to speculation; what he thought of its commercial prospects is not.

Welles envisioned shooting the whole picture from the protagonist's point of view – a technique that had been used for little more than brief shots in previous films, and would not be used extensively until 1947's *Dark Passage* and *Lady in the Lake*. Perhaps to ease concerns, Welles wrote an overture to the film to ease the audience into the technique, involving the POVs of a caged bird, a golfer and a prisoner being electrocuted. He further complicated matters by designing shots so that edits were hidden with invisible wipes. This experimental approach required the use of handheld Eyemo cameras (a favourite of combat cameramen), and pushed the cost of the picture, as estimated by RKO, to north of $1 million. At a time when the studio was struggling financially, that was unacceptable.

Welles attempted to salvage the picture by agreeing to waive his fee on a mooted adaptation of Nicholas Blake's thriller *The Smiler with the Knife*, and to substantially reduce the budget of *Heart of Darkness*. But neither picture materialized, and Welles moved on to *Citizen Kane* (1941).

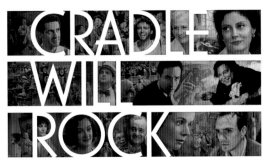

Tim Robbins's 1999 film *Cradle Will Rock* told the story of the 1937 stage production – but, with its focus on US socialist theatre as a whole, Welles (played by Angus Macfadyen) became a marginal character. Marc Blitzstein was played by Hank Azaria and John Houseman by Cary Elwes, with John Cusack and Susan Sarandon also starring. 'It has ironies and dichotomies in it,' Robbins said. 'For example, their unions tell them they can't do this play, which is deeply ironic because it is a pro-union play.'

In the fall of 1984, Welles – armed with the *Rock the Cradle* script – wrote an entirely original one, renaming it *The Cradle Will Rock*. Encompassing the broader events of his life, the script took in his acclaimed interpretation of *Doctor Faustus* (which opened at the Maxine Elliott on 8 January 1937), his meeting Blitzstein and staging *Cradle*, his driving from job to job in New York in a rented ambulance and his eventual resignation from the Federal Theatre Project to form the Mercury Theatre with John Houseman in August 1937. A surprisingly self-critical and reflective piece, the script also dealt candidly with his failed first marriage, from 1934 to 1940, to actress Virginia Nicholson.

PRODUCTION IN PERIL

The production appeared to move ahead smoothly, with Welles handpicking British actor Rupert Everett – recently propelled to stardom by *Another Country* (1984) – to play his younger self and casting Amy Irving as Nicholson. Sets were constructed at the Cinecittà studios in Rome, where the bulk of the picture was to be filmed, and exterior locations in New York and Los Angeles were scouted. However, just three weeks before shooting was due to begin, some of the financing collapsed, putting the production in peril. Welles approached Steven Spielberg – then Amy Irving's partner – for a bailout. When Spielberg refused, Welles retaliated by claiming the Rosebud sledge from *Citizen Kane* that Spielberg had bought at auction for $50,000 was a fake.

Without sufficient funds to proceed, *The Cradle Will Rock* was put on the backburner. Less than a year later, Welles was dead from a heart attack, and the project perished with him. **DN**

WILL IT EVER HAPPEN?

2/10 Michael Fitzgerald continues to harbour ambitions of filming Welles's script, and it would make an intriguing film. But without the man himself involved, it would never be the convincing self-portrait of a great US artist as a young man that the director himself intended.

MEGALO
POLIS

MEGALOPOLIS

Director Francis Ford Coppola **Year** 1984–2005 **Country** US **Genre** Drama

There's no doubt that Francis Ford Coppola is a towering figure in the history of American cinema. His *Godfather* trilogy – especially the Academy Award-winning first two instalments (1972 and 1974) – took the gangster movie to unparalleled realms of operatic grandeur, while *The Godfather: Part III* (1990) earned him a fourth Best Director nomination. The psychedelic horror of *Apocalypse Now* (1979) did for the war movie what *Sgt. Pepper* did for pop music. All, in different ways, transcended their genres magnificently. Coppola is also an acclaimed writer and producer, showered with awards from every respected cinematic institution on the planet. It is, therefore, ironic that he is now regarded with such wariness by Hollywood.

A HEROIC BEING

To cineastes he represents the triumph of art over commerce. But to current executives – despite a solid track record as a director-for-hire (1992's Oscar-winning *Bram Stoker's Dracula*, 1996's *Jack*, 1997's *The Rainmaker*) – Coppola conjures the spectre of a wayward genius for whom the box office is a distraction rather than a goal. For every *Godfather* and *Apocalypse Now* on his resumé, there's a *One from the Heart* (a financial misfire from 1992), a *Cotton Club* (a well-received but budget-busting 1984 offering), a *Youth Without Youth* (which, owing to its avowedly leftfield nature, opened on just six screens in 2007 and consequently grossed barely a quarter of a million dollars on its release). This contrary legacy is what will, barring a miracle, ensure that *Megalopolis*, his tantalizingly epic saga of one man's crusade to transform New York into a modern Utopia, will never see the light of day.

Coppola began work on *Megalopolis*, for which he wrote a labyrinthine 212-page screenplay, around 1984, and nurtured it for nearly two decades: to get it off the ground, he took mainstream directing jobs. The director described the film as reminiscent of author Ayn Rand, whose philosophy of objectivism she summed up as: 'The concept of man as a heroic being, with his own happiness as the moral purpose of his life, with productive achievement as his noblest activity, and reason as his only absolute.' Coppola's script, with plenty to say on the power of human will and the cult of personality, outstrips

FRANCIS FORD COPPOLA
The famed director acknowledged his estrangement from Hollywood in 2009. 'My attitude is, "Who cares about them?"' he told the *New York Times*. 'It's an industry that just makes the same movie over and over again and rules out a climate of experimentation.'

even Rand for narrative complexity and, like her, employs architecture as an inherently phallic symbol of vaunting ambition.

THE BIG ISSUES

Megalopolis charts a power struggle between tortured architecture genius Serge Catiline and New York Mayor Frank Cicero, both intent on rebuilding the city – or rather, building an idyllic city-within-a-city – as a monument to themselves. 'Modern New York – which is to say modern America – is, amazingly, the counterpart of Republican Rome,' Coppola explained to *Scenario Magazine*. 'I've taken a very famous and very mysterious incident in Roman history from the period of the Republic, not the Empire, called the Catiline Conspiracy. . . No one knows too much about who Catiline was, because all we read about him is from the people who were ultimately his enemies. I've taken the characters of the Catiline Conspiracy and set them in modern New York. . . So, in many ways, what it's really about is a metaphor – because if you walk around New York and look around, you could make Rome there.'

The New York of *Megalopolis* resides in the future, but harks back to the shattered, financially ravaged city of the 1970s. 'What I remember from *Megalopolis* is the big issues – New York City politics, architecture, race, the struggle between past and future – and how metaphysics ties all these things together,' producer Linda Reisman, who worked with Coppola, told *Vanity Fair*.

'The future world we're going to live in is being negotiated today. . .' said the director in the mid 2000s. 'It's kind of a shape-of-things-to-come film in which the characters are concerned with artists, businessmen, proletariat all having a stake in the future.' That is to put things in a very small nutshell. *Megalopolis*

DESIGNING DECADENCE

Below *Megalopolis*'s architectural anti-hero Serge Cataline, as envisaged by artist Karl Shefelman, a conceptual illustrator and a film-maker in his own right. Shefelman has also produced storyboards for Jonathan Demme, Martin Scorsese, Ridley Scott and Barry Levinson.

KARL SHEFELMAN 2001

– populated by a vast cast of characters – features myriad subplots, usually driven by Catiline's debauched lifestyle (one early draft included his sex tape with a Britney Spears-esque pop star). Reading the screenplay, you emerge dazed, unable to decide whether a film spawned by it would have been a work of genius or the kind of folly that brings studios to their knees. Of course, the same could be said about the script for *Apocalypse Now*, and we know how that turned out. 'It was very difficult even to get feedback on it,' Coppola told aintitcool.com. 'The sort of notes I would get would be related to the project's financial or pop-value. I didn't want that kind of narrow movie feedback, because I was trying to write a script that was [more] ambitious.'

> *'It's a movie that costs a lot of money to make and there's not a patron out there.'*
>
> Francis Ford Coppola

TRAGEDY STRIKES

Russell Crowe, Nicolas Cage, Robert De Niro, Paul Newman, Kevin Spacey, Edie Falco and Uma Thurman were rumoured to be involved, although no actors were ever attached to the project. However, Coppola shot a reported thirty hours of test footage in New York and, by 2001, things seemed to be making progress: it was speculated that United Artists might be handling distribution. Then tragedy struck. The 9/11 attacks on the World Trade Center abruptly rendered a film about the rebuilding of an idealized New York more than a little hard to swallow. 'It made it really pretty tough. . .' the director admitted. 'All of a sudden you couldn't write about New York without just dealing with what happened and the implications of what happened. The world was attacked and I didn't know how to try to deal with that. I tried.'

Until 2005, Coppola continued to harbour hopes that it would one day get the green light. His conviction never faltered – after all, no one objected when Fellini routinely made expensive art-house movies – but, in the now financially and conceptually conservative Hollywood, no studio with appropriate resources was likely to give him $100 million to make a monumentally ambitious movie about architects. (United Artists was swallowed up by Sony in 2005.)

Megalopolis remains one of cinema's great what-ifs. Had Coppola been given the opportunity to realize his dream, would it have been a film to rank alongside *The Godfather* and *Apocalypse Now*? **SB**

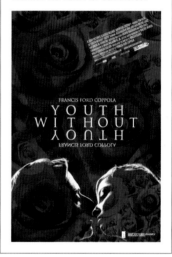

WILL IT EVER HAPPEN?

3/10 It seems not even Coppola thinks so. 'I feel pleased to have written something,' he told Movieline in June 2009. 'Then I'm done with it and I want to go on and write something else. Someday, I'll read what I had on *Megalopolis* and maybe I'll think different of it, but it's also a movie that costs a lot of money to make and there's not a patron out there. You see what the studios are making right now.'

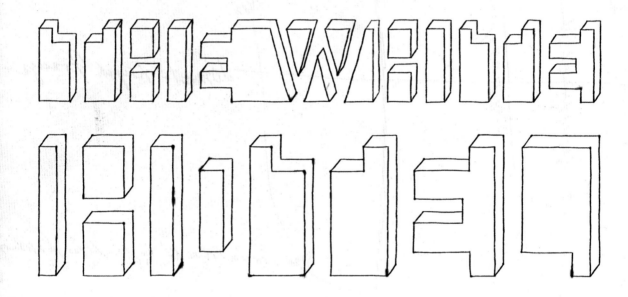

BASED ON THE BOOK BY
D.M. THOMAS

COMING SOON

THE WHITE HOTEL

Directors Mark Rydell, Bernardo Bertolucci, David Lynch, Emir Kusturica, Simon Monjack **Starring** Isabella Rossellini, Juliette Binoche, Anthony Hopkins, Brittany Murphy **Year** 1988 onwards **Genre** Drama

The story of the attempted making of *The White Hotel* is as surreal as the book on which the film would have been based: begun at the behest of a superstar songstress and ending with the premature death of a rising starlet. Even the author, D.M. Thomas, conceded that the novel, published in 1981, was not for all tastes. It concerns a nineteenth-century Odessa woman, Lisa, and her treatment by Dr Sigmund Freud. Her quest for self-knowledge reveals her history and fears – concerns that are devastatingly realized in the book's final stretch, when the spectre of the Holocaust rears its terrifying head.

SEX AND VIOLENCE

Thomas says he imagines the film of his novel as a patchwork of what might have been: a kaleidoscopic vision uniting all the great directors who were attached, then almost immediately withdrawn. Then there are the stars tipped to play Freud and Lisa – starting with Barbra Streisand, who bought the rights to the book after a friend at a dinner party recommended it. Perhaps emboldened by Meryl Streep's recent success with Karel Reisz's adaptation of John Fowles's novel *The French Lieutenant's Woman* (1981), Streisand took the project to producer Keith Barish, who produced Franco Zeffirelli's *Endless Love* (1981). To direct, Streisand chose Mark Rydell, whose recent work included *The Rose* (1979) and *On Golden Pond* (1981) – the first of which boded better than the second for Thomas and his work, which he freely admitted contained lots of sex and violence, often at the same time.

After Rydell, the rights passed to US producers Robert Michael Geisler and John Roberdeau. The pair were obsessed with reclusive US director Terrence Malick, but he would not be tempted (after 1978's *Days of Heaven*, he wouldn't direct a new movie until 1998's *The Thin Red Line*). Next to be attached was Bernardo Bertolucci. He seemed perfect, having directed the groundbreaking, explicit *Last Tango in Paris* (1972) and, according to the director himself, had been briefly involved in the Streisand years. The latter deal apparently came unstuck when the actress asked, 'How are we going to deal with all the sex, Bernardo?' Bertolucci replied, 'I have this idea for glass fiber optics to enter the woman's vagina.' The subject was never mentioned again.

BARBRA STREISAND
The starry roll call of names associated with *The White Hotel* began with the singer. When her involvement with the production ended, Streisand instead took an award-winning role in 1983's *Yentl* (above).

HOSTEL RECEPTION

Cornish novelist, poet and biographer D.M. Thomas, although exhausted by his futile trek though development hell on behalf of *The White Hotel*, initially bore Hollywood no ill will. 'After all, this is not The Somme,' he wrote in the *Guardian* in 2005. 'One thing is certain: the imagined movie is wonderful. . . I never tire of seeing Lisa in the train, a blue lake outside, and hearing the first crashing chords of *Don Giovanni*. . . Or perhaps clowns tumbling in a circus ring, with Nazi officers gazing up at Lisa, swinging through the air.' Four years later, in the *Telegraph*, he was in a less charitable mood: 'The movie-making business is like sex. Constant tumescence, detumescence, tumescence, and then again detumescence. . .' Thomas's 2008 book *Bleak Hotel* chronicles his and the movie's tribulations.

Bertolucci's ideas for *The White Hotel* began with celluloid itself. It was to be shot using Showscan, a precursor to IMAX, which projected the film at 65mm and at sixty frames per second. The idea was ahead of its time, which suited the book, and the writer, producer and director-to-be were treated to a showcase of Showscan's capabilities, involving car chases and roller coasters. 'Can you imagine how the sexual fantasies will look in Showscan?' Geisler enthused afterwards, as a motion-sick Bertolucci fumbled to the bathroom.

It became apparent that the director would be demanding. Some sources say he wanted too much money, others that he placed too much emphasis on Freud and psychoanalysis for the producers' liking. His nine Oscars for 1987's *The Last Emperor*, including Best Picture and Best Director, perhaps made the decision for him, and he walked. Geisler and Roberdeau promptly revised their opinion of Bertolucci's masterwork, *Last Tango in Paris*: 'overrated', they said.

SURREAL FETISHES

David Lynch – a visionary well suited to *The White Hotel*'s surreal fetishes and horror – was next to be involved, with British dramatist Dennis Potter attached to write the script. The combination of two artists adept at translating the intellectual into something real and visceral was so great that even Potter felt it. At his first meeting with Lynch, the writer grabbed his lapels and told him that, if they got it right, 'This movie will be the *Madame Bovary* of our time.'

However, wrote Thomas, 'When I was sent Potter's screenplay, I was dismayed to find Freud and Vienna deleted, and my operatic heroine now a high-wire act in a Berlin circus. Don Giovanni and Eugene Onegin had given way to jaunty Potteresque tunes from the '30s. Geisler and Roberdeau explained that Lynch didn't feel he could deal with European high art. He liked the lively Potter screenplay, and so, with reservations, did they.'

Thomas's fears were allayed when, in 1991, Lynch split with his lover and muse Isabella Rossellini, who was lined up to play Lisa. Lynch couldn't do it without her, and so exited the project. However, shortly after Potter's death in 1994, the script did come close to life when, for a commemorative charity event at New York's Lincoln Center, the screenplay was given a staged reading, with Rebecca De Mornay as Lisa and Brian Cox as Freud.

Their dream once again in ashes, Geisler and Roberdeau returned to Malick, by this time deep in preparation on his 'comeback', *The Thin Red Line*. But, by 1998, a new contender had appeared: Serbian director, double Palme d'Or winner and political firebrand Emir Kusturica. (Potter's script was adapted by Serbian playwright Dušan Kovacevic.) He had great plans for the film, which he imagined would be shot in the former Yugoslavia. The producers wanted Juliette Binoche, but Kusturica allegedly regarded her as insufficiently sensual.

Nicole Kidman, Lena Olin, Irene Jacob, Catherine McCormack and Rachel Weisz were all reported to have met with the director and *The White Hotel* was back on track – until an attack by NATO on Belgrade in 1999 almost killed Kusturica's son. He duly bowed out of the film and all commercial dealings with the United States. (Thomas wryly noted that Kusturica resurfaced in 2000's *La veuve de Saint-Pierre*, acting alongside none other than Binoche.)

ELECTRIFYING EROTICISM

Spanish auteur Pedro Almodóvar entered the fray, only for a court case over the rights of ownership – between Geisler and Roberdeau, and investor Gerard Rubin – to close things down. The red tape took its toll: John Roberdeau died of a heart attack in 2002 and when, in 2003, director David Cronenberg expressed interest, he cancelled his contract within a matter of hours, having received a legal notice from Rubin's hardball lawyer.

Thomas finally negotiated a one-year option and, in 2005, French-born, Australian-raised director Philippe Mora stepped up to the bar. Juliette Binoche was interested again, and the project was successfully launched at the Cannes film festival, where investors were enticed by 'a dream of electrifying eroticism and inexplicable violence'. The pitch worked: soon $15 million was in the pot, and Anthony Hopkins was on board to play Freud. Within months, Binoche had gone, and offers went out to Kate Winslet and Tilda Swinton. Winslet passed, as did Hopkins, the latter quickly replaced by Dustin Hoffman.

As Swinton exited owing to creative differences, many more actresses came into the frame: Naomi Watts, Hilary Swank and Milla Jovovich – the latter, like

> *'I have this idea for glass fiber optics to enter the woman's vagina.'*
>
> Bernardo Bertolucci

Thomas's Lisa, a genuine Ukrainian. Then Hoffman left, and bitter disputes over money ensued. After a clash with producer Susan Potter, Mora was replaced in 2006 by British writer-director Simon Monjack. He was very much a dark horse but, in the wake of his attachment, Kirsten Dunst was reported to be interested, with, as Freud, Geoffrey Rush. Penélope Cruz was also mooted.

Monjack – nicknamed 'Con-Jack' – was viewed with scepticism by the industry, having directed only one film (2001's *Two Days, Nine Lives*) and having sued the producers of George Hickenlooper's Edie Sedgwick biopic *Factory Girl* (2006) – which he claimed, without any apparent basis, to have written. Monjack brought with him a new Lisa: Brittany Murphy, who rose to fame in the teen comedy *Clueless* (1995) and latterly starred in *8 Mile* (2002) and *Sin City* (2005). Despite Monjack's sketchy track record, Murphy's involvement held faint promise. It proved, however, to be the project's last gasp: the option on the novel lapsed and both Monjack and Murphy withdrew, rendering *The White Hotel* once again closed for business. **DW**

WILL IT EVER HAPPEN?

2/10 Although it was reported as late as 2009 that Philippe Mora 'insists he has not given up the project yet', there has been no further talk of Thomas's novel making it to the screen. There have been many precedents – J.G. Ballard's *Crash*, William Burroughs's *Naked Lunch* – but *The White Hotel* remains the very definition of the unfilmable book, the last domino to tumble.

WHAT HAPPENED NEXT. . .

Events turned from frustrating to outright tragic. Two years after the film stalled, with Simon Monjack and Brittany Murphy (below) now married, the actress unexpectedly died of pneumonia and anemia at the age of thirty-two. Within two months, Monjack – eight years her senior – would also be dead, from similar symptoms.

LENINGRAD

Director Sergio Leone **Starring** Robert De Niro **Year** 1989 **Genre** War

SERGIO LEONE
'I [didn't] underestimate the difficulties of
the project,' the director admitted in 1986,
'but I'm drawn toward difficult challenges.
It is not worth the bother of dealing with
a "routine" film in the meantime. You can't
shoot film as if you were putting salami
into its skin.'

Summer 1984 found Sergio Leone at war with Hollywood. Contracted
to deliver a 165-minute cut of his epic *Once Upon a Time in America*,
the Italian director had instead given Warner Bros a version lasting
just under four hours. It was only his seventh (credited) full film and his first
non-Western in twenty years, but he intended it to be his masterpiece. Despite
its gangster theme, he insisted, 'I didn't remake *The Godfather*.' (Leone had
been approached to helm that 1972 classic, but – to his regret – declined.)
Instead, he had made a film about 'time, memory and cinema' that flashed
back and forth as the protagonist, played by Robert De Niro, contemplated
his life, and the life to come, through a drug-induced haze. Throughout the
film, a phone rang, to be revealed at the end as its true framing device, giving
last-minute order to the narrative. Warner, however, was having none of this.
In the US release, the phone rang just once. Out went the flashbacks and
anything that didn't involve blood and bullets – leading Leone to engage Orson
Welles's lawyer, who assured him that his contract, signed on French soil, was
inviolable. Leone, however, didn't stand a chance. Every time Leone lashed
out at an executive, they left, or were fired, or promoted without trace. 'It is
difficult,' he told *Cahiers du Cinéma*, 'to fight an enemy who doesn't exist.'

BLEAKEST OF CIRCUMSTANCES
This experience perhaps explains why the story that was to occupy his mind
until his death was one of warfare in the bleakest of circumstances. The Nazi
siege of the Russian city of Leningrad – now known as St Petersburg – lasted
from September 1941 to January 1944. Some forty percent of its population
was killed, but their resilience was more than a match for Hitler's ambition.
Screenwriter Sergio Donati encouraged Leone to think small, perhaps make a
film noir, but he *couldn't* think small. And it didn't get bigger than *Leningrad*.
Leone didn't commission research, much less a script. Instead, he listened to
the *Leningrad Symphony* (Symphony No. 7 in C major), completed by Russian
composer Dmitri Shostakovich in 1941 and premiered the following year.
Through the music, and also the history of the performing of it, Leone began
to form an idea, inspired not just by images of the war-torn city but by two

BASED ON THE PULITZER PRIZE-WINNING BOOK BY HARRISON SALISBURY

LENINGRAD
THE 900 DAYS

A FILM BY SERGIO LEONE

THRICE UPON A TIME
Between 1968's *Once Upon a Time in the West* and the similarly entitled but otherwise unrelated *Once Upon a Time in America* (1984), Leone made only one film (although he played uncredited roles in the making of others): 1971's *Giù la testa* – the second of the *Once Upon a Time. . .* trilogy – aka *Duck, You Sucker* or, more popularly, *A Fistful of Dynamite*. James Coburn (above left) and Rod Steiger (above right) starred.

photographs of Shostakovich. One showed him as a bookish composer; the other found him in full fireman's outfit, doing his bit for the resistance.

Leone's biographer, Sir Christopher Frayling, suggests that the production the director envisaged was, 'A love story involving a cynical American newsreel cameraman and a young Soviet girl, against the epic background of the siege. The heroic self-sacrifice of three million people in defence of their city would [in Leone's words] "open the American's eyes" . . . The cameraman would be commissioned to "spend twenty days in Leningrad covering the battle" but would stay for the rest of the siege, even though "he doesn't give a damn about the cause." But love would change his mind.'

Leone poured all of his imagination into the film's opening scene, which would begin with the fingers of the actor portraying Shostakovich at his piano. The camera would pull back through the window and – in the most ambitious tracking shot ever attempted – through the ravaged city, to the trenches where Russian snipers lay in wait. Across the steppe, in the same single take, hordes of German Panzer tanks would stand ready, one firing a single shell that would trigger the first cut of the movie. Leone proposed shooting the whole scene on location, somehow evacuating Leningrad's entire population while he did so.

While Leone fleshed out the idea in the early 1980s, Russia's leadership passed from Leonid Brezhnev, to Yuri Andropov, then Konstantin Chernenko

> '*He always had this dream of doing a picture about Leningrad, and he never could pull it together.*'
> Clint Eastwood

and finally Mikhail Gorbachev. None of them, progressive or not, were open to turning the world's attention back to a conflict – often confused with Stalingrad, the scene of a devastating battle in 1942 – that would show the Russian people in stricken circumstances: starved into desperation, forced to eat their own pets and even worse.

Nevertheless, Leone continued his pitch to whoever would listen, confronting obstacles thrown up by the Communist Party and courting the press. 'Rarely,' commented journalist and cinephile Gilles Gressard, 'has a filmmaker spoken so much and so often about a film that was not yet made.'

In 1984, Leone suggested in *Screen International* that MosFilm – Russia's oldest and biggest studio – was on board and hinted that De Niro might play the cameraman. 'I have promised the Russians,' he said, 'it will be an epic film that highlights the heroism and human qualities of the Soviet Resistance when the Nazis entered their country.' In 1988, things became more serious with an announcement in Communist newspaper *Pravda*. The following year, Leone held a press conference in Moscow. He revealed that a co-production deal had been agreed with Sovifilm, Sovexportfilm and Lenfilm Studios, underwritten by his own production company and Italy's RAI. His former classmate Ennio Morricone would write the score, and the film would be shot by Leone's regular director of photography, Tonino Della Colli.

Frayling records Leone declaring, 'Think of *Gone with the Wind*. A love story, against the backdrop of a war. This will be a huge cinematic fresco, at least three hours' screen time. . . There will not be an emphasis on war, although I have to say that I asked for 400 tanks when in fact I will be requiring at least 2,000.' Leone estimated that the film – from script to editing – would be ready in less than three years. To *Première*, he mused, 'The production is so immense that I don't just need a production house – I need a state.'

ALMOST IMPOSSIBLE

Leone claimed it would cost $30 million, but industry projections ran to three times that. He was burning up pre-production time and had yet to provide a title, let alone a cast (De Niro denies ever being offered the part). All Leone had was that opening sequence – which, he was reminded by Della Colli, was almost impossible to shoot in an unbroken take, as camera magazines held only about 980 feet of film. As far as anyone can tell, no script was ever written.

In 1988, Clint Eastwood, star of Leone's *Dollars* trilogy (1964–66), asked the director what he was doing next. 'Well,' said Leone, 'I'm still preparing this movie about Leningrad.' Says Eastwood: 'He was always interested in pictures that had revolution. That's why, on *The Good, the Bad and the Ugly*, he had the Civil War as the background. So he had dreams about doing it, but I don't know whether he ever conquered the script. . . he just never was able to get to the point to pull the trigger on it. The reason, I think, Sergio became less prolific is because he had a rough time making a decision on what stories to do next. Once he'd done *Once Upon a Time in America*, and one or two films where he was associated as a producer, he started kinda losing his interest. He always had this dream of doing a picture about Leningrad, and he never could pull it together. I think it was just kind of a dream that sat there.'

Despite a heart condition diagnosed during the *Once Upon a Time in America* shoot, Leone continued to pursue that dream. But in 1989, he died at the age of sixty – two days before a planned visit to Los Angeles to make one last attempt to nail down finance for the film that had eluded him. **DW**

WILL IT EVER HAPPEN?

2/10 In 2011, Tornatore said his *Leningrad* project was still in negotiations. A deal was announced with producer Avi Lerner, who had hits in the 1980s with the likes of Steven Seagal, and who suggested changes to raise the desired $100 million budget. 'We have agreed,' he said, 'to make it more upbeat.' Tornatore downplayed Kidman's involvement: 'She was the one who talked to the journalists.' As of late 2012, Al Pacino was the only actor attached, but imdb.com listed Leone as the author of the screenplay and Morricone as the composer.

WHAT HAPPENED NEXT. . .

Hopes for Leone's *Leningrad* project were briefly revived at the Cannes film festival in 2004. Italian film-maker Giuseppe Tornatore (left, with, on the right, Leone's composer Ennio Morricone) – who helmed the hit *Cinema Paradiso* (1988) – announced an English-language historical epic called *Leningrad*. Implicitly referencing Leone's working title *The 900 Days*, producer Gianpaolo Letta noted, 'The 900-day German assault on this major Soviet city, now known as Saint Petersburg, has become memorable because Hitler thought it would be quickly reduced to rubble. But, in the end, the Nazis were forced to retreat.' It was, he added, 'a key World War II episode never seen before on Western movie screens.' A-list stars were promised, with a rumoured role for Nicole Kidman.

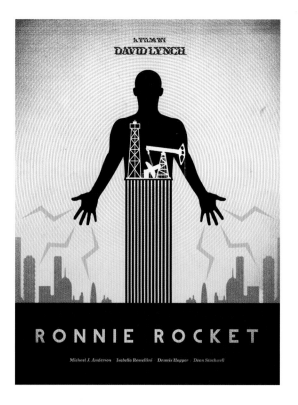

Chapter 5
The Nineties

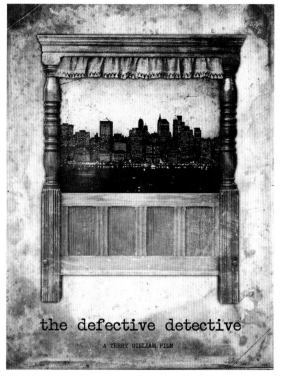

THE ARYAN PAPERS
A STANLEY KUBRICK FILM

CRUSADE
ARNOLD SCHWARZENEGGER
A PAUL VERHOEVEN FILM

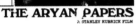

THE HOT ZONE
JODIE FOSTER ROBERT REDFORD WRITTEN BY JAMES V HART DIRECTED BY RIDLEY SCOTT

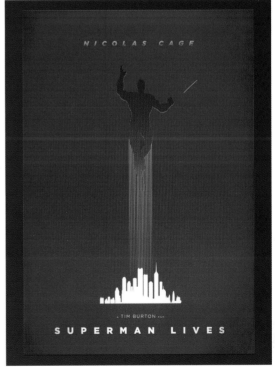

NICOLAS CAGE

A TIM BURTON FILM
SUPERMAN LIVES

RONNIE ROCKET

Director David Lynch **Starring** Michael J. Anderson, Isabella Rossellini, Dennis Hopper, Dean Stockwell
Year *c.*1990 **Country** US **Genre** Mystery

DAVID LYNCH
'I've been writing *Ronnie Rocket* for ten years, since I finished *Eraserhead*,' the idiosyncratic director revealed in the 1980s. 'I need,' he admitted, 'to work with people on it who are not looking for a tremendous commercial return.'

The shortlist for 'David Lynch's strangest film' would actually be a fairly long list, encompassing virtually everything from *Eraserhead* (1977) to *Inland Empire* (2006). The US auteur is acclaimed as the contemporary master of surrealism and dreamlike imagery, beloved by fans and critics. But *Ronnie Rocket* might have been the strangest of all. Its script begins: 'Black. . . fade in a giant stage. . . enormous with black curtains – open. The entire stage is filled with a wall of fire 200 feet high. Within the fire are thousands of souls screaming out silently. . . only the roaring of the fire.'

METAPHYSICAL MYSTERY
At the American Film Institute Conservatory in Los Angeles, Lynch assembled his debut, the underground sensation *Eraserhead*. Conceived at the same time was his metaphysical mystery and science-fiction oddity *Ronnie Rocket*. In the wake of *Eraserhead*'s impact, producer Stuart Cornfeld – who assisted Mel Brooks on 1977's *High Anxiety* and would later be Ben Stiller's production partner – approached Lynch about new projects. *Ronnie Rocket* was discussed but dismissed as being too unlikely to find funding. Cornfeld and Lynch instead collaborated on *The Elephant Man* (1980), a critical and commercial hit.

Riding high, Lynch returned to the idea, but two other sci-fi films came his way: 1983's *Return of the Jedi*, which he declined ('It's your thing!' he told George Lucas. 'It's not my thing.'), and 1984's *Dune*, which, somewhat unfortunately, he accepted. And so a pattern emerged: Lynch revisiting *Ronnie Rocket* after each new endeavour, but never managing to launch it.

The director has described the film as being 'about a three-foot tall guy with red hair and physical problems, and about sixty-cycle [per second] alternating current electricity' – making its failure to secure financing a great deal more explicable. From the abstract ideas to the casting of the titular character, *Ronnie Rocket* would have been an ambitious and difficult project.

The film is set in a dark, oppressive, industrial city, where smoke spews from factories and the air hums with electricity. A detective travels here, the very end of the line. He has come to investigate an ambiguous case involving the centre of the city, where no one is allowed in or out. The detective also possesses the

Poster: Matt Needle

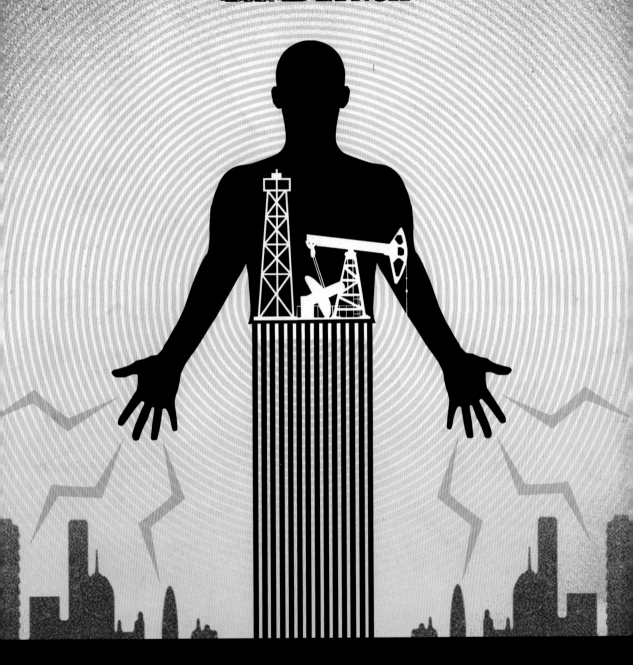

A FILM BY
DAVID LYNCH

RONNIE ROCKET

Michael J Anderson · Isabella Rossellini · Dennis Hopper · Dean Stockwell

THE SOULS AND THE FIRE

Jonathan Caouette, director of 2003's *Tarnation* – a documentary about his mother Renee's (above) schizophrenia – told aintitcool.com about wanting to direct *Ronnie Rocket* himself: 'It's one of the most mesmerizing screenplays I've ever read in my life. It's just so brilliant. I would love to do it. With the souls and the fire. . . and the knitters, and the inability to concentrate because the electricity is going in reverse – Jesus Christ, it would be the perfect metaphorical schizophrenic film to make! It's such an expression of what schizophrenia – I think – is like. . . I'm not schizophrenic, but I get the gist of it because I've seen it firsthand'.

ability to stand on one leg, making him something of a prodigy to the folk he meets. He journeys deeper, falling in love with the beautiful and pure Diana and learning that, to avoid being killed by the sinister 'donut men' and bad electricity, one must maintain a state of pain – achieved by stabbing oneself with knitting needles. Meanwhile two delusional scientists, Dan and Bob, are experimenting on the deformed Ronald De Arte, trying to make him into 'The Average Handsome Man'. With patronage from wife/mother figure Deborah, they instead succeed in installing into Ronald a power pack that means he has to plug himself into the mains every fifteen minutes or lose his charge. (Similar to the dynamics in *Eraserhead* and 1986's *Blue Velvet*, the scientists, Deborah and Ronald form a twisted take on the US nuclear family.)

Stumbling upon a struggling rock band during practice, Ronald is lured into the group by their unscrupulous manager. His bizarre warblings and screams – powered by high voltage – make the band an overnight success. These

> *'I want to have time to go into that world and live in it for a while, and that costs money.'*
>
> David Lynch

vocal outpourings wear Ronald down but the band insist on pushing him to extremes. His family try to save him but are killed. Then they come back to life. Together with the detective and his newfound sidekicks, Terry and Riley (a nod to the minimalist composer Terry Riley), they all set out to destroy the evil overlord Hank Bartells and bring light and good electricity back to the city.

The story is part *Frankenstein*, part rock 'n' roll fable and part old-fashioned tale of good versus evil. It is packed with bizarre occurrences (villains whose shoelaces prove their undoing; women exposing themselves to the detective; obscure hypotheses on circles, closed circuits and the universe) and Lynchian motifs (mystery, sensuality, love, violence, oppressive industry, pompadours and surreal musical performances). It veers wildly between lighter moments, like the detective and Terry's philosophical banter, and extreme darkness, such

RON FROM ANOTHER PLACE

Seemingly ideal for David Lynch's story of 'a three-foot-tall guy', the 3 foot 7 inch (1.1m) Michael J. Anderson instead found fame as 'the man from another place' in the director's 1990 TV series *Twin Peaks*. The actor told braddstudios.com how he came to work with Lynch in the mid 1980s: 'The ad placed in *Variety* was in reference to *Ronnie Rocket*. *Twin Peaks* came along by surprise, years after *Ronnie Rocket* had been shelved. . . . It was a bizarre and amazing script. Interestingly enough, I began writing "The Secret Diary of Ronnie Rocket" – but, in the absence of the movie, it seemed rather moot'. Anderson also graced *Mulholland Dr.* (2001).

Lynch's unrealized projects mounted up, among them one written in 1987 with *Twin Peaks* co-creator Mark Frost (with Lynch, left). *One Saliva Bubble* is set in Newtonville, Kansas ('Lightning capital of the world. . . We're zappy to see you!!!'), where a stray saliva bubble in a military base has catastrophic consequences. A cast of characters including a crackpot genius, an asylum inmate and Chinese acrobats are subjected to a body-swap crisis. It seems to be a stab at mainstream comedy, but is not without Lynchian elements: a man who talks in rhyming couplets, a magazine called *Detectives in Love*, a tap-dancing ketchup bottle and unusual happenings in small-town America. It was to star Steve Martin and Martin Short, but production never began. Other Lynch projects that never came to pass include his thinly veiled Marilyn Monroe biopic *Goddess* (aka *Venus Descending*), his self-described 'existential Marx Brothers' comedy *Dream of the Bovine* and a rumoured but highly unlikely sequel to *Mulholland Dr.* (2001).

as people collapsing into seizures, bleeding and stabbing themselves to stay alive. Far too odd to have mass appeal, it is Lynch to the max – heaven for his fans but a headscratcher for the rest of the world.

Ann Kroeber – the wife and sometime assistant of Lynch's late sound designer Alan Splet – said, 'He used to talk with my late husband and I, any chance he could get, about *Ronnie* during breaks of shooting *The Elephant Man. Ronnie Rocket* was the subject that was near and dear to his heart.'

It would easily be Lynch's biggest production since *Dune*. The script describes giant buildings and a psychedelic climax featuring an auditorium of clones and a stage of damned, burning souls. 'I want to have time to go into that world and live in it for a while,' Lynch said, 'and that costs money. I don't really want to have a normal eleven-week shooting schedule on *Ronnie Rocket*. I'd rather go with a smaller crew, and build the sets and live in them for a while.'

The closest it came to life was in the director's early 1990s heyday, circa *Twin Peaks*. A potential cast included Michael J. Anderson, and *Blue Velvet*'s Isabella Rossellini, Dennis Hopper and Dean Stockwell. After working on Lynch's *Dune* and *Blue Velvet*, Dino De Laurentiis considered producing it, as did Francis Ford Coppola's American Zoetrope. Sadly, both went bankrupt.

Ronnie Rocket remains the missing link between the nightmarish sci-fi of *Eraserhead* and the dreamy mystery and romance of Lynch's later works. **SW**

WILL IT EVER HAPPEN?

5/10 In 2012, the director told salon.com that he looks at his script 'from time to time. . . there's always something I haven't figured out yet. I want to make it – I love that world'. With fans craving a fresh film, he could use an initiative such as Kickstarter to get the ball rolling. And the prospect of what Lynch might accomplish with 3D or motion capture is mouthwatering.

NOSTROMO

Director David Lean **Starring** Marlon Brando, Alec Guinness **Year** 1991
Budget $46 million **Genre** Drama **Studio** Columbia TriStar

Considered one of author Joseph Conrad's masterworks, the 1904 novel
Nostromo is also notoriously difficult. Its labyrinthine plot is populated
with dozens of characters and shrouded in a moral fog. Conrad scholar
Jacques Berthoud called it a 'novel that one cannot read unless one has
read it before' – a view David Lean would have recognized given that, as he
confessed, it took him three attempts to get past the first hundred pages. Set
against a backdrop of revolution in an 'imaginary (but true)' Latin American
country, *Nostromo* charts the fortunes of a sailor renowned for his loyalty. He
is trusted by the ruling regime to guard a hoard of silver against rebel forces,
but succumbs to the temptation of stealing it. When Lean finally finished the
novel, he was excited by its portrayal of a society in chaos, and its exploration
of tumultuous events and how those involved are corrupted by greed and lust.
Fellow director Michael Powell had already judged an adaptation of *Nostromo*
as impossible – the very reason, he suspected, that Lean wanted to do it.

CLASSIC LITERATURE
No stranger to bringing classic literature to the screen, Lean cut his teeth with
acclaimed adaptations of Dickens and Coward, and cemented his reputation
with epic versions of T.E. Lawrence, Pasternak and Flaubert. In 1986, he
commissioned playwright and screenwriter Christopher Hampton to work on a
screenplay for *Nostromo*. Hampton was familiar with the novel, having written
a script for an unrealized TV version. The duo worked for a year in London and,
after six drafts, shaped a screenplay with which the director was happy.

Lean contacted Steven Spielberg – who, having been 'pulverized' by 1962's
Lawrence of Arabia, described the British film-maker as his 'greatest influence'
– in the hope of enlisting him as producer. Spielberg agreed and won backing
from Warner Bros to the tune of $30 million. Actors including Alec Guinness
(star of Lean's 1957 classic *The Bridge On the River Kwai*, another Spielberg
favourite), Marlon Brando, Peter O'Toole, Anthony Quinn, Isabella Rossellini,
Alan Rickman, Julian Sands and Dennis Quaid were connected to key roles.
(The lead was to have been played by the relatively unknown French actor
Georges Corraface, whom Lean had discovered in a Parisian theatre company.)

DAVID LEAN
'I hope I'll be able to make this film,'
David Lean (above) told fellow British
director John Boorman, shortly before
he died, 'because I feel that I'm just
beginning to get the hang of it.'

BOX OF DELIGHTS

Production sketches by John Box (foot of page and overleaf) give a sense of *Nostromo*'s scale. At Lean's memorial service in 1991, the production designer described the director as 'a craftsman'. Box himself died in 2005.

Unfortunately, things grew rocky early on. Lean, under the impression that he was being granted free rein on the picture, was taken aback when, at a meeting Spielberg had organized, he was presented with a list of changes to the script. Although Spielberg thought it was brilliantly written, he and the studio believed the myriad plots and characters would have to be clarified to attract a wide audience. Furious, Lean returned to London and raged at Hampton about the meeting. Spielberg, not wanting to fall out with a director he admired, withdrew from the project. Without him, Warner's commitment evaporated. Having initially promised half the budget if Lean could raise the rest, they dropped the project entirely. Lean was undeterred, but Hampton – who had been offered the chance to adapt his play *Les Liaisons Dangereuses* for the screen (hence 1988's *Dangerous Liaisons*) – wanted six months off. Lean reluctantly agreed and approached Robert Bolt to replace him.

The pair had collaborated memorably on *Lawrence of Arabia*, *Doctor Zhivago* (1965) and *Ryan's Daughter* (1970), and it was Bolt who first suggested Lean read *Nostromo*. Their relationship had turned frosty when Lean dropped out of their *Mutiny on the Bounty* project (Bolt's script was ultimately filmed by Roger Donaldson in 1984 as *The Bounty*), but the director invited the writer to his eightieth birthday and they rekindled their friendship.

Finding new financing proved more problematic. Hollywood studios saw the film as a money pit: a big-budget art-house picture with little chance of

recouping its costs. Lean's advanced age also raised insurance concerns that would only add to the budget. Lean managed to attract Serge Silberman, the producer of Luis Buñuel's later films, who had financed Akira Kurosawa's *Ran* (1985). In 1989, he brought Columbia TriStar to the table. It offered $46 million with the proviso that Lean select a standby who could take the reins if his health failed during the shoot. He opted for Guy Hamilton, director of *Goldfinger* (1964), who began in the industry as an assistant to Lean's friend Carol Reed. Lean also asked Hugh Hudson, best known for *Chariots of Fire* (1981), to adopt the film should he fail to put it into production. (He also encouraged the directorial ambitions of TriStar executive Jonathan Darby, his chief liaison with the studio for *Nostromo*. The result – 1992's *Contact*, which Darby wrote at Lean's house and which starred Brad Pitt – was Oscar-nominated in the Best Short Film, Live Action category.)

Even with financing in place, there were obstacles to negotiate. Bolt was in poor health and unable to continue work on the script. Lean was unhappy with the screenplay as it stood, so enlisted Maggie Unsworth, who had done uncredited work on the scripts for *Brief Encounter* (1945), *Great Expectations* (1946), *Oliver Twist* (1948) and *The Passionate Friends* (1949). He approached John Box – production designer on *Lawrence*, *Zhivago* and *A Passage to India* (1984) – to craft the sets, and asked cinematographer David Watkin, who had won an Oscar for *Out of Africa* (1985), to shoot the picture.

Serge Silberman, rattled by the delays, threatened to pull out. But Lean, famed for his sweeping vision, would not be rushed. Ever the perfectionist, he deliberated over which film stock to shoot on. He favoured Showscan – a 65mm process that photographed and projected at sixty frames per second, for a clearer image – but needed to see what it could do. Lean conducted test shoots in Spain with David Watkin, but, although impressed by the Showscan stock, found the cinematographer worked too quickly for his liking. Lean preferred to take his time, pausing for reflection between set-ups; Watkin tended to light a set once for multiple shots. Lean replaced him with Alex Thomson, known for his work on *Excalibur* (1981), *Legend* (1985) and *Labyrinth* (1986).

Content at last with the screenplay, Lean and Silberman worked out a schedule. Principal photography was to begin in May 1991 in Almeria, Spain,

> *'I hope I'll be able to make this film, because I feel that I'm just beginning to get the hang of it.'*
>
> David Lean

near where Lean shot some of *Lawrence*. Millions had already been spent, with John Box building sets and Lean conferring on the music with Maurice Jarre, who had scored all his pictures since *Lawrence*. All the stages at France's Côte D'Azur studio La Victorine had also been booked for the production.

CLASSIC LITERATURE

Ready to roll, Lean was in good spirits. In December 1990, he married art dealer Sandra Cooke, his sixth wife, but their honeymoon was short-lived. In January, Lean fell ill, was diagnosed with a tumour in his throat, and underwent radiation therapy. He forged ahead with the film nonetheless, and initially showed signs of recovery. But when pneumonia set in, it became clear there was no road back. Columbia pulled the plug on *Nostromo*, instructing Box to halt work on the sets. The production designer himself contacted Lean to report that the film had been cancelled. The news crushed Lean and, on 16 April 1991, at the age of eighty-three, he passed away in London.

Christopher Hampton maintains that, were it not for the exacting standards Lean set himself and everyone around him, the film could have been made in 1987 at Warner. Lean was incapable of moving ahead until every phase of production was perfect. But his ambition and determination made him the only director with the true vision to bring Conrad's masterpiece to the screen. **DN**

WILL IT EVER HAPPEN?

1/10 Conrad's brand of adventure is out of favour in Hollywood. *Atonement* (2007) showed that middling budget pictures aimed at adults can make money, but it lacked Lean's flair for grandeur. It would be a shame to see a *Nostromo* shot digitally with green-screens, but film-making has changed since Lean's heyday and on-location 70mm spectacles are an extinct species.

the defective detective

A TERRY GILLIAM FILM

THE DEFECTIVE DETECTIVE

Director Terry Gilliam **Starring** Nicolas Cage, Robin Williams **Year** 1993 onwards **Country** US **Genre** Fantasy adventure

Terry Gilliam is almost as well known for the movies he has not made as for the ones he has. He was the first to attempt Alan Moore's supposedly unfilmable *Watchmen* (with producer Joel Silver). He struggled to get Mel Gibson to the screen in an adaptation of Dickens's *A Tale of Two Cities*. (When that fell apart, he declined Gibson's offer to helm the actor's pet project about a Scottish warrior, name of William Wallace). And, like Orson Welles (see page 77), he spent so many years struggling to breathe life into *Don Quixote* that a documentary about his attempt (2002's superb *Lost in La Mancha*) remains as close as he will probably ever get to realizing that particular Quixotic vision. It doesn't make him a happy man. 'When something doesn't happen, I go into a spin,' he has said. 'And those spins seem to go on forever when I'm in them. It's the problem of not living in the future or the past, but living in the eternity of "now." And if now is good and jolly – great. If not – whoops!'

CINEMATIC MISFORTUNE

Gilliam's cinematic misfortune is in part down to a reputation and a legacy he has carried with him since the late 1980s. The reputation is not deserved. The legacy bears the name *The Adventures of Baron Munchausen*.

He began as a film-maker in New York in the mid 1960s, raiding bins for film stock, onto which he would draw and scratch images. Dissatisfaction with the United States, at the time in the midst of the Watts riots and the onset of Vietnam, led him to decamp to England and turn his artistic skills to animation. A unique style (and, allegedly, his exotic Afghan coat) brought him to television and a collaboration with the future *Monty Python's Flying Circus*.

Gilliam co-helmed (with Terry Jones) Python's big-screen venture *Monty Python and the Holy Grail* (1975). Sticking with a medieval theme, he left most of his fellow Pythons behind, in favour of the long-held influence of Lewis Carroll, for 1977's *Jabberwocky*. In 1981, he hit the big time with the box office smash *Time Bandits*, the first instalment of what he would later view as a fantasy trilogy. Part two, the Oscar-nominated *Brazil*, followed in 1985. And then in 1988 *Baron Munchausen* happened. The film was originally budgeted at a not inconsiderable $23 million. By the time its troubled shoot was over,

TERRY GILLIAM
As late as 2011, the death rites had not been read on *The Defective Detective*. 'I'm just dredging up an old script. . .' the director said. 'And we are just snooping around to see if there is any way we can move that one forward.'

THE BIGG TIME

Opposite These three pieces of concept artwork – 'Bar in the Forest', 'Cityscape aka The Bigg Time' and Recyclable Trees' – were made in 1993 when Terry Gilliam first conceived *The Defective Detective*. Together they chart the changing appearance of the fantasy land that Joe must save. Gilliam was still referring to them in a draft of the script dated 1996.

that had doubled to $46 million and rising, offering the press an opportunity to write damningly about the film's budget rather than its considerable merit.

Conceived a few years after *Munchausen*, *The Defective Detective* was in many ways the fourth part of his fantasy trilogy. But before he could make it, Gilliam had to redeem himself. The budget-busting loose cannon needed to show Hollywood he could play nice. He did so in spectacular fashion with 1991's *The Fisher King*. It broke all his rules: he didn't write it, he was offering himself as a director for hire for the first time and he was working in the country he had left behind in the mid 1960s. But Gilliam took a relatively low budget film and delivered a box office hit, netting numerous Academy Award nominations (and a win for Mercedes Ruehl as Best Supporting Actress).

KINDRED SPIRIT

Richard LaGravenese's screenplay for *The Fisher King* could have been written with Gilliam in mind. It had medieval knights in New York, a *Parsifal* figure, a castle on the Upper East Side – it even had a Holy Grail. Needless to say, Gilliam felt he had found a kindred spirit. 'I remember on a plane ride to promote *Fisher King*,' LaGravenese recalls, 'he said to me, "*Fisher King* was me coming into your world. Now let's see what you do working in my world."'

By 1993, the pair were heavily into the world of *The Defective Detective*: the tale of middle-aged cop Joe Foster succumbing to an overwhelming sense of failure. A chance encounter with a ten-year-old girl – who appears to be whisked away on a bed that files over night-time Manhattan – leads Foster on a journey to another world: a world of two-dimensional cutout forests, newspaper trees, valiant knights, a virgin damsel in distress, three-headed

TERRY HITS THE WALL

One of Gilliam's trademarks is hiding his movies in plain sight: in most cases, pinned to the wall. Look closely at Kevin's bedroom wall in *Time Bandits* and you'll see the movie laid out before you, with pictures of knights, warriors, Napoleonic battles and even a fire engine. When Jeff Bridges finds his way into Parry's basement lair in *The Fisher King*, pasted among the pipes are his heraldic visions and images of the Grail, plus news clippings about his wife's murder. And in *Twelve Monkeys* (1995), when Bruce Willis is being interrogated, the wall behind him is covered with clippings that tell the story of the twelve monkeys.

In *The Defective Detective*, when Joe Foster enters the missing girl's bedroom, he finds the walls adorned with pressed flowers, pictures of animals, wild forests and fairy-tale kingdoms:

```
A collage of colour and fantasy. . . Joe feels deeply affected
by the room. . . as if he has entered some sort of womb. For a
moment, he feels almost elated.
```

Later, as Joe begins to grasp the meaning of the fantasy world he finds himself in, he realizes it's the girl's bedroom wall. As with all of Gilliam's movies, it's all there. You just have to look closely.

dragons, a corporate Mr Bigg capable of dividing into twelve duplicates of himself and a young boy who may well be the innocent hopeful Joe before the world dragged him down. 'This is a hero who has gone sour,' says Gilliam. 'He's a guy from the Midwest who came to New York to take on the Big Apple. He's a good cop and has an early initial success. He's a hero, and then life goes on and he doesn't get to be a hero again. He's reaching the point where he's right on the edge of a breakdown, and he finds himself in this fantastical world, having to rediscover how to be a kid again, to play, because all this tough guy stuff doesn't work in this world.'

Gilliam and LaGravenese went all out in early drafts. Once, the director had found economical ways to create amazing effects (see *Brazil*); here, he let his imagination run riot. After a brief establishing sequence in the real world, Joe is transported to a universe that cries out for computer-generated effects, years before the technology was up to snuff. As the film progresses, Gilliam's vision becomes more unbound: the pastoral otherworld, in which the boy always wins the battle and good always triumphs over evil, is laid waste by Joe's sexual desire for the damsel. After a brief, hung-over sojourn in the real New

CASTLES IN THE AIR – GILLIAM'S GORMENGHAST

Mervyn Peake's gothic fantasy trilogy – *Titus Groan*, *Gormenghast* and *Titus Alone* – was published between 1946 and 1959. It focused on the world of Castle Gormenghast: a vast, sprawling citadel in decline, populated by a cast of grotesques – including the central figure of Titus Groan – who are torn between a desire for personal freedom and centuries of tradition and duty.

Terry Gilliam read the books in the early 1970s. Identifying with both the themes and the imagery, he instantly wanted to film them – particularly *Gormenghast*, charting the rise of Titus Groan to power, and his battle with the Machiavellian former kitchen boy Steerpike. The director also identified with Peake himself, an acclaimed artist who had once illustrated Lewis Carroll's *Alice's Adventures in Wonderland*, a key influence on Gilliam. The film rights not being readily available, Gilliam opted instead to adopt a few of Peake's ideas. '*Jabberwocky* was, in a sense, my attempt to do *Gormenghast*,' he later said.

In the early 1980s, rock musician Sting (a London neighbour of the director) secured the property and was at pains to persuade Gilliam to helm the project, with himself in the role of Steerpike. 'At that time, to be honest,' admitted Gilliam, 'I didn't feel he was quite right for the part.' Nonetheless, Sting played Steerpike in a 1984 BBC radio adaptation.

For many years, the notion of a big-screen version of *Gormenghast* haunted Gilliam, who kept a copy of the book jacket pinned to a bulletin board in his workspace. 'It keeps coming at me and scripts keep coming up,' he said. 'I think it's a hard thing to do because there's not much of a story there. It's the atmosphere and characters that are wonderful. Ultimately, I think I'd rather steal from things than make them. It's only been later in life that I've been foolish enough to actually make the thing. It's always been better to steal.'

Gormenghast eventually made it to the screen as a four-part BBC miniseries in 2000, starring Jonathan Rhys Meyers (right), Celia Imrie and Christopher Lee. Coincidentally, that same year, a short film adaptation of Peake's Titus novella *The Boy in Darkness* was narrated by Gilliam's Python cohort, Terry Jones.

York, he returns to find that Mr Bigg has turned the cutout forest into a neon-soaked, overcrowded, overgrown and decaying city. Then things really get wild. Mr Bigg drags Joe to Hell, where they battle demons who subdivide on contact. An ever-present floating tree has its roots chained and pulled towards Earth; we see the sky being dissected into cubes and removed piece by piece. The film ends back in what may have been the 'real' world all along: today's New York exploding into a spectacular *Metropolis* (1927)/Garden of Eden hybrid.

FIRE-BREATHING DRAGON

Many of these ideas and images had run through Gilliam's previous work (the knight even has a touch of Python in his dialogue). 'The way I approached it,'

> *'I went through all the stuff I had thrown out of all the other films. . . a bit of recycling, nothing wasted.'*
>
> Terry Gilliam

he says, 'was I just went through all the stuff I had thrown out of all the other films and said, "I've got to use this shit" – a bit of recycling, nothing wasted.'

Given its gigantic scale and Gilliam's reputation, however undeserved, *The Defective Detective* was never going to be an automatic green light. However, Nicolas Cage loved it and attached himself to the role of Joe, giving the project a degree of traction. *Fisher King* star Robin Williams agreed to play Mr Bigg as well as, possibly, the Devil and at least one third of a three-headed, fire-breathing dragon. But, to Gilliam's frustration, the film constantly foundered on budget issues. Despite interest from Bruce Willis in the late 1990s, he eventually put it on hold. Since then, he has talked sporadically about reviving *The Defective Detective*, although there is an element of his and LaGravenese's screenplay that has always troubled him: not its scale or ambition, but the fact that Joe Foster – one of the director's alter egos – doesn't make it to the end.

'That's one of the reasons it scares me to do it,' he says, 'because I kill myself at the end. There's a side of me that doesn't want to, because my films and the making of my films become one and the same thing. . . It scares the shit out of me because it brings back all the nightmares of *Munchausen*.' **BM**

WHAT HAPPENED NEXT. . .

In 1995, exhausted by his constantly thwarted efforts to get *The Defective Detective* off the ground and the collapse of *A Tale of Two Cities*, Gilliam retook the route he'd taken with *The Fisher King*: someone else's script, US setting, director for hire. The result was another huge box office hit: the excellent *Twelve Monkeys*. He then replaced Alex Cox on 1998's *Fear and Loathing in Las Vegas*, planning to make *The Defective Detective* directly afterwards.

WILL IT EVER HAPPEN?

3/10 Not likely, although visual ideas and conceits from *The Defective Detective* did find their way into Gilliam's 2009 *The Imaginarium of Doctor Parnassus*. 'I'm beginning to think these films are never meant to be made,' he later reflected. 'They're your workouts between real films. You explore ideas and characters and then the right script comes along and you incorporate the ideas that have been tried out on these other things. In a way, the picture I have in my head is of an artist's studio with all these half-finished canvases all around the place. And he keeps coming back to them a year later and saying, "Oh shit. That was the wrong red!"'

THE ARYAN PAPERS

Director Stanley Kubrick **Starring** Johanna ter Steege **Year** 1994 **Country** Slovakia, Czech Republic
Genre Historical drama **Studio** Warner Bros

STANLEY KUBRICK

'He kept looking for different ways to tell stories. . .' recalled Steven Spielberg, who played an unwitting role in the end of *The Aryan Papers*, in 1999. 'He never made the same picture twice.'

Stanley Kubrick, in his later years, garnered a deserved reputation as a reclusive obsessive who spent more time immersed in exhaustive research for film projects than he did actually making movies. The sheer weight of pre-production material he amassed is legendary and fills a vast archive. This monument to perfectionism and procrastination provides tantalizing and frustrating evidence of the brilliance to which we might have been treated, had Kubrick got out of the library and back behind the camera.

MOVING AND HARROWING

One of the projects that absorbed his time and energy in the early 1990s was *The Aryan Papers*, an adaptation of *Wartime Lies*, Louis Begley's semi-autobiographical 1991 novel set during the Holocaust. Kubrick had wanted to make a film about the Holocaust for decades, but was daunted by the enormity of the subject and the inadequacy of a mere movie to encapsulate its horror. Rejecting the idea of a documentary, he had considered a film focusing on Nazi propaganda minister Joseph Goebbels but could not find a suitable script.

In 1976, he invited Isaac Bashevis Singer – author of the story on which *Yentl* (1983) was based – to write an original screenplay. Singer declined, on the grounds that he was not a Holocaust survivor – the implication being that he therefore had neither the facility nor the right to dramatize it (a puzzling response as he wrote 1972's *Enemies, a Love Story* – filmed in 1989 – about Holocaust survivors). Undeterred, Kubrick continued his research, eventually settling on Begley's book as the perfect vehicle for him to address the subject.

Based on the author's experiences in Nazi-occupied Poland, *Wartime Lies* charts the heartrending plight of Tania and Maciek, a Jewish woman and her nephew, who evade the death camps by obtaining Aryan identities and posing as Catholics. The moving, often harrowing book is narrated by the adult Maciek, whose life has been shaped by the lies he was forced to tell to survive. Kubrick wrote a typically dense adaptation. 'It's a big, risky topic,' Jan Harlan, his brother-in-law and producer said in the *Independent*. 'It is not a drama that is over-the-top and has lots of action. It is a very silent film, a very serious film.' In other words, a Stanley Kubrick film – and one that the director seemed

THE ARYAN PAPERS

A STANLEY KUBRICK FILM

determined to actually make rather than just tinker with. He even elected to shoot on location in Slovakia and the Czech Republic, despite having not made a film outside England since *Spartacus* in 1960, owing to his fear of flying.

NO ORDINARY AFFAIR

The script written, Kubrick put his energy into assembling a cast. Among front-runners for the key role of Tania was Uma Thurman, who later told MTV: 'It would have been the part of my career – the best part I ever had been offered or had written for me.' However, the actress Kubrick settled on was Johanna ter Steege, who had enjoyed moderate success in her native Holland, appearing in George Sluizer's 1988 thriller *The Vanishing*. She was about to appear alongside Gary Oldman in the Beethoven biopic *Immortal Beloved* (1994), but was hardly a star. *The Aryan Papers* would have changed that.

'[Kubrick] phoned me. . .' she told the *Independent*. 'He asked me questions about the films I had done – very specific questions.' She was subsequently summoned to England for a screen test. It was, characteristically of Kubrick, no ordinary affair. The meeting took place in Jan Harlan's kitchen and began with the director quizzing ter Steege not on her acting career or her thoughts on the character but on sport, particularly Dutch tennis player Richard Krajicek.

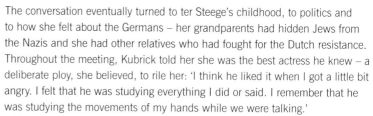

'The ending was very painful. . . it felt like a huge balloon was suddenly burst.'

Johanna ter Steege

FILM OF THE FILM THAT NEVER WAS
In 2009, artists Jane and Louise Wilson unveiled *Unfolding the Aryan Papers*, an installation at the British Film Institute's Southbank Gallery in London. This employed production stills, archive photographs and a wealth of other material culled from the Kubrick archive to give audiences an abstract inkling of what the finished film might have been. The centrepiece of the installation was a film of Johanna ter Steege (above), talking about the character of Tania and bringing to life original stills from her wardrobe test.

The conversation eventually turned to ter Steege's childhood, to politics and to how she felt about the Germans – her grandparents had hidden Jews from the Nazis and she had other relatives who had fought for the Dutch resistance. Throughout the meeting, Kubrick told her she was the best actress he knew – a deliberate ploy, she believed, to rile her: 'I think he liked it when I got a little bit angry. I felt that he was studying everything I did or said. I remember that he was studying the movements of my hands while we were talking.'

The meeting culminated in Kubrick filming ter Steege with a variety of lenses – some of which, she recalled, made her look very young, others much older than her thirty-two years. Finally, late in the evening, Kubrick called a halt and, popping a bottle of champagne, told her she had got the part.

THE BOMBSHELL DROPS

Ter Steege returned to Holland and waited. And waited. Then, seven months after her meeting with Kubrick and, later, extensive costume tests and detailed preparations for the location shoot, the bombshell dropped. Mere weeks before production was due to begin – and after, by Louis Begley's recollection, he had 'spent about ten million dollars' – Kubrick had decided not to make the film. His principal reason was Steven Spielberg's future Academy Award-winning *Schindler's List*, which premiered in November 1993 and opened worldwide in 1994. The public, Kubrick believed, would not have the fortitude for two

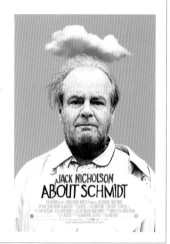

Schindler's List won seven Academy Awards and widespread praise, albeit not from Stanley Kubrick. 'Think that's about the Holocaust?' he said to writer Frederic Raphael. 'That was about success, wasn't it? The Holocaust is about six million people who get killed. *Schindler's List* is about 600 who don't.' Kubrick worked on what would become *A.I. Artificial Intelligence*, before putting it on hold to focus on *Eyes Wide Shut* in 1999. He died in March that year. Louis Begley's 1996 novel *About Schmidt* became a movie in 2002, starring Jack Nicholson. Johanna ter Steege starred in European shorts and feature films, while Uma Thurman enjoyed a rather more prominent profile thanks to another 1994 classic: Quentin Tarantino's *Pulp Fiction*.

Holocaust movies in the space of a year. 'He'd already had this experience with *Full Metal Jacket* [1987], which came out the year after *Platoon*,' Harlan told the *Guardian* in 2000, 'and that hurt us, there's no question about it.'

With the prospect of stardom and a collaboration with one of cinema's greats snatched from her grasp, ter Steege took to her bed for two days. For years she refused to talk about *The Aryan Papers*. But she broke her silence in 2009, telling the *Independent* that she had no regrets and that it was a compliment to be even considered. 'It was a wonderful experience,' she said. 'The ending was very painful. There was a huge future. . . then it felt like a huge balloon was suddenly burst. Then, that's it. You have to go on. Not for the first time in my life, I realized that personal happiness has nothing to do with success.' (Thurman had evidently assumed that she was still in the running too. 'I was contracted to do it and things happened and he shelved the film. . .' she told MTV. 'It was devastating because it was an incredible part.')

His decades-long plans for a Holocaust movie in ruins, Kubrick went back to work on another project to which he'd dedicated countless hours and untold resources: *A.I. Artificial Intelligence*. This time the film *would* be brought to the screen, but – somewhat ironically – by Steven Spielberg in 2001. **SB**

WILL IT EVER HAPPEN?

3/10   Warner Bros owns the rights to the property, Kubrick's script exists and his family have no objections to a film being made with the right director. In 2005, *Variety* reported that *Kingdom of Heaven* (2005) screenwriter William Monahan had been hired to adapt Begley's book, but this too came to nothing. In 2009, Jan Harlan said how delighted he would be if a film-maker of Ang Lee's calibre chose to revive the project, leading excitable members of the blogosphere to report that Lee was actively circling the project. He wasn't.

CRUSADE

ARNOLD SCHWARZENEGGER

A PAUL VERHOEVEN FILM

CRUSADE

Director Paul Verhoeven **Starring** Arnold Schwarzenegger, Robert Duvall, Jennifer Connelly, John Turturro
Year 1995 **Budget** $100 million **Genre** Historical drama

One star bestrode the 1980s and 1990s like a movie colossus. His name – hard to remember, impossible to forget – was Arnold Schwarzenegger. By 1989, when he was making *Total Recall* with Dutch auteur Paul Verhoeven, both director and star were at the top of their game. A string of hits including *Conan the Barbarian* (1982), *The Running Man* and *Predator* (both 1987), and *Twins* (1988) had put Schwarzenegger among the world's biggest box office attractions, and he relished his ability to wield star power. Verhoeven, meanwhile, had crossed the Atlantic in fine style, catching everyone's attention with 1987's *RoboCop*. Based on a Philip K. Dick story, *Total Recall* had brought new meaning to the term 'development hell', with its torturous evolution wearing out a succession of stars and directors, while its screenplay ran to more than forty drafts. When the De Laurentiis Entertainment Group – the original producers – went bust, Schwarzenegger, who had been eagerly eyeing the project, chose his moment to pounce. Persuading buccaneering production outfit Carolco to take on the project, he assigned himself the lead role and insisted they hire Verhoeven to direct.

FAKING A MIRACLE

While filming *Total Recall*, Schwarzenegger mentioned to Verhoeven that he had seen a screenplay about the Crusades. He didn't like the script much, but was interested in the subject matter. Verhoeven shrewdly engaged Walon Green as writer. Most famous for his work on Sam Peckinpah's milestone Western *The Wild Bunch* (1969), Green was something of a legend in the screenwriting community – a status that would be sensationally underlined by *Crusade*.

The tale takes place in 1095. Pope Urban II makes the proclamation that leads to the first Crusade: a holy war bent on recapturing the sacred city of Jerusalem from the clutches of the Islamic empire. Caught up in the ensuing Christian fervour is Hagen, a sharp-witted thief who escapes execution by faking a miracle and getting himself drafted into the military campaign.

Aided by his wily sidekick Ari – a mercurial shyster who changes sides (and religions) at will – Hagen journeys to the Middle East while under a permanent threat of death from his sadistic half-brother, a nobleman named Emmich.

SCHWARZENEGGER, VERHOEVEN
The director (above right) insisted that he and the star would create 'a lighter version of the Crusades' – presumably one with the kind of dark humour that elevated his *RoboCop* (1987) and *Total Recall* (1990) above their ultraviolent contemporaries.

As the screenplay's epic sweep takes us to its monumental final battle and the conquest of Jerusalem, Green strews the pages with a stunning – often shocking – avalanche of rape, castration, slavery, decapitation and slaughter. In the most infamous sequence, Hagen is stitched into the carcass of a donkey and left to the mercy of a pack of slavering hyenas. 'Take a deep breath,' Hagen harangues the Crusaders after the climactic butchery, 'and, with the stench of death in your nose, go tell God you've restored His kingdom!'

THOUGHT-PROVOKING SMART BOMB

Written at the time of the first Gulf War, amid a renewed escalation of tension between the Christian and Muslim worlds, Green's screenplay promised a thought-provoking smart bomb of a movie. The Catholic Church is depicted as irredeemably corrupt, and the European knights as rampaging, opportunistic psychopaths, while Muslims and Jews are often portrayed sympathetically. 'The Pope instigates this complete slaughterhouse. . .' Verhoeven explained, 'that started with pogroms against Jews, and which ultimately had only one goal: to destroy as many Arabs as possible. In the movie the Arabs are the good people and the Christians are the bad ones.' However, the director had reservations about the script, and brought in Gary Goldman, writer of *Big Trouble in Little China* (1986) to give it a polish, as he had with *Total Recall*.

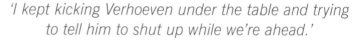

'I kept kicking Verhoeven under the table and trying to tell him to shut up while we're ahead.'

Arnold Schwarzenegger

'I'LL BE BACK. POSSIBLY.'
Fans have long wished for Arnie's return as Conan, preferably directed by *Conan the Barbarian*'s John Milius (above, with Schwarzenegger in 1982). In 2001, Milius prepped *King Conan: Crown of Iron*. His huge script saw our hero ascending to a long-promised throne. But Arnie quitting movies to become Governor of California was the final nail in its coffin. In 2012, however, Universal announced that *The Legend of Conan* (2014) would feature the superstar as an older, wiser, more regal Barbarian, bowing out with the mother of all battles. 'I always loved the Conan character,' Schwarzenegger commented, 'and I'm honoured to be asked to step into the role once again.'

In an illuminating account of *Crusade* in his book *Tales from Development Hell*, David Hughes observes that the gentlemanly Goldman left Green's best stuff intact but added vivid, giant-sized flourishes of his own, giving the film its best shots at cinematic immortality. Perhaps the most talked-about sequence occurs during the final showdown between the Crusaders and the Muslims. The workings of fate see Hagen fighting for the Christians and, during a frenzied assault, an apparently miraculous event takes place: the light of the setting sun projects a gigantic silhouette of the battling Hagen onto a cloud of smoke. This optical illusion has the effect of unnerving the Muslims while affording the Christians a much-needed shot of divine inspiration.

Bankrolled by the production company Carolco, which had hit with *Total Recall* and 1991's *Terminator 2: Judgment Day*, and with a cast including Robert Duvall and Jennifer Connelly, *Crusade* was due to begin shooting in Spain in the summer of 1994. But Carolco's finances were perilously over-stretched, not unconnected to the huge fees given to stars like Schwarzenegger.

Crusade, Carolco mainman Mario Kassar told *Entertainment Weekly* in 2004, 'was ready to go. There was only one thing. The budget. I asked Verhoeven, "We were supposed to make this movie at $100 million. Now I'm hearing 125. What is the budget of this movie?" And the answer was, "Well, I don't know if it's 125 or 135 or 175." I said, "Well then, I can tell you one

WHAT HAPPENED NEXT. . .

Despite cutting its losses with *Crusade*, Carolco lost its shirt on Renny Harlin's pirate mega-flop *Cutthroat Island* (1995). The company went bankrupt and the rights to *Crusade* fell into Arnold Schwarzenegger's hands. Recognizing a legend-making role when he saw it, the man who would be Hagen had a decent crack at getting the movie onto the big screen. However, it was still a giant financial undertaking and, in the mid 1990s, Schwarzenegger and Paul Verhoeven's fortunes fluctuated. They never again had the golden touch of the *Total Recall* (and, in the director's case, the 1992 *Basic Instinct*) glory days, although Verhoeven's *Starship Troopers* (1997) owed something to the vision of *Crusade* – in both its amazing battle scenes (Verhoeven directs, left) and its blackly comedic appraisal of man's motives for going to war.

thing: it's not going." So I stopped it.' Schwarzenegger confirmed this account in an interview with *Empire*: 'Paul started going crazy. We had the final meeting with the studio and we were all sitting at this boardroom table. They said, "So the budget is $100 million. That's a lot of money. What kind of guarantees do you have that we will get it for 100 and it won't go up to 130?" He says, "What do you mean, guarantees? There's no such thing as guarantees! Guarantees don't happen. . ." I kept kicking him under the table and trying to tell him to shut up while we're ahead. But he just wouldn't, and that was it.'

In retrospect, the script for *Crusade* resembles one of Robert E. Howard's Conan chronicles. Was Hagen a cipher for Conan? Like him, Hagen is a thief and a mercenary. He's a serf who has noble blood – Conan is a barbarian who rises to become king. He's a brutal berserker but he's also a hit with the ladies.

Even given this resemblance to one of his on-screen alter egos, could Schwarzenegger have pulled off such a character? The script demanded a man who was fleet of foot and sharp of mind as well as an unstoppable slayer. On that level, Hagen has more in common with Kevin Costner's Robin Hood or Mel Gibson's William Wallace than Conan and Terminator. However, the star passed himself off as an ordinary joe in *Total Recall*, countering violent heroics with humour – a technique used to even greater effect in 1994's *True Lies*, so maybe Hagen would have been a cinch. Whatever, Schwarzenegger believed he could play the part, and his self-belief is not to be underestimated. **PR**

BE WITHOUT FEAR. . .
Carolco balked at paying $130 million to make *Crusade*. But 20th Century Fox gave that amount to Ridley Scott to make *his* Crusading epic, 2005's *Kingdom of Heaven*, starring Eva Green (above).

WILL IT EVER HAPPEN?
4/10 As Walon Green's screenplay remains one of the most lauded works in all fandom, there's no good reason why *Crusade* couldn't find an audience. 'The story of the Crusades is the murderous attack of the Christians on the Arabs and the Jews,' Verhoeven observed during the 'War on Terror' in 2002, adding wryly, 'Do you think that's a politically interesting situation?'

THE HOT ZONE

Director Ridley Scott **Starring** Jodie Foster, Robert Redford **Year** 1995
Budget $25 million **Country** US **Genre** Thriller **Studio** 20th Century Fox

RIDLEY SCOTT
Five months before the plug was pulled, the *Los Angeles Times* reported rumours that the director Ridley Scott (above) might be replaced by Sydney Pollack or John McTiernan. 'They're still making their deals,' said a Fox source. 'Everybody is hanging in.'

Hollywood caught its own Millennium Bug when rival pandemic pictures went head to head in the twentieth century's closing years. But, in the battle of the 'iller' thriller, *Outbreak* (1995) zipped Dustin Hoffman into a hazmat suit and topped the US box office. *The Hot Zone* didn't even make it out of the Fox studio lot, leaving Ridley Scott, Jodie Foster and Robert Redford disoriented, quivering and coughing up stage blood. The film's failure bears all the scars of a classic Hollywood brawl – studios at war, ego clashes – but, in the final diagnosis, it was death by Terminal Indecision.

CHEST-BURSTING VISCERA

Like *Top Gun* (1986), *Saturday Night Fever* (1977) and *The Killing Fields* (1984), *The Hot Zone* took its inspiration from a magazine article. First published in the *New Yorker* in 1992, Richard Preston's 'Crisis in the Hot Zone' told the chilling true story of the US Army's attempts to contain the lethal Ebola virus, smuggled in via a shipment of green monkeys, and discovered just miles from Washington DC. It made for contagious reading, thanks to the gruesome virus that made leprosy look like a head cold. Highly infectious, Ebola took just days to munch away the body's cells until its victim died from a 'bleed out', hemorrhaging from every orifice – the Brian De Palma of tropical diseases.

When Stephen King described the piece as 'one of the most horrifying things I've ever read', Hollywood quickly flicked out the chequebook. In the resulting bidding war, 20th Century Fox producer Lynda Obst won the auction – after pledging not to rewrite the female protagonist – leaving Arnold Kopelson, representing Warner Bros, fuming into his cigar. 'Preston's piece wasn't a movie,' he observed to *Entertainment Weekly*. 'It was about one hundred monkeys, and all of them end up getting killed. I'd have the animal rights activists all over me. And it didn't have a beginning, middle, or end.'

As facts are public property, Kopelson figured Preston didn't 'own' them, and set about making the film that would become *Outbreak*. For Team *Hot Zone*: director Ridley Scott. For Team *Outbreak*: Wolfgang Petersen, hot from 1993's *In the Line of Fire*. Both studios stoked for a fight, the starting pistol was fired on the kind of ridiculous spectacle only Hollywood could invent: a writer's race.

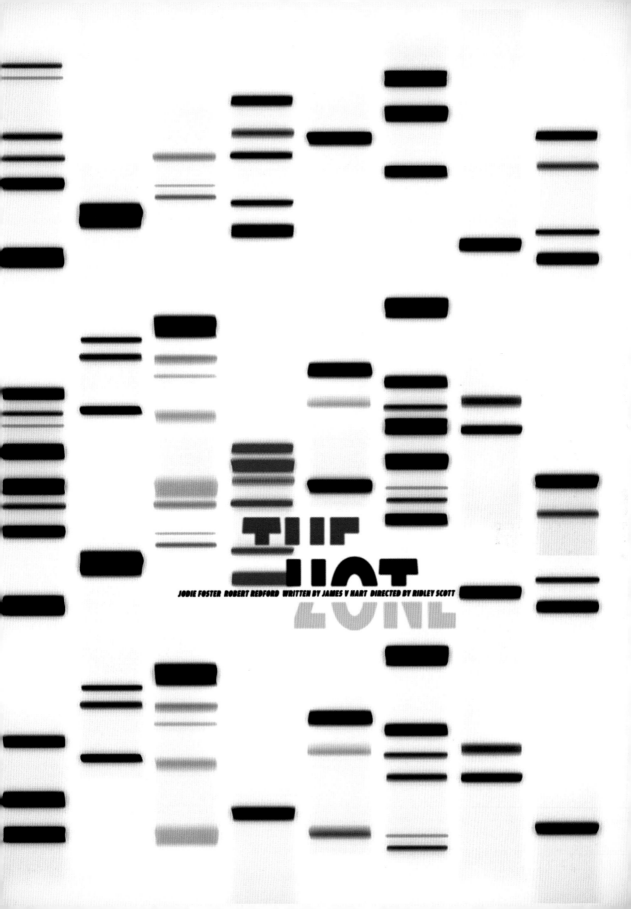

JODIE FOSTER ROBERT REDFORD WRITTEN BY JAMES V HART DIRECTED BY RIDLEY SCOTT

THE HOT ZONE

Kopelson was right: Preston's piece had science on its side, but didn't have a beginning, middle or end. His solution was to hire writer Ted Tally of *The Silence of the Lambs* (1991) for the first draft. But while *Outbreak* was free to dramatize its viral a-cough-alypse, Scott pledged fidelity to his source. And *The Hot Zone* was a big deal. The director had chosen Preston's piece as the first in a multi-picture deal with 20th Century Fox. 'It was a science-fact thriller, one of those rare projects that was actually about something,' he said. 'We also got a very good script from [*Bram Stoker's Dracula* writer] James V. Hart.'

Hart's script certainly opens well, with 'legendary field virologist' Ken Johnson witnessing the aftermath of an Ebola outbreak in Zaire: 'A silhouette of bodies, mud walls spattered with blood – as if a bomb had gone off.' Threat established, the action shifts to the United States, where Nancy Jaxx of the Army's Infectious Diseases unit is investigating a virus that's liquefying green monkeys at the Synergy research centre. After suspenseful lab sequences – pounded glass, rips in suits, much sweating – the film becomes a race to quarantine Ebola, find the host monkey (nicknamed 'Super Monk'), and locate a vaccine before citizens become a mass of 'viral bombs'. Jodie Foster was to play Jaxx. Robert Redford – written in so Fox could boast a double A-list poster hit – was to be virologist Johnson. The student–guru relationship was to be strictly platonic. There were, after all, more than enough bodily fluids on show.

> *'I would have liked to see Dustin Hoffman bleed out of his nipples.'*
> Richard Preston

A bloody good shockbuster was on the cards. With its claustrophobic hazmat suits, chest-bursting viscera, grisly autopsies and gloopy horror, it's easy to imagine Scott visualizing *The Hot Zone* as an earthbound *Alien* (1979) – particularly during a tense sequence in which a bio-army, armed with 'kill syringes', hunt the host monkey, rendered 'rabid and raptor-like' by Ebola.

Yet while the science is authentically technobabbly ('The immunoglobulins won't clone!' 'He spun the plasma's phoresis in the chopper'), the characters are, as a Fox source noted in the aftermath, 'just too average'. Which is one way of putting it. Lumbered with dire-logue like, 'I can't die! I don't have a babysitter!' Nancy comes across on paper as a soccer mom with a centrifuge. Ken, meanwhile, amounts to little more than Mr Science Bit.

The result? As *Outbreak* sprinted into production (to compound the panic, both sides were feverishly reading each other's leaked scripts), *The Hot Zone* found itself mired in internal squabbles. 'Redford and Ridley are not getting along,' gossiped a studio source. 'They couldn't see eye to eye on changes in the script.' Further issues were reported between Foster and Scott, and between the two leads. Redford, it was alleged, brought in his own writing team to beef up his part. The agitated game of script ping-pong reached such a manic state, Foster was reportedly sent 115 pages of rewrites just a fortnight before the shoot was due to start. Utterly fed up, she quit. Redford followed.

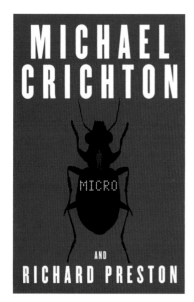

MICRO MANAGEMENT
Having specialized in viral thrillers (such as *The Hot Zone*'s fine follow-up, 1998's *The Cobra Event*), Richard Preston was ideally suited to complete the late Michael Crichton's unfinished *Micro* (2011). In an interview for the e-book edition, he talks about 'poking around the rain forest on Oahu, learning the biology of micro-monsters and doing the detective work with Michael's notebooks and materials, figuring out what Michael intended. . .'

Ridley Scott boarded the good ship *White Squall* (1996), while Robert Redford retreated to 1996's romantic drama *Up Close & Personal* (left). Jodie Foster took on another scientist role in 1997's *Contact* (right), which had languished in development hell since 1985. (Coincidentally, its script was written by *The Hot Zone*'s James V. Hart.) 'I would have loved to work with Jodie,' Scott said later. Sadly, he again failed to do so when she declined to grace his *Silence of the Lambs* sequel, *Hannibal* (2001).

Outbreak had its own problems – Donald Sutherland's villain was scrawled in as a last-minute replacement for Joe Don Baker – but at least it was filming. *The Hot Zone* looked cryogenic by comparison. Fox was defiant, but the movie was haemorrhaging cash. The budget ballooned to $45 million – an estimated $11 million alone had already been spent on sets ('To my knowledge,' sighs Preston, '[the sets are] still sitting in a pile at the Fox lot in LA'). In August 1994, the studio finally pulled the plug. *The Hot Zone* was in the Dead Zone.

MELTING NUNS

Although audiences were denied the spectacle of Redford delivering lines like, 'A man's testicles swell up to the size of footballs,' the best character in the would-be movie is the virus itself, whether gazed at through a microscope ('Black holes grow in the carpet of cells as if eaten by moths') or, during the memorable opening sequence, melting nuns into blancmange. In contrast, the feel-good climax, featuring Foster saving her own daughter from the virus, feels tacked on, probably due to film's sheer number of feel-bad monkey autopsies.

Scott described the experience as 'traumatic'. To rub salt into his wounds, *Outbreak* stormed the box office, eventually coining $190 million for Warner. Bad blood played out through the pages of *Entertainment Weekly*. 'I sat there laughing,' Preston told *EW* after watching *Outbreak*. 'The scabs looked like Gummy Bears. In a real Ebola attack, the men bleed out of their nipples. I would have liked to see Dustin Hoffman bleed out of his nipples.' **SC**

1/10 **WILL IT EVER HAPPEN?**
Unlikely, unless Ebola hits the headlines again. *Outbreak* stole its thunder and audiences are immune to the once-novel concept of pandemic thrillers: Danny Boyle's *28 Days Later. . .* (2002) offered a zombie spin on a primate-spread infection, while Steven Soderbergh's *Contagion* (2011) captured the pandemonium of a pandemic with supercharged realism.

SUPERMAN LIVES

Director Tim Burton **Starring** Nicolas Cage **Year** 1998
Budget $190 million **Country** US **Genre** Superhero fantasy **Studio** Warner Bros

KEVIN SMITH

'They said to me, "Kevin. . . this is a corporate movie,"' the film-maker recalled of his encounter with Warner Bros. '"It doesn't matter how good the dialogue is. . . it's about how many toys we can sell." That was real soul-killing, man.'

Superman is one of the jewels in the Warner Bros crown. The DC Comics icon got his first big-screen treatment in 1978 at the hands of director Richard Donner and star Christopher Reeve. The smash spawned two entertaining sequels before running out of steam with *Superman IV: The Quest for Peace* (1987). Batman became Warner Bros' new favourite son, thanks to gothic-flavoured hits by Tim Burton and family-oriented offerings by Joel Schumacher. But by 1995, Warner was looking to revive Kal-El and handed the property to *Batman* (1989) producer Jon Peters. With the sound of cash registers ringing in his ears, Peters sought an accessible approach with merchandising potential. The 1992 comic *The Death of Superman* was the basis for a script by Jonathan Lemkin (the highlight of whose résumé was TV's *21 Jump Street*), rewritten by Gregory Poirier. Unconvinced by the writer of the 1995 *Wild Malibu Weekend!* screenplay, Warner called for a fresh angle on the film, then known as *Superman Reborn*. Enter comics fan Kevin Smith.

GAY ROBOTS AND GIANT SPIDERS

Then basking in the success of his feature debut *Clerks* (1994), Smith trashed Poirier's script. As detailed in his stand-up DVD *An Evening with Kevin Smith* (2002), the writer-director met with Peters and studio executives and drafted what was very much a script-by-committee. According to Smith, elements of the story introduced by Peters included a new costume, a no-flying rule, a gay robot assistant and a climax that would see Superman battle a giant spider (an idea Peters recycled for 1999's Will Smith-starring *Wild Wild West*). Smith turned in a script entitled *Superman Lives* in March 1997.

In it, archvillain Lex Luthor teams up with an alien called Brainiac to block out the sun and render Superman, fuelled by sunlight, powerless. A machine called the Eradicator, sent by the hero's father to protect him, is activated. Brainiac wants to absorb the Eradicator's lifeforce, making him all-powerful. Using beats from *The Death of Superman*, Brainiac sends a monster called Doomsday to kill Superman in his depleted state. Our hero sacrifices himself to destroy the monster, the Earth is bathed in moonlight and Lex is victorious. But the Eradicator resurrects Kal-El and the two return to Metropolis with a mortal

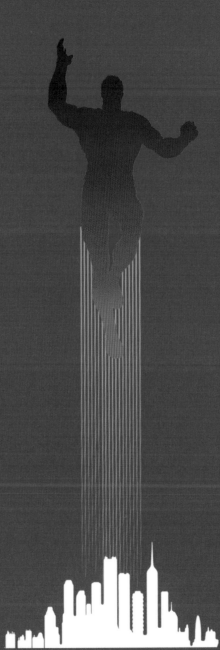

NICOLAS CAGE

A TIM BURTON FILM

SUPERMAN LIVES

Superman wearing a suit that simulates his powers (which suited Peters's request for a revamped costume, ideal for a line of toys). Brainiac attacks the city, the Eradicator destroys the satellite blocking the sun and Superman's powers return. As a final roll of the dice, Brainiac holds Lois Lane hostage and pits Superman against a biomechanical spider (called a Thanagarian Snare Beast). Ducking in and out of a beam of sunlight to recharge himself, Superman defeats the bio-spider and Brainiac, rescues Lois and sends Lex to prison. With misplaced optimism, Smith left the door open for a sequel.

SUPERNIC

Avid comic reader and collector Nicolas Cage's first foray into his heroes' world came when he changed his name from Coppola to Cage, in honour of Marvel's vigilante Luke Cage. In 2005 he named his newborn son Kal-El, after Krypton's most famous inhabitant. However, a comic book role eluded him until he was attached to *Superman Lives*. After that fell apart, he played Johnny Blaze in *Ghost Rider* (2007) and *Ghost Rider: Spirit of Vengeance* (2012). But his most triumphant foray into comic book adaptations was in 2010's *Kick-Ass*, playing Hit-Girl's unhinged but well-meaning father (above).

BATTLING POLAR BEARS

The script is cartoony and joke-heavy, with a style more suited to comics – a medium Smith would come to write for, working on runs for Batman and Green Arrow, alongside his own 'View Askewniverse' titles. It is very much of its time, featuring 1990s jargon, references to the fledgling internet and a wise-cracking Lois. Seeking a middle ground between himself and the producers, Smith does his best to get around the studio-enforced elements: a nonsensical sequence

'Burton says, "I wanna do my own script." Presumably a version of Superman who has scissors for hands.'

Kevin Smith

of Brainiac battling polar bears in the Arctic is as short as possible, while the no-flying rule is morphed into Superman travelling via a sonic boom. Reluctant to stray from comic lore, Smith describes the redesigned costume as simply 'Superman. . . '90s style.' More inventively, he deploys a more creative villain – Brainiac – rather than simply Lex Luthor (who also appears) or General Zod. There are geek references galore, including a character named after Superman co-creator Joe Shuster and a cameo by Batman.

Smith's passion for the character is evident and, for the first time in the franchise, the versions of Lois and Clark are aware of Superman and his

SMITH'S ASKEW SUPERMAN

Kevin Smith's proposed cast included stars of his own 'View Askewniverse' movies like *Mallrats* (1995), *Chasing Amy* (1997) and *Dogma* (1999): Ben Affleck (right, in *Daredevil*, 2003) as Superman, Jason Mewes as Jimmy Olsen, Jason Lee as Brainiac and Linda Fiorentino as Lois Lane. The oddest suggestion came from producer Jon Peters – who, after seeing Dwight Ewell in *Chasing Amy*, said (in Smith's words): 'The gay black guy – I liked that, I liked that a lot, I liked his voice. . . We need that voice, that character – somebody like him – in our movie. Can't Brainiac have a sidekick? Give him a little robot sidekick and give him that dude's voice. . . That's what this movie needs: a gay R2D2.'

history. Despite Smith's brand of knowing, juvenile humour, there are moments of gravitas: the world being cut off from sunlight and plunged into darkness is powerful and beautiful. Equally effective is the description of Superman bloodied and beaten by Doomsday. The most impressive, sorrowful section in the script, this is as heartfelt as anything in a Superman film so far. Arguably there is more emotion in Superman's death than in any of Smith's own films.

AN ODD FIT

Impressed, the studio attached a director: Tim Burton. He seemed an odd fit: could the man responsible for the whimsical and monochrome *Edward Scissorhands* (1990) find a footing in colourful Metropolis? *Batman* (1989) was a success but its hero is an altogether darker proposition than the Man of Tomorrow. Nevertheless, production proceeded and a summer 1998 release date was set. Eschewing Jon Peters's suggestion of Sean Penn, Nicolas Cage was cast as Superman. Both he and Burton signed pay-or-play deals – meaning both would collect their multi-million dollar fees whether or not the film was made. Rumoured co-stars included Kevin Spacey as Lex Luthor (a role he would eventually play in 2006's *Superman Returns*).

An art designer was hired, costume fittings were undertaken and shooting was scheduled to begin in Pennsylvania. However, Burton commissioned a new screenplay by Wesley Strick, writer of 1994's *Wolf*. 'He says, "I wanna do my own script,"' suggests Smith. 'Presumably a version of Superman where he has scissors for hands.' (Strick's version was itself rewritten by Richard Donner's protégé Dan Gilroy, who had a hand in 1992's *Freejack*.)

But too many elements pulled the project in different directions: the money; the idiosyncratic writer, director and producer; the merchandising; Superman's legacy. Warner, Burton suggested to writer Edward Gross, 'were a little sensitive because they were getting a lot of bad press that they had screwed up the Batman franchise. [In] the corporate environment, all of the decisions are basically fear-based. So I think one of the aspects that led to their decision was that somehow they were going to fuck up another franchise.'

With the budget rising, a release date looming and Burton disillusioned, Warner threw its weight behind *Wild Wild West*. *Superman Lives* collapsed. After more abortive stabs at a script and fruitless overtures to directors from Brent Ratner to Oliver Stone, Cage dropped out in 2000. Another new take was conceived by writer and director J.J. Abrams in 2002. *Superman: Flyby* was, reportedly, an origin tale featuring a black-suited hero in *Matrix*-style fights. But as the budget shot north of $200 million, the film failed to take flight. **SW**

WHAT HAPPENED NEXT. . .
Director Bryan Singer, fresh off the *X-Men* movies (2000, 2003), came on board. His *Superman Returns* (2006), starring Brandon Routh, was not a hit and the series again faltered. When *Batman vs. Superman* (see page 190) and George Miller's team-up movie *Justice League* came to nought, the studio turned to director Christopher Nolan who, like Burton, had resurrected Batman. With co-writer David Goyer, he conceived *Man of Steel* (2013), directed by Zack Snyder.

3/10 **WILL IT EVER HAPPEN?**
The more bizarre elements of the plot are now too notorious to ever be realized on film. If the 2013 reimagining, *Man of Steel*, proves a big enough hit, it is feasible that a *Death of Superman*-inspired storyline could be used in future instalments. But the giant spider fight and toy-inspired sidekicks are certainly banished to the Fortress of Solitude.

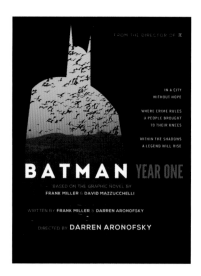

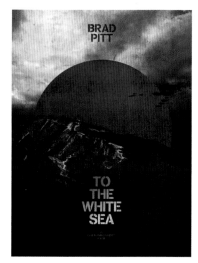

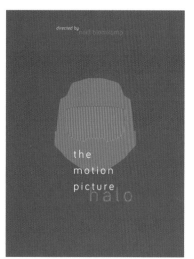

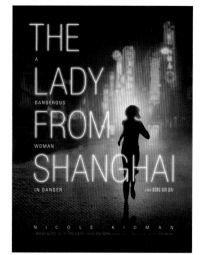

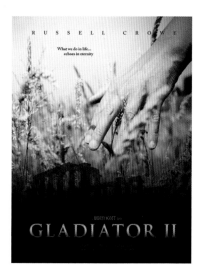

Chapter 6
The Two Thousands

WHITE JAZZ

GEORGE CLOONEY
CHARLIZE THERON
JASON BATEMAN
RAY LIOTTA
CHRIS PINE

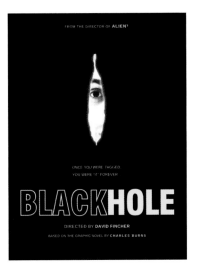

FROM THE DIRECTOR OF ALIEN³

ONCE YOU WERE TAGGED
YOU WERE 'IT' FOREVER

BLACKHOLE

DIRECTED BY DAVID FINCHER

BASED ON THE GRAPHIC NOVEL BY CHARLES BURNS

YOU CAN'T JAIL THE REVOLUTION

A STEVEN SPIELBERG FILM

CHICAGO

OF THE

THE TRIAL SEVEN

JOHNNY
DEPP

AMITABH
BACHCHAN

The true story of eight years
in the Bombay underworld

shantaram

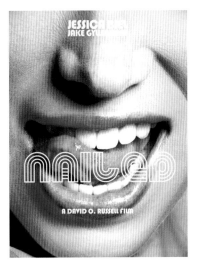

JESSICA
JAKE GYLLENHAAL

NAILED

A DAVID O. RUSSELL FILM

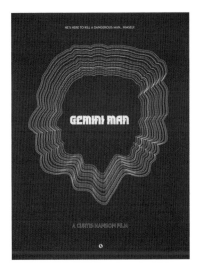

HE'S HERE TO KILL A DANGEROUS MAN... HIMSELF.

GEMINI MAN

A CURTIS HANSON FILM

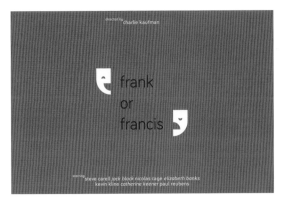

directed by
charlie kaufman

frank
or
francis

starring steve carell jack black nicolas cage elizabeth banks
kevin kline catherine keener paul reubens

FROM THE INTERNATIONAL BEST- SELLER

DIRECTED BY
TONY SCOTT

STARRING
MICKEY ROURKE
JAVIER BARDEM
CHRISTOPHER WALKEN
JOHNNY HALLYDAY

POTSDAMER PLATZ

FROM THE DIRECTOR OF *π*

IN A CITY
WITHOUT HOPE

WHERE CRIME RULES
A PEOPLE BROUGHT
TO THEIR KNEES

WITHIN THE SHADOWS
A LEGEND WILL RISE

BATMAN YEAR ONE

BASED ON THE GRAPHIC NOVEL BY
FRANK MILLER & **DAVID MAZZUCCHELLI**

WRITTEN BY **FRANK MILLER** & **DARREN ARONOFSKY**

DIRECTED BY **DARREN ARONOFSKY**

BATMAN:
YEAR ONE

Director Darren Aronofsky **Year** 2000 **Country** US **Genre** Superhero drama **Studio** Warner Bros

With so many adaptations of *Batman* over the years, both live action and animated, you could be mistaken for thinking that by the late 1990s he really did have nowhere left to go. Clearly Warner Bros, the studio behind the film franchise, believed that – and, with the shine wearing off Tim Burton and Joel Schumacher's take on the legend, it looked like it might indeed be time for The Dark Knight to hang up his cape for good. Enter Darren Aronofsky, a director who at that point had only a handful of shorts and one feature film (admittedly, 1998's hit *Pi*) to his credit. Born in 1969, the director, producer and screenwriter had studied film theory at Harvard before specializing in live action and animation at the American Film Institute. This pedigree and his penchant for disturbing themes made him perfect to inject new life into the flagging franchise.

TOSS OUT EVERYTHING

Among the greatest of all Batman graphic novels, *Batman: Year One* – written by the legendary Frank Miller, author of 1986's iconoclastic *The Dark Knight Returns* – originally appeared in DC Comics in 1987. With artist David Mazzucchelli (first renowned for his work on *Daredevil*), Miller created a story explaining the origin of Bruce Wayne's career as a masked avenger and his troubled relationship with Gotham City Police Commissioner Jim Gordon.

This provided fodder for Warner to take the legend back to its roots, but initial discussions with Aronofsky didn't quite go to plan. 'I told them I'd cast Clint Eastwood as The Dark Knight, and shoot it in Tokyo, doubling for Gotham City,' he recalls in David Hughes's *Tales from Development Hell*. 'That got their attention.' Whether he was joking isn't clear. Nonetheless, he got the job.

Miller had already developed a treatment of his original story. However, his collaboration with Aronofsky on a screenplay continued the evolution. Their efforts, the director told *Empire*, would 'be very different than anything in [the graphic novel], and anything you've seen. Toss out everything you can imagine about Batman! Everything! We're starting completely anew.'

DARREN ARONOFSKY

'I don't even really know what me and Frank are going to do,' the director told dailyradar.com in 2000. 'I will be working with Frank Miller if I do it. . . if it happens. Things look good, but you never know.'

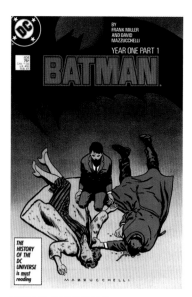

Aronofsky and Miller's version imagines Bruce Wayne not as a millionaire playboy but as a kid, wandering the streets of Gotham after seeing his parents murdered. He's taken in by a mechanic, Little Al, who teaches him about cars as Bruce watches the city's darkness encroach on his life. Latterly, as a vigilante with psychotic tendencies, Bruce scours Gotham for trouble, driving around in a blacked-out Lincoln Town Car that becomes the Batmobile. The bat connection is made when he punches a wrongdoer in the face with his father's signet ring: the initials T.W. – Thomas Wayne – leave what looks like the image of a bat on the perp's forehead. A cape and hockey mask hasten his transformation into Batman. Catwoman and The Joker, introduced in Miller's original, were also to feature. However, the central tone owed more to *Dirty Harry* (1971), *Death Wish* (1974) and *Taxi Driver* (1976) than the caped crusader of old.

SPIKY APPENDAGES

It was hardly the Batman that the mainstream knew and loved, although the studio's concept art for the characters and the Batmobile had a more traditional look. The tremendous amount of artwork proves how far the project progressed, although the bulk of it has little in common with Aronofsky and Miller's vision of a down-at-heel, streetwise kid. In it, Batman looks like a warrior from the Middle Ages, albeit with a distinctly futuristic slant. Along designs that hark back to the familiar streamlined appearance is a set depicting him in gleaming armour and swathed in what looks like a slippery latex cloak (think Iron Man gone kinky). The medieval look continues with Catwoman, while the Batmobile is so covered in spiky appendages and propulsion units that you can hardly see the car beneath – so much for Aronofsky and Miller's souped-up limo.

That Warner's designs, although a radical break from anything seen before, were poles apart from what Aronofsky and Miller were envisaging flags up the fundamental differences in how they each saw the character developing. It's

THE MILLER'S TALE

In addition to their reinterpretation of *Batman: Year One* (above), Aronofsky and Miller planned to adapt the latter's 1983–84 comic *Ronin* (unrelated to the 1998 John Frankenheimer thriller of the same name). Sadly, as Aronofsky admitted, 'We never really quite nailed it.'

BATMAN VS. SUPERMAN

'The Superman/Batman clash, putting them together in one film, would be absolutely fantastic,' Wolfgang Petersen told SuperHeroHype.com in 2006. Warner Bros agreed: after *Superman Lives* (see page 182) and *Batman: Year One* faltered, it announced in 2002 that Petersen would direct a Caped Crusader/Man of Steel mash-up. The script, by Andrew Kevin Walker of *Se7en* (1995), was rewritten by *Batman Forever*'s (1995) Akiva Goldsman. As Goldsman wrote *Batman & Robin* (1997), that's like getting Stephenie Meyer to rewrite Edgar Allan Poe. Still, Christian Bale and Colin Farrell were in the running for Batman, as was Jude Law for Superman. (Although Law – mindful of the calamitous campification of Warner's Batman franchise – was reportedly worried that sequels, to which he would be contractually committed, wouldn't measure up.) The project collapsed when Petersen opted to direct *Troy* (2004). 'I hope it still will happen because they are so different. . .' he told SuperHeroHype. 'The dark Batman and the sort of goody-goody Superman. It's so nice to play with both and see how the dynamic between the two – also including fighting between the two – would work.' A teaser poster survived in *I Am Legend* (2007, right), an inside joke by or for its screenwriter: Akiva Goldsman. **SB**

likely these divergences of opinion were responsible for Warner parting ways with Aronofsky, effectively putting the final nail in the coffin of a live action *Year One*. Another theory is that Aronofsky and Miller's vision just wasn't commercial enough. With a bleak storyline and few fancy vehicles and gadgets, the chances of snagging the valuable younger demographic were slim.

A review of the screenplay – described by Aronofsky as a 'gritty urban crime drama with an underground guerrilla flavor' – by Jett, the founder of batman-on-film.com, observed: 'It would make a hell of a film – it just shouldn't be a Batman film.' Noting its lack of relation to the graphic novel (which ultimately foreshadowed Christopher Nolan's 2005 film *Batman Begins* instead), Jett says that the script had Batman taking on, and eventually killing, corrupt police commissioner Gillian B. Loeb. 'The number one reason why it fails for me is that I didn't care much for this Bruce Wayne. . .' he adds. 'His voice-over dialogue – letters to his dead father – are particularly cheesy [and] his intentions – his "mission" – and his actions are all about self-gratification. He's not donning the Bat-suit to save Gotham, he's putting it on to beat the living hell out of criminals to make himself feel better. What kind of hero is that?'

> *'I told them I'd cast Clint Eastwood and shoot it in Tokyo. That got their attention.'*
> Darren Aronofsky

The studio was well aware that, following the debacle of Joel Schumacher's *Batman & Robin* (1997), a rethink was needed to save the franchise, but it seems it was not ready for such a fundamental overhaul. Aronofsky himself was quoted as saying he believed Warner always doubted whether his and Miller's take was even filmable, let alone commercially viable. And a decade later, at the Edinburgh International Film Festival, he admitted: 'I never really wanted to make a Batman film. It was a kind of bait-and-switch strategy. I was working on *Requiem for a Dream* [2000] and I got a phone call that Warner Bros wanted to talk about Batman. At the time I had this idea for a film called *The Fountain* [2006], which I knew was gonna be this big movie and I was thinking, "Is Warners really gonna give me $80 million to make a film about love and death after I come off a heroin movie?" So my theory was, if I can write this Batman film and they could perceive me as a writer for it. . .' **CP**

WHAT HAPPENED NEXT. . .

Year One's transition to the screen did not end with Aronofsky. In 2011, Warner and DC united for a sixty-four-minute animation (below), based on the comic by Frank Miller and David Mazzucchelli. Directed by Sam Liu and Lauren Montgomery, its minimalist style perfectly suited the bleak story of revenge, retribution and introspective self-analysis. Voices were provided by *Breaking Bad*'s Bryan Cranston (Gordon), *Southland*'s Ben McKenzie (Wayne/Batman) and *Dollhouse*'s Eliza Dushku (Selina Kyle/Catwoman).

WILL IT EVER HAPPEN?

2/10 It's highly unlikely a live action version of *Batman: Year One* will see the light – and certainly not by Aronofsky. Time and Hollywood wait for no man, especially where big-budget superhero films are concerned. Miller's novel tells the story of Bruce Wayne and what led to him becoming the hero – in other words, what we saw in Christopher Nolan's *Batman Begins* (2005). And, as Nolan's *The Dark Knight Rises* (2012) proved, there are plenty of places to take the Caped Crusader without revisiting the past.

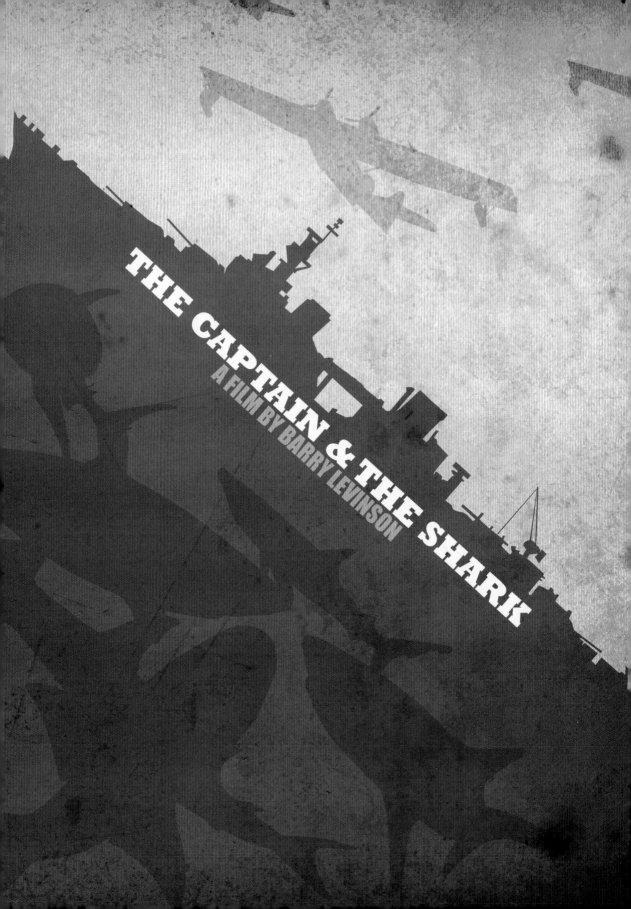

THE CAPTAIN & THE SHARK

A FILM BY BARRY LEVINSON

THE CAPTAIN AND THE SHARK

Director Barry Levinson **Starring** Mel Gibson **Year** 2001 **Country** US **Genre** Historical drama **Studio** Warner Bros

Halfway through *Jaws* (1975), police chief Brody, ichthyologist Hooper and grizzled sea dog Quint are on the hunt for the shark, trying to forget their worries through drinking and comparing scars. When Hooper quizzes Quint about a tattoo on his arm that has been removed, the old salt reveals he was a survivor of the USS *Indianapolis*, the Second World War ship sunk carrying components for the Hiroshima/Nagasaki bombs in the South Pacific, resulting in one of the largest known recorded shark attacks: 'Eleven hundred men went into the water. Three hundred and sixteen men come out. The sharks took the rest. June the twenty-ninth, 1945.' The speech makes the hitherto monstrous Quint seem human, gives the hunt an even greater sense of purpose and broadens the scope of the movie into the real world. Yet the four-minute monologue exposes only a fraction of the drama surrounding the USS *Indianapolis*. Over the decades since *Jaws*, some of the biggest film-makers and movie stars in the world have tried to bring the whole sorry tale to life.

CHOPPED TO PIECES

The key focus that Quint's retelling omits is the story of the ship's captain, Charles McVay. McVay was unaware of the true nature of the payload the *Indianapolis* had delivered to the air base on the island of Tinian. On its way back to join the fleet at Leyte in the Philippines for gunnery practice and refresher training before the expected invasion of Japan, the *Indy* was slammed by two torpedoes from a Japanese submarine: one in the bow, one in the gas tank (on 30 July, rather than the date in *Jaws*). Many of the sailors sleeping on deck to keep cool were thrown overboard as the ship took on water and listed to forty-five degrees. As the order was given to abandon ship, crewmen who jumped from the keel were chopped to pieces by the ship's propeller blades.

Over 800 men went into the water. With the lifeboats unreachable, they formed clusters to stay afloat, the largest group numbering around 300. The sinking ship spewed gallons of fuel into the sea, coating the sailors in black goo. It didn't take long for the men to start turning on each other – fifty were killed in a ten-minute burst on the first morning. Drinking seawater turned the sailors maniacal, then comatose. Fever and hallucinations became the norm.

BARRY LEVINSON
The director of the much-loved *Diner* (1982) also helmed *Good Morning, Vietnam* (1987) and *Rain Man* (1988). But over a decade after *The Captain and the Shark* sank, he hit the water for the equally grim *The Bay* (2012).

Then the sharks arrived. Tigers, makos and whitetips began picking off sailors from the edge of the clusters. For some, being covered in black fuel saved their lives as the sharks were drawn to the pale skin of the unaffected bodies. Eventually, a Navy plane spotted the survivors. Against orders, the pilot landed his plane on the sea without knowing the nationality of the men and began a rescue. Many of the men, tired through treading water, drowned from exhaustion just after slipping off their life jackets. Fifty-six survived by lashing themselves to the plane's wings with parachute cords. But more than 500 died.

NASTIER ELEMENTS

Yet the nightmare was not over for Captain McVay. Despite testimony from survivors that his actions had saved lives during the ordeal, the Navy made him a scapegoat after families of the deceased demanded to know why authorities lost track of the ship. In fact, the *Indy* sent three signals that

> *'Hey,* this *is a movie. Somebody someday should do a movie just about the* Indianapolis.*'*
>
> Steven Spielberg

were ignored. The first recipient commander was drunk, the second had put a Do Not Disturb sign on his cabin door and the third signal was deemed a Japanese prank. To cover its tracks, the Navy doctored claims about McVay's inability to plot a zigzag pattern to avoid the torpedoes. Court-marshaled and receiving death threats, he committed suicide in 1968, aged seventy.

'I remember just saying, "Hey, *this* is a movie!"' Spielberg told aintitcool.com. 'Somebody someday should do a movie just about the *Indianapolis*.' The idea was nixed by Universal studio president Sid Sheinberg, who remarked, 'That's a different kind of shirt than we want to wear.' The incident finally made it to the screen as a 1991 TV movie with the unwieldy title *Mission of the Shark: The Saga of the U.S.S. Indianapolis*. With Stacy Keach as McVay and Richard Thomas (*The Waltons'* John-Boy), the CBS film didn't shy away from nastier elements like the madness from drinking salt water, and the crew turning on each other. But budget limitations and the restrictions of television meant it was a tepid retelling of the tale. Only a big-screen adaptation would do it justice.

RAZOR-SHARP WRITING
The writers credited for the screenplay of *Jaws* were Carl Gottlieb and the source novel's author Peter Benchley. However, Steven Spielberg reported that Quint's monologue scene (above) was written by Howard Sackler and John Milius and refined by actor Robert Shaw.

DISGRACE AND SUICIDE

In 2001, Warner Bros announced *The Captain and the Shark*, a screenplay by John Hoffman (author and screenwriter of the play-turned-1997-TV film *Northern Lights*), based on Doug Stanton's 2001 book *In Harm's Way*, a chilling retelling of the incident. Mel Gibson was pencilled in as McVay and Barry Levinson was in the frame to direct. Known for both small-scale chamber pieces (1982's *Diner*, 1987's *Tin Men*) and awards-friendly star vehicles (1987's *Good Morning, Vietnam*, 1988's *Rain Man*, 1991's *Bugsy*), Levinson had shot the underwater thriller *Sphere* (1998) for Warner and looked a good bet to create exciting spectacle without overpowering McVay's personal story.

WHAT HAPPENED NEXT. . .

In 1997, twelve-year-old Hunter Scott wrote a school report about the *Indianapolis* after seeing *Jaws*. His research, which included interviews with survivors and fully vindicated McVay, led to an inquiry in 2001 that persuaded the Navy to exonerate the captain. The resolution was signed by President Clinton. The saga reinvigorated Universal's appetite for the project and, in 2006, Robert Nelson Jacobs – screenwriter of *The Shipping News* (2001) and *The Water Horse* (2007) – was hired to rework *The Good Sailor*. Weaving a fictional story around the schoolboy and a survivor of the disaster, it used flashbacks to retell the yarn. Perhaps ignited by *The Good Sailor*, *The Captain and the Shark* resurfaced with a new director: Chris Kentis, who attracted attention with 2003's *Open Water* (left), about two divers abandoned in the ocean at the mercy of circling sharks. Yet *The Captain and the Shark* failed to move forward and the film was once again all at sea.

As is often the way in Hollywood, a rival *Indianapolis* project was doing the rounds. At Universal, *The Good Sailor* was written by Brent Hanley, who had penned the ingenious thriller *Frailty* (2001). Courted for both projects, Gibson apparently opted for *The Captain and the Shark*, only for it to stall.

The Good Sailor managed to stay afloat, with directors such as Peter Weir and Ron Howard (reputedly looking to cast Russell Crowe as McVay) circling the project. In January 2005, it was announced as the big-screen directorial debut of J.J. Abrams – at that point best known for the TV series *Felicity* and *Alias* – with *American Pie* (1999) producer Chris Moore. The project had momentum until Tom Cruise recruited the director for *Mission: Impossible III* (2006).

That it failed to launch may be down to factors inherent in the story. The sinking of the ship is the kind of spectacle usually reserved for James Cameron and would require a huge budget. Anyone familiar with the making of *Jaws* knows the nightmares of shooting on water in general and involving sharks in particular. And, given the money and logistics involved, the huge loss of life and McVay's subsequent disgrace and suicide, make it a downer for any audience. There are few studios that would be prepared to take the risk. **IF**

WILL IT EVER HAPPEN?

4/10 In 2011, Robert Downey Jr. and his wife/producing partner Susan enlisted Pulitzer Prize winner Robert Schenkkan, a writer for HBO's *The Pacific* (2010), to script the project for Warner Bros. While Warner owns the rights to *The Captain and the Shark*, it is believed that Schenkkan is writing a screenplay from scratch encompassing both the *Indianapolis* and Hunter Scott (see What Happened Next. . ., above) strands of the tale. Given Downey Jr.'s A-list status, and the Oscar-friendly potential of the story, it can only be a matter of time before the *Indianapolis* sets sail on its fateful final voyage once more.

TO THE WHITE SEA

Directors Joel and Ethan Coen **Starring** Brad Pitt **Year** 2002
Budget $50 million **Country** US **Genre** Adventure **Studio** 20th Century Fox

THE COEN BROTHERS
'No one was interested in financing this expensive movie. . . in which there's no dialogue,' rued Joel (left). 'And,' observed his brother Ethan (right), 'it's a survival story, and the guy dies at the end.'

Following the success of their then highest-grossing film *O Brother, Where Art Thou?* (2000) and the low-key noir *The Man Who Wasn't There* (2001), directorial brothers Joel and Ethan Coen conceived their most ambitious project yet. *Miller's Crossing* (1990) had been inspired by Dashiell Hammett's *The Glass Key*. *The Big Lebowski* (1998) leaned on Raymond Chandler's *The Big Sleep*. *O Brother, Where Art Thou?* referenced Homer's *Odyssey*. *The Man Who Wasn't There* owed a clear debt to James M. Cain. But *To the White Sea* was the Coen brothers' first *official* literary adaptation.

ADVENTURE AND ALIENATION

Author James Dickey served in the Second World War and the Korean War, then became a lecturer and writer. His work is clean and economical with flourishes of brutality. More famous for his poetry than his prose, he was awarded the Poet Laureate Consultant in 1966. However, he is defined by his savage 1970 thriller *Deliverance*. This became an Oscar-nominated film in 1972, directed by John Boorman. It remains Dickey's only work to make it to the big screen.

To the White Sea (1993) is less famous than *Deliverance,* but is an even more brutal and challenging story. It follows the epic journey of Muldrow, once an Alaskan hunter, now a US Air Force pilot stranded in Japan during the Second World War. When Tokyo is firebombed by his own forces, he escapes, making his way through Japan towards the safety of the frozen, desolate island of Hokkaido. His violent odyssey takes him through hostile territory and bitter weather, as he endeavours to keep one step ahead of the soldiers pursuing him.

The tale revisits familar Coen motifs. They plotted an adventure and odyssey through a dark chapter of US history in *O Brother, Where Art Thou?*, and – barring the 1910s, 1950s and 1960s – have set a film in every decade of the twentieth century. *To the White Sea* would have ticked the Second World War box. Despite Joel and Ethan's skill with intricate, idiosyncratic dialogue, *To the White Sea* was to feature little speech. Scenes played out in silence as the pilot trekked through a largely deserted landscape. Such people he did encounter would speak in their native Japanese. These exchanges would have no subtitles, leaving the audience as alienated from the world as Muldrow himself.

The Coens, determined to keep their films under two hours, turned the book into a lean, eighty-nine-page screenplay, with a first draft by David Webb Peoples (Oscar-nominated for 1992's *Unforgiven*). It is a faithful adaptation, with many passages transferred wholesale, including a stand-off with a blind swordsman and the murders of soldiers and innocent civilians who hinder Muldrow's progress. In places, however, the Coens went deeper than Dickey's original work, adding a voice-over and creating flashbacks to Muldrow's youth.

BLEAK WHITE

The project was announced in 1999 as being under the aegis of producer Jeremy Thomas, who won an Academy Award for 1987's *The Last Emperor*. Hopes were high that the Coens would return to the bleak, white landscapes of *Fargo* (1996) and that such a prestige picture would deliver them a Best Picture Oscar to go with their Best Original Screenplay for that movie. Similarly, it seemed that Brad Pitt could cement his evolution from underappreciated actor to award-winning movie star by playing the part of Muldrow.

The blackly comic violence of *Fargo* and the brothers' feature film debut, *Blood Simple* (1984), is alive and well in the script, especially in a scene taken directly from the novel. Muldrow comes upon a pond filled with swans and sees an opportunity to use their feathers to bulk out a coat and insulate himself against the cold. First, he dispatches a man by the water, then sets about killing a swan, which goes less smoothly than he would like:

```
The old man feebly beats the water but is too weak to
offer much resistance. The swans glide away from the
churning water but continue to paddle serenely around
the old man, pecking at the grain that floats on the
surface of the pond.

MOMENTS LATER

At the cut a cacophony of honking and splashing water.

Muldrow is waist deep in the pond, wielding a short
heavy stick, clubbing the swans.

The swans at the periphery move only to the extent that
they are crowded out by the retreating swans near the
middle. They bunch up in confusion.
```

BLEAK VISIONS
Roger Deakins, the Oscar-nominated cinematographer of *Fargo* (starring Steve Buscemi, above) was slated to take the same role on *To the White Sea*. It is tantalizing to imagine what he would have made of the similarly bleak landscapes.

With producer Richard Roth – the first to be attached when the property was set up at Universal in 1993 – also on board, the project proceeded smoothly at 20th Century Fox, which was apparently undaunted by the prospect of a near-silent movie. January 2002 was mooted as the start date for filming. But, in September 2001, *Variety* reported: 'Like its protagonist, the picture seems to have been shot down over a disagreement. . . Sources familiar with the

The Coen brothers reteamed with *O Brother* star George Clooney for *Intolerable Cruelty* (2003) – a contemporary and rather disappointing take on a screwball comedy. However, it was better than what followed: their first undisputed failure, *The Ladykillers* (2004). After a three-year hiatus in which they recharged their batteries and wrote new projects, the Coens returned with *No Country for Old Men* (2007). This adaptation of a Cormac McCarthy novel, starring Tommy Lee Jones, shares traits with *To the White Sea:* it is a sparse, brutal, bleak chase movie with worldly, pragmatic characters. Four Academy Awards were their reward. As for Brad Pitt, he and the Coen brothers found the right project for their combined talents with 2008's espionage comedy *Burn After Reading.*

deal said that the Coens and the studio could not come to agreement on the budget for the pic, which was to have been filmed on location in Japan – never a cheap prospect.' A large portion of the budget would have been spent on recreating the firebombing of Tokyo: a four-page sequence of chaos as napalm rains from above. Further location shooting was to take place in Canada. ('Don't set a movie in Tokyo during the firebombing unless you have lots of money to pay for it,' Joel Coen told Creative Screenwriting in 2011.)

COSTLY MISFIRE

The Coens' only real experience of a big budget had produced a costly misfire: 1994's *The Hudsucker Proxy*. Expensive, R-rated pictures are difficult to green-light at the best of times and even Pitt's star power could not convince Fox to take the risk. When Ethan Coen was asked by an empireonline.com visitor about the film's chances of resurrection in 2011, he was pessimistic: 'Jeremy [Thomas] came very close to getting us the budget. . . But he came up short even with Brad Pitt doing the movie for free. So if we failed under those circumstances I don't know that we'll ever succeed. Also, Brad's too old now'.

Even with their stock high after the Oscar success of *No Country for Old Men* (2007) and the box-office triumph of *True Grit* (2010), *To the White Sea* seems destined to remain the Coens' great unmade masterpiece. **SW**

BRAD PITT
The star (right), said Ethan Coen (left), 'has this sort of remorse or regret' about the collapse of *To the White Sea*. Pitt did, however, work with Ethan and Joel (centre) on *Burn After Reading* (2008).

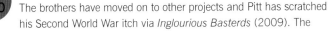

2/10 **WILL IT EVER HAPPEN?**
The brothers have moved on to other projects and Pitt has scratched his Second World War itch via *Inglourious Basterds* (2009). The Coens proceeding with the film with a younger member of their acting troupe is an option but the muted reception for Peter Weir's similar survival epic, *The Way Back* (2010), is likely to discourage studios' interest.

directed by
neill blomkamp

the
motion
picture
halo

HALO

Director Neill Blomkamp **Year** 2005 **Budget** $128 million **Country** US **Genre** Sci-fi **Studio** Universal, Fox

Video games don't have the greatest track record when it comes to being transformed into film. There have been occasional hits, like *Lara Croft: Tomb Raider* (2001) and the *Resident Evil* franchise (2002–present) – but, even when financially successful, these films tend to be vilified by the very fans they're seeking to attract. *Halo*, for a while, looked like being different.

BIGGER THAN MOVIES

Microsoft's flagship franchise is fundamental to the success of its Xbox console. Remaining to this day exclusive to Microsoft – so PlayStation owners can only weep in frustrated jealousy as they load up another methadone session of *Resistance* – it was the title that gamers simply had to have, and had to buy the machine to play. And it's no exaggeration to say the franchise – which has raked in over $3 billion to date – is bigger than movies. *Halo: Reach* (2010) took $200 million on its day of release, more than double any Hollywood blockbuster. The achievement broke its own records: *Halo 3*'s first twenty-four hours brought in $170 million in 2007, and *Halo 2* (2004) $125 million.

In the much-imitated sci-fi first-person shooter game, the player usually controls a genetically engineered super-soldier called Master Chief, who doesn't speak and is never seen out of his face-obscuring combat suit. The general setup is an interstellar war between Earth and an alliance of dastardly alien races called the Covenant: religious fanatics led by holy 'Prophets' who worship an ancient civilization called the Forerunners, who were wiped out by a race of tentacular parasites called the Flood.

The halo of the title refers to the vast, habitable, ring-shaped super-weapons created by the Covenant to combat the Flood: a concept familiar from Larry Niven's *Ringworld* novels, and from Iain M. Banks's books about the Culture. The gameplay revolves around much shooting of aliens, on foot and in various vehicles, while uncovering secrets and fending off galactic invasions.

The *Halo* narrative has also included spin-off media such as novels and comics, so a film based on an action spectacular with dense mythology and a fan base of millions was a no-brainer. Microsoft itself began the process of bringing Master Chief to the screen in 2005, commissioning a screenplay –

NEILL BLOMKAMP
'I wanted it to feel like the most brutal, real version of science fiction in a war environment that you've seen. . .' the young film-maker told creativity-online.com. 'It would have been a unique take. . . science fiction in a dirty, organic way.'

HALO LEGENDS

Halo has found success as a straight-to-DVD anime. *Halo Legends* (2010) is an *Animatrix*-like collection of short films. The project was overseen by Shinji Aramaki (the artist behind the *Appleseed* saga). All the episodes are considered canonical in *Halo* mythology, bar one: the parodic *Odd One Out*, featuring Spartan 1337, the Frank Drebin of Master Chief's unit.

with strict guidelines – from Alex Garland (writer of *The Beach*; *28 Days Later. . .*, 2002 and *Dredd 3D*, 2012) for a cool million dollars. The result was shopped to the Hollywood studios, the scripts delivered by couriers in *Halo* suits. With Microsoft naturally keen to maintain creative control and earn a hefty chunk of the eventual profits, most studios immediately passed, citing low risk and high gain for the company, and the opposite for themselves. The exceptions were Universal and Fox, whose unusual joint approach – Universal grabbed the domestic US stake, Fox took the foreign territories – eliminated much of Microsoft's leverage. They were obliged to accept a relatively paltry $5 million for the option on the property and ten percent of the eventual gross.

Microsoft's desire for a big-name director led to the hiring of Peter Jackson (*The Lord of the Rings*, 2001–03). However, he signed on as a co-producer only, and – after a brief flirtation with Guillermo del Toro (who eventually moved on in favour of 2008's *Hellboy II*) – controversially decided to give the film to the then untested Neill Blomkamp. The South African had a background in flashy, high-profile commercials for the likes of Nike, Adidas and Citroën, but it was his short film *Alive in Joburg* (2006) that had caught Jackson's eye. Shot in grainy, handheld, documentary style, *Alive in Joburg* involved aliens landing and integrating in 1990s Soweto – an idea that would be developed and expanded for his *District 9* (2009) – and suggested the arrival of an unusual and creative voice in sci-fi.

THE WHOLE CREATIVE UNIVERSE

'I was busy directing commecials and always knew I wanted to get into features,' recalled Blomkamp. 'My agent in LA connected me with Mary Parent, who was producing *Halo*. She said, "Jackson's seen your work and he wants to meet you. You have to fly down to New Zealand so he can see if you're viable." I was extremely interested in doing *Halo* because that whole universe I find very awesome and stimulating. So I immediately got on a plane and met him

WAR IS HALO: A LOOK AT *LANDFALL* 2007

'The legacy of a film that never was' is how Microsoft described the three advertising shorts shot by Blomkamp for *Halo 3*, later edited into the online short *Landfall* (right). 'I went about starting to make those three pieces back with a lot of the guys from [Jackson's studio] Weta, who had made the original film,' the director told creativity-online.com's Nick Parish. 'All of the design and everything that we'd made for the film is just locked up in some locker somewhere, so all of the stuff for the shorts is specifically for the short films, from scratch.' Filming took place in a landfill, in New Zealand's capital, Wellington. 'I just needed a chunk of land with some architecture,' Blomkamp explained. As theshiznit.co.uk opined, 'If the *Halo* movie is to be resurrected, pray it looks as good as this.'

and Fran [Walsh, Jackson's partner] and everyone at [Jackson's studio] Weta, and saw the whole creative universe he's set up down there. And I just stayed!' The studios were happy to go with Jackson's instinct – doubtless it didn't hurt that the untried Blomkamp would be cheaper to hire than the man who was paid a record-breaking $20 million to direct *King Kong* (2005).

However, Microsoft's relationship with the developing film did not improve when it became clear that Blomkamp's grainy aesthetic was being applied to their signature property. 'Directors always want to make something their own,' Blomkamp explained. 'But there's already a foundation to whatever that creative property may be. You have to build on top of that, while giving the fans what they want – and, to a certain extent, also giving whoever owns the intellectual property what they want. So *Halo* was an exercise in thousands and thousands of pieces of artwork that had my filter on top of what [the game's developer] Bungie had already designed. The guys at Bungie liked what I was doing and where I was going – I'm fairly confident of that. But artwork

> *'I was extremely interested in* Halo *because that whole universe I find very awesome and stimulating.'*
> Neill Blomkamp

was getting back to Microsoft – and reportedly Microsoft, the corporate entity, was not happy with it because it was too unconventional.'

Frustratingly, Blomkamp's desire to radically depart from the glossy but empty video-game-to-movie spectacles of the past was precisely what prompted dissatisfied rumblings from higher up the corporate food chain. But, ultimately, money killed the project. Costs were rising and – with Microsoft expecting as much return from its intellectual property as the studios producing the film – it was decided that slices of the pie would be too thin for each of the recipients.

'The lack of progress and the lack of decisiveness just wore on everyone,' says Blomkamp. 'I was an untested director, doing a movie that was pretty big, so I think things would have been different if Peter had been directing it. The fact that he had one layer of removal from it was impeding its ability to move forward. But there's no question that, the way my career has turned out, I owe a massive amount of gratitude to Peter Jackson.' **OW**

WILL IT EVER HAPPEN?

5/10 It's hard to imagine that it won't. But with the studios' option long since lapsed and the rights back with Microsoft, it won't be Blomkamp's vision. A new script submitted in 2009 by Stuart Beattie (writer of *Collateral*, 2004, and the first three *Pirates of the Caribbean* films) apparently found great favour at Microsoft, so it's unclear if Garland's draft remains in contention. The company's franchise development director, Frank O'Connor, told a San Francisco conference in 2010, 'We're going to make a movie when the time is right.' *Halo* continues to dominate its industry, so there's time yet.

WHAT HAPPENED NEXT...
Jackson shepherded Blomkamp's feature debut, *District 9* (2009), through production and release. 'The day after *Halo* collapsed, Fran Walsh suggested we make something else that we could control, and that it be based on *Alive in Joburg*,' says Blomkamp. 'After all the hard work on *Halo* and that bottoming out, we just transitioned straight into *District 9*.' Among an extraordinary awards haul, the result was nominated for four Oscars, including nods for Jackson and Blomkamp himself.

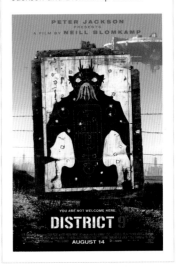

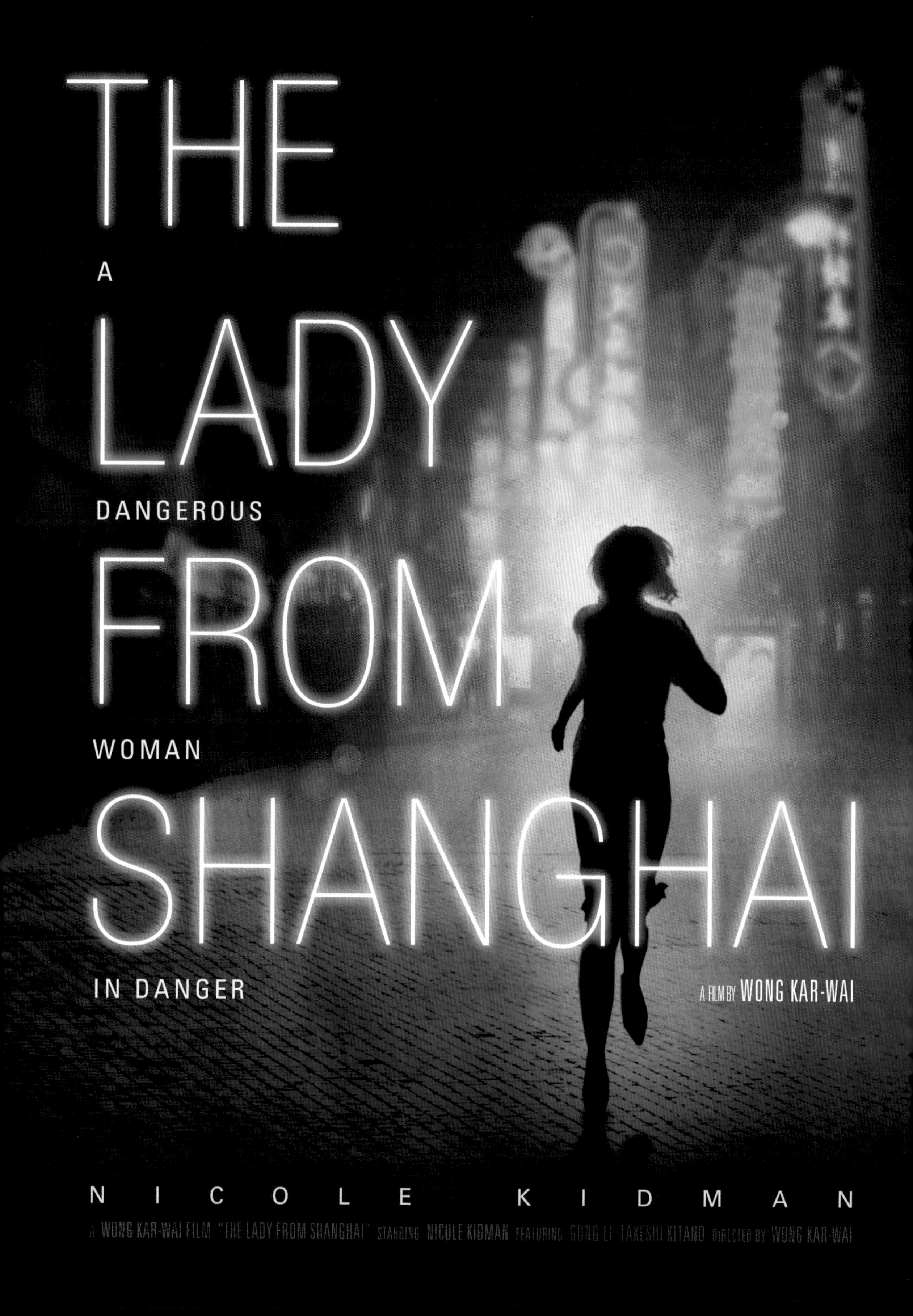

THE
A
LADY
DANGEROUS
FROM
WOMAN
SHANGHAI
IN DANGER

A FILM BY WONG KAR-WAI

NICOLE KIDMAN

A WONG KAR-WAI FILM "THE LADY FROM SHANGHAI" STARRING NICOLE KIDMAN FEATURING GONG LI TAKESHI KITANO DIRECTED BY WONG KAR-WAI

THE LADY FROM SHANGHAI

Director Wong Kar-wai **Starring** Nicole Kidman **Year** 2005
Budget $30 million **Country** China, US **Genre** Thriller **Studio** Studio Canal

As the unwieldy production histories of *2046* (2004) and *The Grandmaster* (2013) illustrate, Chinese director Wong Kar-wai is not a man of decisive action. The former was filmed over four years in gauzy secrecy, halted mid-shoot by the 2003 SARS epidemic and returned to the editing room for months of tinkering after its nick-of-time Cannes premiere. The latter's comparable years of delay and recess have become the stuff of arthouse-geek mythology. The natty overlord of second-wave Hong Kong cinema keeps his face determinedly hidden behind trademark sunglasses, and his working processes are scarcely less inscrutable. But if Wong has a difficult time finishing his appropriately languid projects, starting them hardly seems any easier. No film demonstrates this better than *The Lady from Shanghai*, the longest and least fulfilled tease of a brilliantly exasperating career.

FAMOUSLY FANTASTIC FACES
One could argue that the project sounded a rather distant dream from the get-go. In the autumn of 2003, word travelled that Wong was developing his first English-language project for none other than Nicole Kidman, who was then on something of a creative hot streak. That year, she had taken the Best Actress Oscar for Stephen Daldry's chamber drama *The Hours* (2002), in which her improbable casting as Virginia Woolf paid off both dowdily and handsomely. Three months after that Academy Award triumph, she wooed the auteurist crowd when *Dogville*, in which she impressively subjected herself to the punishing whims of Dogme 95 director Lars von Trier, was unveiled at Cannes.

The actress's artistic leaps seemed to have grown more reckless and less commercially minded following her 2001 divorce from Tom Cruise. So the news that Kidman was eyeing a collaboration with a subtitle-dwelling critics' pet from the Far East wasn't as surprising as it might once have been.

For Wong, however, *The Lady from Shanghai* seemed a step into another dimension. He had certainly dabbled in Asian celebrity: *In the Mood for Love* (2000), his most broadly celebrated film, was built on the superstar cheekbones of Maggie Cheung and Tony Leung, while *2046* would prove to be equally dependent on the power of famously fantastic faces, such as

WONG KAR-WAI
'We have to work up a schedule with Nicole [Kidman],' the Chinese director, lauded by the likes of Sofia Coppola, told aintitcool.com in April 2008. 'She is the reason I wanted to start this project.'

WONG AND THE WOMEN

Had Wong and Nicole Kidman teamed up, it might not have been a one-off: the director is famous for reusing actors. Tony Leung has featured in seven of his films, but Wong's work is also distinguished by a rotating company of female stars. Maggie Cheung was invaluable to his first three features – as well as *In the Mood for Love* (2000) – but, since her semi-retirement in 2004, he seems to have been grooming suitably iconic replacements. Gong Li and Ziyi Zhang (above) have each worked with him twice. Norah Jones seems less likely to make a second appearance, although he built *My Blueberry Nights* (2007) around her, much as he conceived *The Lady from Shanghai* for Kidman.

singer Faye Wong and model Ziyi Zhang. Still, Kidman's was a star name that superceded Wong's, taking *The Lady from Shanghai* into a realm of online buzz and rumour-mongering that proved more inquisitive about the director's typically fragile conception than he would probably have liked.

In late 2004, Wong reportedly predicted that the film would be shot the following year and finished 'in three months'. But if the director, never a rigorous believer in final drafts, ever even completed a script, there's little to show for it. A 2005 *Inside Film* report alleged that Kidman had been presented with a secret story idea, and that the director would be using scriptwriters on set. Two years later, he claimed to be still mired in the first-draft stage.

Whatever the secret was, he has successfully kept it guarded beyond the most succinct of summaries, allowing little more than that Kidman would be playing 'a dangerous woman in danger' in 1920s Shanghai, with diversions in Russia and the United States. That terseness enabled fast-and-loose speculation across the blogosphere, of which the most widespread misconception was that the film was conceived as a remake of Orson Welles's 1947 film noir of the same name. Wong admitted taking inspiration from the title, but this purported espionage romance was to be his own creation.

The script, in any event, was less of a concern for the director than the star. Having told Italian newspaper *Corriere della Sera* that he elected to work with

> *'Nicole has the character of the Hitchcockian star: [she] is elegant, dangerous and in danger.'*
>
> Wong Kar-wai

Kidman – whom he had admired in Gus Van Sant's black comedy *To Die For* (1995) – because she had 'the character of the Hitchcockian star', he later insisted that he had no desire to complete the film without her. 'There is no reason to do it,' he told the *New York Times* in November 2006, responding to word that Kidman, who reportedly cleared six months in her calendar as early as 2004, had pulled out of the repeatedly postponed shoot. Around the same time, the actress, newly married to country music star Keith Urban, told *The Advocate*, 'I want to be close to the person I love, and that does not mean sitting in China. So you give up a lot so that you can have your love.' (Wong's proposed locations for exterior shots included Harbin in northeast China, New York and St Petersburg in Russia.)

PROCRASTINATION AND PERFECTIONISM

The Lady from Shanghai may simply have fallen prey to the most banal causes of shelved cinema: 'scheduling conflicts' and 'personal reasons'. But Wong's own combination of procrastination and perfectionism was evidently an aggravating factor. Stories leaked of further delays being caused by Wong's concern about Kidman-induced media intrusion, revisions to the script and his inability to settle on a suitable male lead for the film – his first choice of Tony Leung being deemed too short to star opposite his 1.8 metre-tall leading lady.

WHAT HAPPENED NEXT. . .

Wong never renounced *The Lady from Shanghai* but, after more than four years of dangling, it quietly left the conversation. Perhaps the critical and commercial failure in 2007 of the project that became his first English-language film – *My Blueberry Nights*, a pretty but fatuous US road movie starring Jude Law, Rachel Weisz, Natalie Portman and jazz singer Norah Jones – put him off further collaborations with

Hollywood stars. The long-delayed martial arts biopic *The Grandmaster* (2013) sees him returning both to home comforts and Tony Leung. Nicole Kidman, for her part, has maintained her commitment to exotic directors looking to spread their wings: South Korean genre ace Chan-wook Park successfully nabbed the star for his first non-Asian directorial feature, 2013's mystery *Stoker* (right).

Whether these tales were true or the fabrication of the Asian media gossip mill, they were indicative of the aura of difficulty that surrounds the director.

Other star names connected to the project at one point or another include Chinese actress Gong Li, who endured the *2046* waiting game with Leung, *Crouching Tiger, Hidden Dragon* (2000) star Chang Chen and Japanese actor/director Takeshi Kitano. None of these attachments were ever concrete, although all were more plausible than far-fetched talk that posited Hugh Jackman as Wong's leading man of choice. The hulking *X-Men* (2000) star, who would eventually star opposite Kidman in *Australia* (2008), professed amusement at the rumour, dryly admitting, 'I just hope it gets back to him.'

With names like Jackman being aired, and Kidman repeating her reluctance to commit, it seems *The Lady from Shanghai* had jumped the reality shark by 2006. By that time, Wong was ensconced in a starry project that *did* come to fruition: 2007's *My Blueberry Nights*. As late as 2008, however, he was still telling interviewers about his plans for the Kidman film – until *The Grandmaster* came along and hogged the next four years of his creative energy.

'I dream with open eyes,' he had told Italian newspaper *Il Messaggero*, admitting that ideas for *The Lady from Shanghai* were keeping him awake at night. One assumes, with disappointment, that he has since closed them. **GL**

HUGH MISTAKE

False rumours of Jackson's involvement may have sprung from his casting with Kidman in *Australia* (2008, above) or from a press trip he took to China to promote *X-Men* (2000). 'I was really upset because I think [Wong Kar-wai is] brilliant,' the actor told *Latino Review*. 'If you know him, can you put in a word for me?'

WILL IT EVER HAPPEN?

2/10 Probably not, though forecasts are ill-advised in a career as singular and unrestricted as Wong's. Perhaps, with *The Grandmaster* finally off his plate, the idea will be resurrected, or transmuted into another project. Perhaps another game international star will tickle his fancy, although his fixation on the project as a bespoke Kidman vehicle has remained steadfast. This much we know: if anything does happen, it won't happen quickly.

GATES OF FIRE

Director Michael Mann **Starring** Bruce Willis **Year** *c.* 2006 **Country** US **Genre** Historical drama **Studio** Universal

MICHAEL MANN

'It was a people's army that defeated the Persians, ultimately,' the director told *Empire*. 'It wasn't the elite. . . Some of that is what I find fascinating. But it will only work as a film if you can make it into a personal experience.'

A defining moment in history arose in 480 BC. Three hundred Spartans and disparate allies took a stand against the 100,000-strong Persian army sweeping through Asia and Europe. Facing incredible odds, the Spartans held the narrow pass at Thermopylae – the 'hot gates' – in Greece for three days. The enemy eventually won, but not before losing thousands of men. It was a crucial blow, halting Persia's advance across the globe.

DYING TO DO IT

Two thousand, four hundred and eighty years later, it was announced that director Michael Mann was to film a version of the epic tale. The project was based on Steven Pressfield's exhaustive 1998 novelization, *Gates of Fire*. David Self – then best known for writing *Thirteen Days* (2000), but later acclaimed for his adaptation of *Road to Perdition* (2002) – was tasked with creating a script. George Clooney's Maysville Pictures were to produce and Bruce Willis was rumoured for a lead role. Mann was coming off the critical success of *The Insider* (1999), nominated for seven Academy Awards. With a buzz building around *Gladiator* (2000), sword-and-sandal epics were suddenly all the rage. Universal, which had optioned *Gates of Fire* in 1998, had a hot property on its hands. '*Gladiator* was my favorite film of the year,' Clooney told *Empire* at the end of 2000, 'but I think *Gates of Fire* is a better story. Bruce Willis calls me about every two months, asking what's going on. He's dying, dying to do it.'

Waiting for the film to take shape, Mann moved on to *Ali* (2001), while Clooney and Willis filmed *Ocean's Eleven* and *Bandits* respectively (both 2001). Two years after the initial announcement, Mann assured Empire Online that the film was a going concern: 'I might do it, yes. I just got the screenplay. . . I haven't read it yet.' He added that he was undertaking a great deal of research, discussing the lives of the Spartans with a classics professor from Yale University.

This slouching towards production began to look perilously leisurely when it emerged that 20th Century Fox was planning its own version of the story, using the title of its own 1962 film version of the events: *The 300 Spartans*. Well aware of *Gates of Fire*, Fox chairman Jim Gianopulos told *Variety*, 'You always take into account competing projects but, when you have this kind of story and

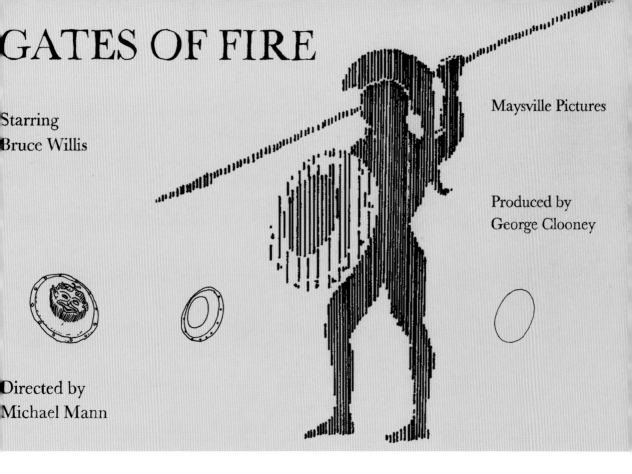

GATES OF FIRE

Maysville Pictures

Starring
Bruce Willis

Produced by
George Clooney

Directed by
Michael Mann

it gathers this kind of momentum, you make your movie, and this is the highest priority.' The writer assigned to the project was Erik Jendresen, who had toiled fruitlessly on *The Hot Zone*, Fox's rival to *Outbreak* (1995, see page 178).

In the post-*Gladiator* box office battlefield, a deluge of sword-wielding epics attacked screens, some successful, some not so much: the *Lord of the Rings* trilogy (2001–03), *Troy*, *Alexander* and *King Arthur* (all 2004). *Gates of Fire* began to feel like an afterthought, arriving late to the party and telling a much less famous tale than that of Troy or Alexander the Great. It also looked ominously expensive. The monumental scenes of Spartans versus Persians – which, in Self's script, filled around forty pages – might have been rendered, at a price, with CGI. But Mann is known for realism – for *Heat* (1995), no less than ninety-five Los Angeles locations were used. Little was heard of the project and Mann returned to his familiar stomping ground of contemporary crime dramas with *Collateral* (2004). Years later, Steven Pressfield would reveal that 'creative differences' between Mann and Universal had put paid to the project.

While *The 300 Spartans* also withered on the vine, a third project reared its head. Producer Gianni Nunnari, whose *Alexander* had battled *Troy*, was 'in love' with Pressfield's book, but lost the race for the rights. Instead, he secured Frank Miller's 1998 comic version of the story, *300*. He united with Miller fan Zack Snyder, and the sensational *300* (2007) was born. Graciously conceding defeat, Pressfield said, 'They beat us out of the blocks fair and square.' **SW**

WILL IT EVER HAPPEN?

2/10 With *300*'s sequel *Rise of an Empire* scheduled for 2013, there's no room for *Gates of Fire*. 'Realistically, I think it's doomed to remain in development hell, unless and until that magical "decisive element" appears,' Pressfield told 300spartanwarriors.com. 'Ridley Scott, are you listening?'

RUSSELL CROWE
What we do in life...
echoes in eternity
A RIDLEY SCOTT FILM
GLADIATOR II

GLADIATOR 2

Director Ridley Scott **Starring** Russell Crowe **Year** *c.*2006 **Country** US **Genre** Historical drama **Studio** DreamWorks

A n old-fashioned epic about heroism, nobility and the fate of empires, *Gladiator* (2000) was a game changer. It made sword-and-sandal films lucrative for the first time since *Spartacus* (1960), turned Russell Crowe into a megastar, and restored director Ridley Scott's reputation after a trio of 1990s films, culminating in *G.I. Jane* (1997), had earned mixed receptions. The story of a Roman general-turned-gladiator, seeking vengeance for the murder of his wife and son, *Gladiator* took almost $500 million at the box office and netted five Oscars, including Best Picture and Best Actor. This success made whispers of 'sequel' inevitable: sticking with the Crowe–Scott dream team would give audiences more of what they wanted. There was only one problem: Crowe's Maximus Decimus Meridius dies at the end of the film.

A WORK OF MAD GENIUS

In fact, there were few obvious avenues left to explore come the closing credits. Maximus was dead. The evil emperor was dead. The gladiators were freed. The End. Moreover, Scott was already committed to direct 2001's *Hannibal*, the follow-up to *The Silence of the Lambs* (1991), while Crowe had moved on to the John Nash biopic *A Beautiful Mind* (2001). However, online rumours linked the original's writers John Logan and David Franzoni to both a prequel and a sequel. 'It's written,' Scott told *Empire* in 2005 of a script by Logan. 'We've already done quite a lot of work and the draft's in now. The target would be early 2005.' Crowe's return was ruled out: 'It's the next generation. Roman history is so exotic that any part of it is really fascinating. History is far more exotic than anything you can dream up.' The story was to focus instead on Lucius Veras, Lucilla's son and the heir to the Roman empire. 'I wouldn't touch the gladiatorial side again,' Scott insisted. 'We have to go to the next step.'

That 'next step' was in a very different direction. 'I was very cynical about the notion of a *Gladiator* sequel,' Crowe told *Empire*, 'but I've come around. . . We've had other ideas too, where we step off into the metaphysical and you actually acknowledge the fact that Maximus is dead! But that's a hard script to write.' With Crowe, Scott and production company DreamWorks unable to agree on Logan's script, the star turned to a fellow Australian maverick.

RIDLEY SCOTT, RUSSELL CROWE
'Russell and I are very similar,' Scott (with Crowe on the set of 2000's *Gladiator*, above) told the *Telegraph*. 'He's angry all the time and I'm angry all the time as well. We don't mean to be irritable but we don't suffer fools gladly.'

THE CAVE CONNECTION

'Russell Crowe read *The Proposition* and I'd heard that he really liked it. . .' said the rock star. 'I got this phone call: "G'day mate, it's Russell here." I'm like, "Russell who?" "Russell Crowe." I'm, like, to my wife, "It's fucking Russell Crowe!". . . He says, "Are you still interested in writing scripts?" I said, "No, mate, I'm not. I don't wanna do that. He says, "What about writing *Gladiator 2*?" And I'm like, "Alright." And I said, "Didn't you die in *Gladiator 1*?" He goes, "You sort that out, mate."'

Goth troubadour Nick Cave had only one screenwriting credit to his name, 1988's *Ghosts. . . of the Civil Dead*. But he was an inspired choice. His script is a work of mad genius, suffused with religion and violence, and venturing bravely into the supernatural. Scott's verdict: 'I think he enjoyed doing it.'

The story opens with Maximus awaking in a netherworld. He visits the old Roman gods, ruined and dying, who task him with seeking out one of their own – Hephaestos – who has gone his own way, preaching the existence of one true God: the Christian God. If Maximus finds and kills Hephaestos, they will restore his wife and child to him. Maximus does indeed locate Hephaestos, but the god warns him his son is in danger and transports him to the real world, in the midst of a massacre of Christians in Lyon. Leading the charge is Lucius, now grown and violently anti-Christian. Maximus learns that his adult son, Marius, is a follower of Jesus, and journeys to Rome to find him.

The once great city is divided, brimming with hate and intolerance. Plague and famine ravage the countryside. Cassian, a philosophy teacher and leader of the Christians, has adopted Marius and tries to recruit Maximus too, but their approaches prove incompatible. They say love and forgive. He says fight.

People recognize Maximus in the streets, gazing at him with fear and awe. 'They say you are the great gladiator, returned from the dead,' he is told. 'And, for once the people are right.' He meets old ally Juba, now a blacksmith, who

> ### 'We step off into the metaphysical and you actually acknowledge the fact that Maximus is dead!'
> Russell Crowe

gives him the wooden figurines from the first film, having rescued them from the sand of the Coliseum. The figures are a reminder of what Maximus wants and what is good: his family and love. With the Christians preaching love, they and Maximus have more in common than he initially realized.

Lucius, driven by fear of the Christians and bloodlust, seeks out Cassian. After a ranting speech in which he blames the followers of Christ for 'the earthquakes that have ripped this mighty empire asunder' and 'the hellish pestilence that ravages our land', he murders Cassian and watches as the students mutilate their teacher's body. Marius looks on in paralyzed terror.

Maximus rescues his son and the two descend on Juba's workshop to arm the remaining Christians for battle. The film climaxes as the first began, with a battle in the woods, but Maximus's declarations of war and glory are replaced by the Christians kneeling to pray. In a brutal and bloody climax, Juba falls and Maximus's son kills Lucius. The battle is won but Marius realizes that he has betrayed Christ's teachings, and that bloodshed brings bloodshed. Maximus knows this is not the end. In an echo of the first film, he kneels and rubs earth into his hands. The scene transforms and our hero voyages through time: the Crusades, the battlefields of Europe, fighting alongside tanks, below helicopters in Vietnam and finally rubbing soap into his hands in the twenty-first century. Maximus takes his seat in the modern-day Pentagon and the story ends.

A HERO WILL RISE. . .

Russell Crowe may have balked at the notion of a mortal becoming involved in the wars of the gods, but a similar premise fuelled Tarsem Singh's *Immortals* (above), a US box office chart-topper in 2011.

Crowe and Scott (left, on the set of *Robin Hood*, 2010) reunited on *A Good Year* (2006), *American Gangster* (2007), *Body of Lies* (2008) and *Robin Hood*. The latter came closest, aesthetically, to *Gladiator*, with its grimy battle scenes. Cave was praised for his screenplay for John Hillcoat's *The Proposition* (2005), created a beautiful score for the Ridley Scott-produced *The Assassination of Jesse James by the Coward Robert Ford* (2007), and penned 2012's *Lawless* (which, like *The Proposition*, starred fellow Australian Guy Pearce). Crowe (right) finally embraced the biblical by playing the hero of Darren Aronofsky's *Noah* (scheduled for 2014) – the screenplay was co-written by original *Gladiator* writer John Logan, whose CV also includes *The Aviator* (2004) and *Skyfall* (2012).

Stunning imagery abounds in the 103-page script, notably a scene at the Coliseum: 'The grounds of the arena have been flooded [and] a naval battle ensues. The water roils with one hundred alligators that have been released in the water. Gladiators fire arrows, throw spears, launch fireballs as the two vessels approach each other. Christians kneel on the decks, hands clasped in prayer. Some Christians, impaled on spears and arrows, fall from the vessels and are torn apart by the alligators.' Take that, CGI tiger.

BLOODY BEGINNINGS

There is much to admire in this take on Christianity's bloody beginnings, but it's not hard to see why the project never made it past script stage. Cave's concerns about religion, familiar to fans of his lyrics, are not what audiences loved about *Gladiator* – a good, old-fashioned tale of good versus evil. And, the flooded Coliseum set piece aside, there is little for a studio looking for a summer blockbuster to latch onto. Much of this could have been altered with a rewrite but that would surely have diluted the script beyond recognition.

'It was a major fucking anti-war movie,' Cave declared in 2009. 'And Russell [said], "Nah, mate. Nah. . ." Ridley Scott, to his credit, said, "I love this script, but it's not gonna fly." And then they sent the cheque and that was that. It took, like, two weeks. Don't tell Russell Crowe that.' **SW**

WILL IT EVER HAPPEN?

1/10 *Prometheus* (2012) and a mooted *Blade Runner* (1982) sequel suggest that Scott is interested in revisiting earlier work, but *Gladiator*'s time has apparently passed. It's unlikely that a studio would grant the budget that the epic scope demands, especially for a film arriving over a decade too late. *Gladiator 2* is dead and, unlike Maximus, stands little chance of resurrection.

WHITE JAZZ

Director Joe Carnahan **Starring** George Clooney **Year** 2007
Budget $28 million **Country** US **Genre** Thriller **Studio** Warner Independent Pictures

JOE CARNAHAN
The director is pictured at the premiere of his thriller *Smokin' Aces* in 2006, the year he was linked to *White Jazz*. 'I love that script,' he told filmschoolrejects.com of the latter, as late as 2012. 'I would love to make that film.'

James Ellroy is an acquired taste. His brand of crime noir isn't so much gritty as abrasive – not just hard-boiled but shot through with strychnine. The author's 'LA Quartet' (1987's *The Black Dahlia*, 1988's *The Big Nowhere*, 1990's *L.A. Confidential* and 1992's *White Jazz*) and 'Underworld USA' trilogy (1995's *American Tabloid*, 2001's *The Cold Six Thousand* and 2009's *Blood's a Rover*) are exciting and terrifyingly vivid. In a cinematic landscape dominated by the likes of Tarantino and Fincher, one might expect all seven books to have appeared on screen – especially the 'LA Quartet', given that its mysteries seethe within the home of Hollywood itself. Yet, to date, only two have survived the agonizing vagaries of development: one a towering triumph – Curtis Hanson's shimmering, stylish *L.A. Confidential* (1997); the other a colossal disappointment – Brian De Palma's overblown and miscast *The Black Dahlia* (2006). *White Jazz* is the only other to ever come close.

BLACKMAIL, BURGLARY AND A BILLIONAIRE
Set in 1958, the novel chronicles the destructive tailspin of LA vice cop and attorney Dave Klein (whose name, 'D. Klein', may well have been a deliberate pun on Ellroy's part). It takes in incest, political blackmail, a burglary at the home of a drug baron (also the LAPD's top snitch), the vindictiveness of billionaire Howard Hughes and a federal investigation into police corruption.

White Jazz directly followed *L.A. Confidential* (presenting a continuity issue: one of its key characters, Dudley Smith, was killed in the film version of *Confidential*). Despite its jagged prose and dreamlike first-person narrative, it appeared as a screenplay just a month after *L.A. Confidential*'s US theatrical debut. This 131-page script was drafted by Ellroy himself, the writer having been unimpressed with Brian Helgeland's restructuring of *L.A. Confidential*.

American independent distributor Fine Line Features intended it to form the directorial debut of Oliver Stone's respected cinematographer Robert Richardson, who won an Oscar for 1991's *JFK*. Budgetary concerns forced it into turnaround at Fine Line, but it was salvaged by actor Nick Nolte in 2001. His production company, Kingsgate Films, planned to co-produce with the Los Angeles-based Interlight and German financiers.

Writer Chris Cleveland took a pass at Ellroy's script, while Robert Richardson lined up an enticing cast: Nolte as Klein, John Cusack as his twitchy partner Junior Stemmons and Winona Ryder as Glenda Bledsoe, slumming actress and object of Howard Hughes's lust/wrath. Possibly connected to her arrest in December 2001 for shoplifting, Ryder was soon out and Uma Thurman was in. Then, for reasons unknown – most likely financial – the project collapsed.

'That's why directors go absolutely crazy,' an exasperated Richardson told the *Globe*. 'The development of a project is highly unpredictable and doesn't make tremendous sense. It may happen, but not in my timeframe.'

The second attempt occurred in late 2006. By now, Warner Independent Pictures held the rights and George Clooney was the actor/producer champion, his eye on the role of Klein. It had been a good fit for the weathered Nolte, and must have presented an appealing challenge for Clooney: the perfect opportunity to showcase a then rarely exhibited dark side. New director Joe Carnahan co-wrote the screenplay with his brother Matthew Michael Carnahan.

Carnahan and Ellroy fit together like knuckles on a pair of fists. The director had made his debut with 1998's searing *Blood, Guts, Bullets and Octane*, but it was the follow-up that proved he had the *cojones* to tackle Ellroy. Starring Ray Liotta, *Narc* (2002) concerns damaged cops butting heads in Detroit's urban wastelands. It is cold, stark, relentlessly aggressive and brilliant.

ALL THAT JAZZ

'I'm interested more in grounding it so that it doesn't feel necessarily like [a] period film,' Joe Carnahan told *Cinematical*'s Ryan Stewart. '[In] the visual presentation we put together (below), you're seeing this great, modernist architecture – like what John Lautner was doing at the time, and the art scene with Frank Stella or Miro. . . the West Coast jazz scene, Brubeck: that's the vibe that I'm going for. Miles Davis. Really making this more of that mid-century explosion of art and music, and letting that be the guiding force behind it, as opposed to making it all "period suits".
I want to try to make it as accurate a reflection of LA at that moment in time as I can. It was exceedingly hip and Bohemian and forward-thinking and all that stuff.'

The Carnahan brothers' *White Jazz* script is a compelling read and a very rare example of a screenplay written in the first person. Klein's own lines are credited to 'Me' and, with just a few exceptions, every scene is portrayed from his perspective, feeding into the fever-dream mood of the source material.

The entire narrative is flashback. But how much is reality? How much is the distorted memory of a man consumed by self-loathing? How much is paranoia induced, in part, by Klein's insomnia? The action is occasionally punctuated by 'blipvert' (i.e. very rapid) daymares. 'I drift despite my best efforts,' says Klein at one point, 'and for a split second you see the Hell I see when sleep wins.'

Like Brian Helgeland's adaptation of *L.A. Confidential*, the Carnahans' *White Jazz* was unafraid to rework major swaths of story. It focused on the controversial 1950s Chavez Ravine slum clearance in Los Angeles, and turned the Armenian Kafesjian family of the novel into the Mexican Magdalenas. Characters are recast, too. Owing to his death in *L.A. Confidential*, the Irish-American Dudley Smith (portrayed in that film by James Cromwell) is

> '*It's such a good script. . . It's dirty, nasty, mean. There's nothing nice about it.*'
>
> George Clooney

reincarnated as the German-American Fritz Koenig. Ed Exley, played by Guy Pearce in Hanson's movie, was present in an early draft of the Carnahans' script. However, rights issues surrounding the character – Regency Enterprises were protecting their own potential sequel to *L.A. Confidential* – required his transformation into Exley 'doppelganger' (Joe Carnahan's word) Boyce Bradley.

Gone is Klein's background of incest with his sister, and his moonlighting as a ruthless slum landlord – two negative traits too far, apparently. Nonetheless, the character remains deeply unsympathetic. Just a few pages in, he hurls an innocent man out of a window and frames it as suicide:

```
                    ME
     Sanderline, you gotta see this. . .


Trusting puppy Sanderline steps to the window:

                SANDERLINE JOHNSON
     What'm I-


-smash his head against the frame using his forward
motion. He loses muscle control for the split-second it
takes me to pitch his legs up and out. My face a quick-
change evil mask. Feature Sanderline's nine-story fall.
That Ambassador Hotel robe billows behind him like a
cape. He detonates an overhead streetlight with a bomb
sound, then hits the driveway.
```

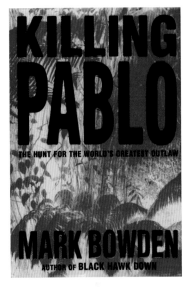

NO-SHOW JOE, PART ONE

White Jazz is not Joe Carnahan's only project to remain unrealized. Of the others, the most likely to come to fruition is *Killing Pablo*, his adaptation of Mark Bowden's book (above) about the life and assassination of Colombian cartel kingpin Pablo Escobar, which he developed in parallel with *White Jazz*. The director had hoped that Spanish actor Javier Bardem would play Escobar. 'I gotta do *Pablo*,' he enthused to IGN in 2006. 'That to me is still my favourite script. . .'

NO-SHOW JOE, PART TWO

Joe Carnahan prepped a remake of Otto Preminger's 1965 psychological thriller *Bunny Lake Is Missing*, which was to shoot back-to-back with *White Jazz*, and star Reese Witherspoon. But the actress (above) bailed out in March 2007 – five weeks before principal photography was to begin – and it was shut down.

Unzip my fly, hustle into the bathroom, screams from outside now. Flush the toilet as Junior and Ruiz pile through the door. Step out, play it baffled: look at the bed where Sanderline sat, then the open window, screams floating up. . .

                    ME
    DID THAT MUTT JUST JUMP?

Klein – described as 'a thug with a law degree' and looking like 'Death taking a shit' – calls himself the 'turd in the punchbowl', but has a perverse morality. 'We're ruining his career, not his soul,' he chides sidekick Junior Stemmons while photographing an unconscious politician in compromising positions with a coerced homosexual, Stemmons having suggested they have their victim performing fellatio. 'It's such a good script,' Clooney enthused to about.com. 'I hadn't read the book. Joe's brother Matt wrote a version of the screenplay that was just. . . dirty, nasty, mean. There's nothing nice about it'.

UNBELIEVABLY GROTESQUE

Carnahan's 'baseline description' for his approach was, 'Imagine an episode of [US documentary series] *Cops* shot in 1958. That'll be the vibe.' Keen to distinguish his film from Curtis Hanson's, he told *Cinematical*, 'We've kind of done the glamour-puss angle.' Not that his movie wouldn't be stylish in its own way: 'I really want to make it as accurate a reflection of LA at that moment in time as I can, and it was exceedingly hip and Bohemian and forward-thinking.'

Carnahan wanted Charlize Theron to play actress Glenda Bledsoe – whom Howard Hughes enlists Klein to investigate – and had Ray Liotta in mind for either the Hughes heavy Pete Bondurant (who became a key character in Ellroy's 'Underworld USA' trilogy) or FBI man Welles Noonan. Jason Bateman (who would later star with Clooney in 2009's *Up in the Air*) and Peter Berg – who appeared in Carnahan's unhinged *Smokin' Aces* (2006) – were attached. Chris Pine – who played a flamboyant neo-Nazi hitman in *Smokin' Aces*, having appeared in Clooney's alma mater *E.R.* in 2003 – was confirmed as Klein's sidekick Junior Stemmons. As for his star, Carnahan spoke enthusiastically of Clooney's willingness to portray Klein as 'unbelievably grotesque and unfathomable and despicable'. 'George wants that,' he insisted.

Yet, by late October 2007, both stars had quit within a week of each other. Pine walked first, to take up a career-transforming role as Captain Kirk in J.J. Abrams's *Star Trek*. This could have occasioned conflict between Carnahan and Abrams, after the latter replaced the former as director of 2006's *Mission: Impossible III* (Carnahan said his version would have 'kicked the shit out' of Abrams's). However, the director blogged, 'I knew how tough the decision had to be for [Pine]. . . I gave him my full support, even if it meant he didn't do *Jazz*. I get it. You don't get opportunities like that often and I told him as long as he could control as much of that process as possible and not get sucked into doing lesser sequels as a result of taking this gig, then good luck and God bless.'

'It was not a no-brainer,' Pine told *Variety*. 'This wild, sociopathic, obsessive-compulsive, latently homosexual, angry young man sounded like a blast.'

Clooney's departure, his producing partner Grant Heslov told *Entertainment Weekly*, 'just simply came down to scheduling. George continues to believe in the project and in Joe.' However, remarked the *Los Angeles Times*, 'Well-connected Hollywood wags think that the faltering fortunes of [the star's 2007 crime drama] *Michael Clayton* might have had a little to do with Clooney getting cold feet about jumping into a period noir piece, the last few of which – *Hollywoodland* and *The Black Dahlia* – have bombed at the box office.'

BITTER AND CYNICAL

It's unlikely Heslov's comments were a complete smokescreen: *Leatherheads* (2008), which Clooney directed and starred in, was pushed back by extensive post-production. 'Something was going to have to give,' Carnahan blogged. 'Also, George is neck deep in the Coen Brothers' film [2008's *Burn After Reading*] at the moment and trying to do *Michael Clayton* press. . . They wanted to see about pushing *White Jazz* back, which I really don't want to do. I've been waiting awhile to make this one and I wasn't content to sit on my hands.'

Meanwhile, *White Jazz* disintegrated. Clooney and Pine's departure caused the film to miss a shooting window that would have seen it roll ahead of the 2007–08 Hollywood writers' strike. In the meantime, Carnahan failed to find a new lead and, while claiming he would never give up on *White Jazz*, decided to give mainstream cinema a try with an adaptation of the 1980s TV show *The A-Team*, which he no doubt felt would be an easier sell for a broader audience.

Ellroy shed no tears, perhaps sensing that Hollywood and its audiences would never stomach material as bitter and cynical as his own, no matter how much movie stardust was sprinkled on it. '*White Jazz* is dead,' he shrugged in 2009. 'All movie adaptations of my books are dead.' **DJ**

WILL IT EVER HAPPEN?

3/10 'I'm still bound and determined to make that movie,' Carnahan told *Cinematical* in 2010, although he conceded that 'there's a lot to be pessimistic about in the business right now because movies like that aren't getting greenlit. I think if we can do it for a number, and that number is gonna be. . . about $12 [million], then we can make that movie. It's a tremendous script, and there's always a place for that kind of movie.'

WHAT HAPPENED NEXT. . .

Joe Carnahan's *The A-Team* (2010), starring Liam Neeson and Bradley Cooper, did not perform as well as hoped, and his popcorn phase seems, for the time being, to be over. He returned to harder-edged, low-budget material with *The Grey* (2011), a thriller that pits air crash survivors, led by Liam Neeson (who would make a great Dudley Smith/Fritz Koenig), against a pack of Alaskan wolves. George

Clooney flirted with darker material for 2010's *The American*, in which he played an assassin, but has never since committed to anything that would test his nice guy image as *White Jazz* would have. Bruce Willis tried fruitlessly to get a TV series based on Ellroy's *American Tabloid* off the ground, while it was announced in 2012 that Luca Guadagnino would direct an adaptation of the author's *The Big Nowhere*.

FROM THE DIRECTOR OF **ALIEN³**

ONCE YOU WERE TAGGED,

YOU WERE "IT" FOREVER...

BLACKHOLE

DIRECTED BY **DAVID FINCHER**

BASED ON THE GRAPHIC NOVEL BY **CHARLES BURNS**

BLACK HOLE

Director David Fincher **Year** 2008 **Country** US **Genre** Horror **Studio** Paramount

High-school kids, navigating the world of adolescence in the 1970s, fall victim to a disease that causes them to shed skin, sprout tails, grow new eyeballs and undergo other terrifying transformations. This is the premise of writer-artist Charles Burns's comic *Black Hole*, first issued in 1995 by publishers Kitchen Sink Press. The story serves as an allegory for sexually transmitted disease and turns a magnifying glass on a Bowie-loving Seventies generation enduring the nihilistic years of Vietnam and the Cold War. Featuring disturbing black-and-white imagery, a melancholy tone and a plot reliant on dreams and introspection, it does not readily lend itself to a film adaptation. Nevertheless, in 2006, film-makers began trying.

DISGUSTING, SO GROSS

First to take a crack at it was Alexandre Aja, the French writer-director of *Haute Tension* (2003) and *Piranha 3D* (2010). *Pulp Fiction* (1994) co-writer Roger Avary and comics legend Neil Gaiman – initially united by an abortive attempt to bring Gaiman's *The Sandman* to the big screen – teamed up to write the script. 'We are trying to stay as faithful as possible to the graphic novel. . .' Aja told chud.com. 'It's just amazing. It's like someone managed to get a very accurate picture of what it's like to be a teenager. We're going to respect that spirit and try to make. . . a very true description of adolescence and what it is to feel as a monster when you are fifteen, sixteen years old. . . I think that if we manage to write a script which is not too expensive, they will let us make the movie under the radar and make the movie as fucked up as the graphic novel.'

By early 2008, however, Aja was out (presumably to the delight of Charles Burns, whose reaction to Aja's involvement was, 'I don't know that it's really appropriate') and director David Fincher was on board, backed by Paramount. A short-lived but quite prescient online rumour mooted the pre-*Twilight* Kristen Stewart – then best known for *Panic Room* (2002) – to star. (Four years later, Stewart told *Elle* magazine: 'I want to do this movie! [The graphic novel] is disgusting, so gross. . . It's so sexual, the desire is so fucking palpable'.)

The production promptly ran into problems, owing to differences between the director and writers. 'David explained his process consisted of having

CHARLES BURNS'S *BLACK HOLE*
'I'm not involved in any of the creative process other than having this book that's the focus of the story,' the artist told *Anthem* of the mooted *Black Hole* film. 'I made a decision that I didn't want to pursue trying to keep control.'

over ten drafts, done over and over,' Gaiman told MTV, 'and Roger and I were asked if we were interested in doing that. And we definitely weren't.' The duo bequeathed their final draft to Fincher. 'We'll wait and see what happens,' said Gaiman. 'I just hope, whatever happens, it's faithful to *Black Hole*.'

Despite its poor box-office results, Fincher's stunning *Zodiac* (2007) was critically lauded, so his stock was still high. However, the second of his two-picture deal with Paramount, 2008's *The Curious Case of Benjamin Button*, strained the director's relationship with his paymasters. Reportedly unhappy with Fincher's refusal to budge on the Brad Pitt vehicle's near three-hour running time, Paramount allowed the rights to *Torso*, one of the director's pet projects (see left) to lapse in January 2009. His fate sealed by *Benjamin Button*'s disappointing box office (despite its thirteen Academy Award nods, three of which would secure wins), Fincher left Paramount for a new home at Sony.

CHALLENGING IDEAS

Fincher was clearly keen to do a graphic novel adaptation. As well as *Black Hole* and *Torso*, he has long been attached as producer to the anthology film *Heavy Metal* (based on the sci-fi/fantasy comics, first brought to the screen in 1981) and *The Goon*, Eric Powell's pitch-black series about graverobbers. As of late 2012, neither of these had reached fruition, although a successful

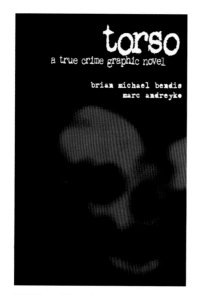

TORS. . . OH

'*Torso* is moving right toward the starting gate,' producer Bill Mechanic (the head of Fox at the time it unleashed Fincher's *Fight Club* in 1999) told collider.com in October 2008. 'David is directing.' The film was to have been 'inspired by' Brian Michael Bendis and Marc Andreyko's 1998 graphic novel rather than be a *Sin City*-esque adaptation, potentially even with a new title. Matt Damon, Gary Oldman and Rachel McAdams were rumoured to be attached. Sadly, the curious curse of *Benjamin Button* nixed Fincher's involvement and, apparently, *Torso*'s graduation to the big screen.

'I want to do this movie! [The graphic novel] is so sexual, the desire is so fucking palpable.'

Kristen Stewart

fundraising campaign for *The Goon* has improved its chances. And as late as December 2011, Fincher was happy to discuss *Black Hole* in an interview with superherohype.com: 'It's a really great script by Dante Harper [writer of 2013's *Hansel and Gretel Witch Hunters*] so the hope is that will win out. It's so weird. It's so great because it would be great to see. It's very tough. There's make-up effects and digital effects that are expensive and, to do it right, you gotta do it just right because it has to challenge your idea of the human body.'

There is no denying that comic-book adaptations can be big business but, outside superheroes, the more difficult, experimental works are far from a guaranteed commercial or critical hit. For every billion-dollar success like *The Avengers* (2012) or *The Dark Knight* (2008), there is the more modest fare of *American Splendor* (2003) or *Scott Pilgrim vs. The World* (2010). With this in mind, it was always going to be difficult to get something as strange as *Black Hole* made at a major studio. Fincher showcased groundbreaking special effects with an ageing Brad Pitt in *Benjamin Button* and the Voss twins in *The Social Network* (2010). The treatment he could have given to the mutated teenagers of *Black Hole* would surely have been both realistic and deeply disturbing. But such effects cost money, and the adult content of the picture would have excluded a large portion of moviegoers, meaning lower box-office takings. And with the director of *Se7en* (1995), *Zodiac* (2007) and

The Social Network (2010) raised Fincher's stock to a new high, but alleged clashes with Sony on *The Girl with the Dragon Tattoo* (2011) meant he turned to the small screen. With *Se7en*'s Kevin Spacey, the director began a remake of the BBC's drama *House of Cards* (1990). If he returns to effects-laden cinema, front-runner is a remake of *20,000 Leagues Under the Sea*, with his *Fight Club* and

Benjamin Button star Brad Pitt (left, with Fincher). Avary and Gaiman brought their take on the poem *Beowulf* to the big screen in 2007, helmed by Robert Zemeckis. Aja hit the big time with a remake of Wes Craven's *The Hills Have Eyes* (2006) and the much-hyped *Piranha* (2010). Charles Burns began a new series, *X'ed Out*, in 2010. Its second instalment, *The Hive* (right), arrived in 2012.

The Girl with the Dragon Tattoo (2011) at the reins, the comic's dark nature was unlikely to be compromised – a risky and not wholly enticing proposition for any major studio that observed the less-than-stellar returns for adult graphic novel adaptations like *Watchmen* (2009) and *Kick-Ass* (2010).

Charles Burns, at least, was open to what Fincher would have brought to the table. 'I made the decision when I signed the option that I didn't try to negotiate and gain any control,' he told shocktillyoudrop.com in 2008. 'I think that I could've tried to write the script, I could've tried to negotiate being involved more, so I think that there's a possibility that I'd be involved, but I don't know. . . I think the story lends itself very well to do in a live action movie [but] for me to try to maintain control I think is nearly impossible.'

Black Hole remained dormant until a short film, directed by Rupert Sanders, appeared online in 2010. (As of late 2012, this version – starring Whitney Able and Chris Marquette – was still available on Sanders's official site.) 'I made a short film with my own money to try and get something to pitch with,' the director explained to Den of Geek!. 'It's kind of a really twisted, hallucinogenic [story] about teenage kids in Vancouver in the seventies who get a sexually transmitted disease that mutates them, so the girl's got a lizard tail and the guy's covered in skin and tadpoles. . . Is it still a possibility? I don't know. I think it's probably gone to someone else now.' Fingers – or tails – crossed. **SW**

BLACK HOLE BELLA
Kristen Stewart would have been ideal for the role played by Whitney Able in Rupert Sanders's version (above). Sadly, the tabloid furore that followed their 'momentary indiscretion' while filming *Snow White and the Huntsman* (2012) may have sounded the death knell for future collaborations by the pair.

WILL IT EVER HAPPEN?

5/10   If Fincher is one thing, it's determined. *Benjamin Button* was a long-time passion project and his list of unmade films is as long as that of his completed projects. Any one has the potential to be revived, but the dark themes limit *Black Hole*'s prospects. Nonetheless, Sanders's version proved that a small budget need be no obstacle to an authentically creepy adaptation.

THE TRIAL OF THE CHICAGO SEVEN

Director Steven Spielberg **Starring** Sacha Baron Cohen, Heath Ledger, Philip Seymour Hoffman, Will Smith
Year 2008 **Country** US **Genre** Historical drama **Studio** DreamWorks SKG

STEVEN SPIELBERG

'We're in the process right now on *Chicago Seven* of doing a feasibility study of what actors are available,' the director told *Vanity Fair* in 2007. 'I don't want to say it's a done deal.'

In the late 1960s, while other US students were getting high on drugs, rock and free love, Steven Spielberg was getting high on film. He was a student at California State College, nominally studying English, but actually spending his days lapping up films at LA art houses ('Anything that wasn't American impressed me,' he later said), making 16mm shorts and hanging out in the editing department at Universal. The times they were a-changing but Spielberg was too in thrall to flickering images to notice. However, some forty years later, he circled back to the decade that passed him by, alighting on an Aaron Sorkin script that dramatized a key episode in 1960s counterculture.

CLASHED WITH POLICE

At the 1968 Democratic Convention, protesters against politicians and the Vietnam war clashed with police in riots shown to millions on TV. Authorities arrested eight of the most vocal activists – Abbie Hoffman, Jerry Rubin, David Dellinger, Tom Hayden, Rennie Davis, John Froines, Lee Weiner and Bobby Seale – and put them on trial seven months later. (If this doesn't feel like Spielberg material, there are antecedents in the director's work: his 1974 debut feature *The Sugarland Express* depicts a media circus, albeit one centred on a hostage situation, and 1997's *Amistad* features his first courtroom drama.)

The incident was perfect fodder for Sorkin, whose screenplay was intended as the first of a three-picture deal with the Spielberg-founded DreamWorks Studios. (Spielberg also produced the writer's play *The Farnsworth Invention*, which premiered on Broadway in December 2007, only to close three months later.) Sorkin's facility for sharp dialogue, appealing liberalism and melding of the political and personal are evident in his scripts for *A Few Good Men* (1992), *The American President* (1995) and TV's *The West Wing* (1999).

It helped that the real-life court case offered plenty of scope for drama. In the early days of the trial, defendant Bobby Seale – a co-founder of the Black Panther Party – called Judge Julius Hoffman a 'fascist dog', a 'honky' and 'a pig'. When Seale refused to be quiet, Hoffman ordered him bound and gagged

YOU CAN'T JAIL THE REVOLUTION

A STEVEN SPIELBERG FILM

CHICAGO
OF THE
TRIAL
SEVEN
THE

ADAM ARKIN
SACHA BARON COHEN
TAYE DIGGS
PHILIP SEYMOUR HOFFMAN
HEATH LEDGER
WILL SMITH
and KEVIN SPACEY
'THE TRIAL OF THE CHICAGO SEVEN'
screenplay by AARON SORKIN
directed by STEVEN SPIELBERG

CARTOON COURTROOM

Although *Trial of the Chicago Seven* stumbled into development hell, the protesters' story did make it to the screen in the form of *Chicago 10* (2007). Director Brett Morgen – who had helmed 2002's *The Kid Stays in the Picture* – conjured a blend of documentary, animation and re-creation. The impressive cast of voices included: as Bobby Seale (left), Jeffrey Wright; as Abbie Hoffman (centre), Hank Azaria; and, as Jerry Rubin (right), Mark Ruffalo. Among the other voices were Nick Nolte and, as the judge, veteran Spielberg compadre Roy Scheider.

THE REAL CHICAGO SEVEN

From left, Jerry Rubin, David Dellinger, Lee Weiner, John Froines, Tom Hayden, Rennie Davis and Abbie Hoffman pose with supporters and a poster of their jailed associate Bobby Seale. More of Hoffman's story is told in Robert Greenwald's *Steal This Movie!* (2000).

in the courtroom. He was subsequently sentenced to four years' imprisonment for contempt of court. The Chicago Eight had become the Chicago Seven.

Seale wasn't the only fly in the establishment ointment. Abbie Hoffman and Jerry Rubin relentlessly mocked legal protocol. On one occasion, they turned up to court in judicial robes. Ordered to take them off, they revealed cop uniforms underneath. Defence attorney William Kunstler used the case to put the Vietnam war on trial, sporting a black armband to commemorate the dead and placing a Vietcong flag on the defence table. The trial sparked a rallying of counterculture heavyweights including singer Phil Ochs, who informed the court he was planning to nominate a pig, Pigasus, for president. When Jerry Rubin began to deliver an acceptance speech for the animal, the police arrested him under an archaic livestock law. Sorkin must have had a field day.

NOT A SURE THING

Spielberg and producers Walter F. Parkes (who worked with the director on *Amistad* and *Minority Report*, 2002) and Laurie MacDonald (*Amistad*; *Catch Me If You Can*, 2002; *The Terminal*, 2004) had the film in development from 2007. The project moved from the backburner after the director wrapped *Indiana Jones and the Kingdom of the Crystal Skull* (2008). Sacha Baron Cohen would be Abbie Hoffman, Heath Ledger Hayden, Philip Seymour Hoffman Kunstler and Will Smith Seale. 'When Steve is ready he will send it,' Smith said. 'He told me the filming dates, so I can be free. . . It's not a hundred percent sure thing yet, but I'm confident.' *Vanity Fair*, interviewing Spielberg for *Crystal Skull*, also spied headshots of Taye Diggs, Adam Arkin and Kevin Spacey.

However, the project, reported *Variety*, 'became sketchy after [the director] could not get rewrites during the [Writers Guild of America] strike'. ('All my writers are on the picket line,' Spielberg noted during the walkout in late 2007.) Its fate was compounded by the threat of another strike, this time by the Screen Actors Guild. The director moved on to *Lincoln* (2012), which had been in development alongside *War Horse* and *The Adventures of Tintin* (both 2011). **IF**

WHAT HAPPENED NEXT. . .

Sorkin (below) told the *New York Times* that the work was now destined for stage rather than screen: 'I'm very eager to go back to work on a new play about the trial of the Chicago Seven (helpfully entitled *The Trial of the Chicago 7*).' Meanwhile, costume designer Mary Zophres put her research for the film to use on Joel and Ethan Coen's 1967-set *A Single Man* (2009).

WILL IT EVER HAPPEN?

5/10 The project passed to *Bourne Supremacy* (2004) director Paul Greengrass, who told chud.com that it was a 'wonderful project' but that 'the timing didn't work out'. Then, in a development that had bloggers' jaws on the floor, talks were reportedly held with Ben Stiller to direct. Later all went quiet, but once linked to so many stars it surely stands a chance of resurrection.

SHANTARAM

Director Mira Nair **Starring** Johnny Depp, Amitabh Bachchan **Year** 2008
Budget $90–100 million **Country** US **Genre** Drama **Studio** Warner Bros

JOHNNY DEPP

'[Johnny] is a humble soul with great curiosity about the world,' director Mira Nair told rediff.com in 2007. 'He loves taking risks. . . You never get the feeling that you are dealing with a movie star when you work with him.'

During a cheery web chat with *Empire* magazine readers to promote *The Way Back* (2010), the usually talkative Peter Weir's mood was spiked by one innocent question posed by a curious fan: 'Are you still in the running for *Shantaram*?' Weir's distinctly undetailed response? A gruff 'No.' Four years after he left the project, *Shantaram* looked like The One That Got Away for the director of *The Truman Show* (1998). But spare a thought for its proposed star, Johnny Depp – he's had his hopes dashed not once, but twice.

POETIC, ALLEGORICAL, SUPER-THICK

Gregory David Roberts's novel was a sensation after its publication in 2003. 'A phenomenon!' screamed the *Sunday Times*. 'A masterpiece!' yelped the *Telegraph*. 'Gigantic!' added the *Daily Mail*. The latter, for the *Mail*, counts as something of a rare understatement: at 936 pages, in small type, *Shantaram* was both an enthralling read and a workout regimen. Adapting it for the screen looked like the cinematic equivalent of a world-record attempt to cram the most people into a Mini. But that, as it turns out, was the least of its problems.

The film rights to *Shantaram* were scooped up by Warner Bros in 2004 for $2 million, as a lure for Johnny Depp – magma-hot after *Pirates of the Caribbean: The Curse of the Black Pearl* (2003) – and his production company, Infinitum Nihil. Depp, it's fair to say, was obsessed with both novel and novelist. 'Roberts has written this absolutely beautiful, poetic, allegorical, super-thick, 1,000-page novel that tore the top of my head off when I read it,' he waxed to Australia's *Herald Sun*. The bad-boy author himself had a similar can-opening effect on the actor. Invited to the Bahamas for six weeks as Depp's guest, Roberts and his famous fan composed and compacted *Shantaram*'s first draft.

Based loosely on Roberts's own experiences, as filtered through his alter-ego Lin, *Shantaram: The Movie* promised a near-uncategorizable saga, spanning continents and genres in a stirring voyage of redemption. The story kicks off in Lin's native Australia, where heroin and bankrobbing habits have landed him in Victoria's Pentridge Prison. Tagged as Australia's Most Wanted after an audacious escape, Lin lands in India. There, despite no previous medical experience, he becomes a doctor in the Mumbai slums, battling cholera

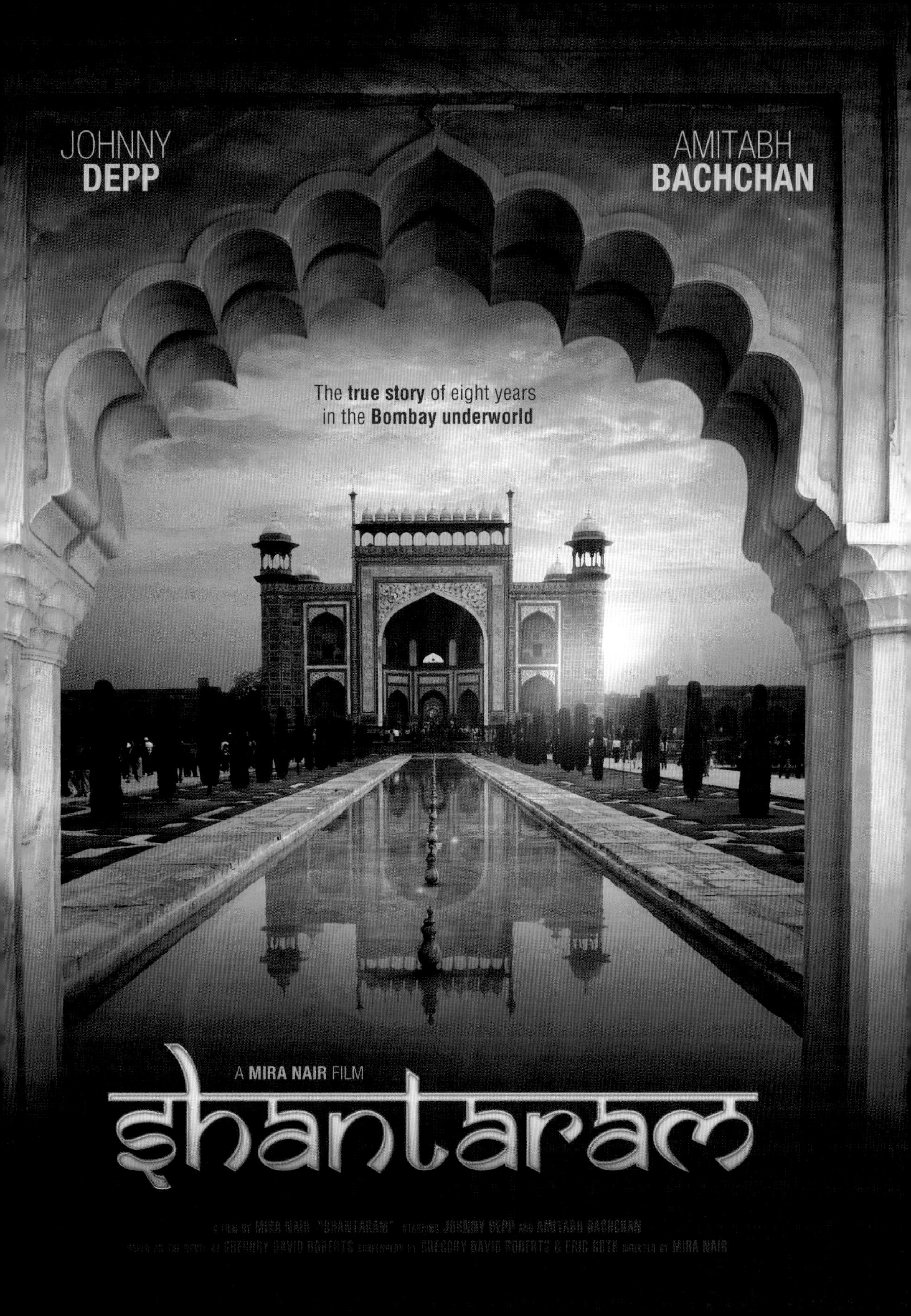
JOHNNY
DEPP
AMITABH
BACHCHAN
The true story of eight years
in the Bombay underworld
A MIRA NAIR FILM
Shantaram
A FILM BY MIRA NAIR "SHANTARAM" STARRING JOHNNY DEPP AND AMITABH BACHCHAN
BASED ON THE NOVEL BY GREGORY DAVID ROBERTS SCREENPLAY BY GREGORY DAVID ROBERTS & ERIC ROTH DIRECTED BY MIRA NAIR

and firestorms, and rediscovering his conscience. But he's soon sucked into the city's teeming underworld, careening through a kaleidoscopic life of crime while trying to win the affections of Karla, a mysterious Swiss-American. Lin's incredible journey – and these are just selected highlights – includes smuggling, run-ins with the mafia, surviving a car crash and an assassination attempt, exploits as a Bollywood extra, a brutal shift in Mumbai's Arthur Road prison, a spell as a passport forger and a climactic stint as an arms dealer aiding the mujahideen in Afghanistan. Keeping up? We haven't even started on the serial killer sub-subplot. . . So (deep breath), that's adventure yarn, romance, prison movie, travelogue, war film, mob drama, buddy movie, Bollywood homage, gun-runner thriller, social drama. . . as many genres as you have fingers. Depp and Warners hoped to capture Roberts's hot, loud, flamboyant depiction of Mumbai life. As *The Beach* (2000) did for Thailand, so this would do for India.

Anybody who has read *Shantaram* will appreciate Depp's physical likeness to the hulking, brawny Lin is about as similar as a parsnip to a dishwasher. (Lin-a-likey Russell Crowe expressed an interest around the time the rights were bought.) But it's easy to see Depp embodying Lin's maverick spirit. Along with the chance of playing an ex-con, ex-addict warrior anti-hero, Depp – who's developed a Streep-like fondness for accents as his career's progressed – also saw an opportunity to chew on a thick Australian drawl.

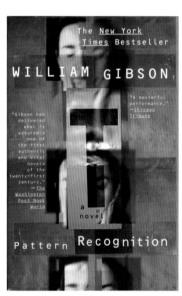

'Roberts has written this absolutely beautiful novel that tore the top of my head off when I read it.'
Johnny Depp

Peter Weir, similarly, seemed the ideal director: an Australian film-maker with extraordinary storytelling skills, regardless of the genre, and the ability to immerse audiences in whatever world he's chosen to enter. *Shantaram* promised a return to his epic, earlier work – the likes of *Gallipoli* (1981) and *The Year of Living Dangerously* (1982). The director duly dipped into Darjeeling during an extensive location scout, and Depp drenched himself in Indian culture. Meanwhile, Eric Roth – whose adaptation of *Forrest Gump* (1994) bagged him an Oscar – was hired to tame the story's hectic sprawl into a manageable script. But on Weir's return, *Shantaram*'s sweet promise soured.

In June 2006, nine months after he was hired, Warner told *Variety* that the director was off the project, citing that old standby, creative differences. 'It's very unfortunate about Peter,' bemoaned producer Graham King, not sounding especially sorry. 'He just had a different vision of the movie which wasn't mine and Johnny's.' It was now clear who was calling the shots. Warner might have the rights, but *Shantaram* belonged to Depp – this was his passion project, as actor, producer and disciple. The shoot was shifted to spring 2007.

Warners secured an inspired replacement for Weir in January 2007: Mira Nair. The director of *Mississippi Masala* (1991), *Monsoon Wedding* (2001) and the Thackeray adaptation *Vanity Fair* (2004), Nair seemed the ideal bridge between Asia and the West, precisely what *Shantaram* called for. 'It's about

OH BROTHER, WEIR ART THOU?
Three more book-based projects slipped from Peter Weir's grasp between *Master and Commander: The Far Side of the World* (2003) and *The Way Back* (2010): *The War Magician*, about an illusionist who 'hid' the Suez Canal from wartime bombers; William Gibson's cryptic *Pattern Recognition* (above), about a psychologist searching for meaning in mysterious online film clips and Robert Kurson's *Shadow Divers*, unlocking the mystery behind the wreck of a German U-boat discovered off the New Jersey coast.

Johnny Depp went back to his comfort zone, teaming with Tim Burton for 2012's *Dark Shadows* (left). Mira Nair, having got over the disappointment of not 'working with Johnny Depp and Amitabh Bachchan in one film,' filmed the Wall Street hostage drama *The Reluctant Fundamentalist* (2012). Weir put his Indian location scouting to good use on 2010's epic *The Way Back* (right). Gregory David Roberts, who planned *Shantaram* as the second in a trilogy, was still toiling on its sequel in 2011. *The Mountain Shadow* is said to feature Lin dragged out of his Sri Lankan paradise to rescue an old pal and features a new character: Navida Der, a half-Irish, half-Indian gumshoe. If you're a whale, hold your breath.

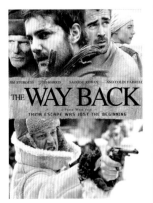

time [Hollywood] got India right,' she told Glamsham.com. 'Authenticity is very important to *Shantaram*. It's the same territory as my film *Salaam Bombay!*, set in my beloved Mumbai during the eighties, when I was in the city.'

GLORIOUSLY GAUDY

Nair lined up one of Bollywood's biggest stars, Amitabh Bachchan, to play Kader Bhai, godfather of the Mumbai mafia and Lin's eventual mentor. 'I can close my eyes and see them together,' she said. Bachchan was even willing to shave his head for the role. She also promised the spectacle of Depp appearing in a gloriously gaudy Bollywood dance number. The vast, five-month shoot, taking in three continents, was set to begin in November 2007. 'It will be an amazing banquet,' Nair told CNBC. But the main course was never served up.

Just as cameras were set to roll, Hollywood's infamous writers' strike hit – a blow compounded, reported *Variety*, by concerns about 'costs and the prospect of shooting in India with monsoon season approaching'. The production had begun to resemble the sprawling novel itself. Interviewed on Indian TV, Depp sounded like a man in denial. 'We've just hit pause,' he sighed. 'Eric Roth and Mira Nair's work is amazing, nearly perfect, but what with the strike, you've got to make sure you've got all your ducks in a row.' Said Bombay ducks had lost the will to quack. *Shantaram* was shelved, and with it an extraordinary, vivid vision of India that could have eclipsed even *Slumdog Millionaire* (2008). **SC**

FAMOUS LAST WORDS

'The movie version of *Shantaram*, purchased by Johnny Depp, Graham King and Warner Brothers, is still very much on track. . .' wrote author Gregory David Roberts (above) in late 2011. 'They are waiting for me to finish this new novel. . . so that I can concentrate on the film of *Shantaram*, and other projects.'

WILL IT EVER HAPPEN?

3/10 As late as March 2011, the *Times of India* reported that *Shantaram*'s production team were to revisit India for (yet another) location scout, with a revised shooting date of June in place. The 'source' claimed Depp and Bachchan had shot for eighteen days in 2009 at the ND studio, with sets built and extras cast. However, since 'everyone had signed confidentiality documents, obviously nobody heard anything'. Obviously.

NAILED

Director David O. Russell **Starring** Jessica Biel, Jake Gyllenhaal, Kirstie Alley, James Marsden, Tracy Morgan, Catherine Keener, Paul Reubens **Year** 2008 **Budget** $25 million **Country** US **Genre** Comedy

A s befits his taste for prickly comedies of conflict, David O. Russell has a reputation for not being the easiest person to work with. That's no insider secret. Tales of an uncharacteristically aggravated George Clooney punching the writer-director on the set of their 1999 Gulf War satire *Three Kings* have become the stuff of Hollywood lore. And Russell's blistering row with Lily Tomlin while filming his ambitious absurdist oddity *I Heart Huckabees* (2004) went one better – it's there for all to see on YouTube.

STRANGENESS AND SEVERITY

The strangeness and severity of the complications that repeatedly halted, and finally scuppered, Russell's 2008 film *Nailed*, however, had very little to do with his own fiery personality. Nor were they due to Russell's creative team or name-heavy cast, led by Jake Gyllenhaal and Jessica Biel. Rather, the blame in this unfortunate case appears to lie with the money men – specifically, film financier David Bergstein, whose company Capitol Films was declared bankrupt in 2010, and his former business partner Ronald Tutor. *Nailed* was just one of the creative casualties of Capitol Films's financial mismanagement. But it was the most high-profile and, arguably, the bloodiest.

What makes *Nailed* a particularly dismaying case of unfulfilled promise is that it doesn't merely exist on the page, or in our collective, hypothesis-driven imagination: the film itself is out there. Ninety-five percent of it is, at any rate – in raw, unfinished form, missing only one crucial scene that looks to remain forever unshot, the production having folded just two days from completion.

How does a star-powered A-list project get so close and yet so far, like a Hollywood cop killed on the eve of retirement? And, given *Nailed*'s nightmarish production history, how did it even get that close? Reflecting on the ordeal in a 2012 Collider interview, producers Douglas Wick and Lucy Fisher estimate that the production was shut down fourteen times en route to its final termination.

This was an undignified end for what was, on paper, a hot project. Russell wrote the script with Kristin Gore, a *Saturday Night Live* satirist whose heritage – she's the daughter of former US vice-president Al Gore – made her an auspicious choice for what promised to be a balls-out Washington satire.

DAVID O. RUSSELL

'I had never seen anything like it,' the director told slashfilm.com about *Nailed* in 2011. 'Our financing got turned on and off like a faucet. . . I spent almost two years trying to get that finished and I just said, "Okay, I got to move on."'

SNAP, CRACKLE, POP

Nailed wasn't Russell's only movie to fall by the wayside after *I Heart Huckabees*. *The Grackle*, he explained to slashfilm. com of a comedy mooted to star Matthew McConaughey (above), 'was written by the guys who wrote *Bad Santa*, [John] Requa and [Glenn] Ficarra. . . I was talking about making that. . . when my dear friend Mark Wahlberg came to me with *The Fighter* [2010]. So, as much as I thought that was really a funny project, if I have to pick between someone who's a little like a brother to me and that other project, I'm going to have to go with *The Fighter*'.

Furthering the adventures of Sammy Joyce, a character Gore had depicted in two novels, *Nailed* cast Jessica Biel as a small-town waitress who, after being accidentally shot in the head with a nail gun, is overcome with hypersexual urges. (It was, Biel told the *Orlando Sentinel*, 'something I could not say "No" to – I am a huge David O. Russell fan'.) When the uninsured nymphomaniac finds the US health care system unwilling to treat her, she embarks on a crusade to Congress for the rights of the 'bizarrely injured' – joined by *30 Rock* comic Tracy Morgan as a priest with an irreversible erection, and aided by Gyllenhaal as a morally challenged congressman with no qualms about exploiting her condition. Adding to the star wattage were Catherine Keener as another Washington politico and James Marsden as Biel's dim-bulb boyfriend.

Pitched between *The Happy Hooker Goes to Washington* (1977) and *The Wizard of Oz* (1939) – the latter cited by the producers themselves – *Nailed* also looked to benefit from a certain topicality in its dissection of the pre-Obamacare United States. It was a bold choice for the producing team of Wick (an Oscar-winner for *Gladiator*, 2000) and Fisher's first foray into independent production, while Russell – who made his big-screen directorial debut with *Spanking the Monkey* in 1994 – seemed ideal to steer this raunchy high-concept farce.

From the first day of shooting, however, the farce seemed mostly to unfold *behind* the camera. Accustomed to confirmed finances on big studio

> *'I am no longer the writer-director of* Nailed.
> *This has been a painful process for me.'*
>
> David O. Russell

projects, the producers found themselves having to work around the whims of an independent financier. That Russell's own tricky temperament had already resulted in James Caan, cast as the Speaker of the US House of Representatives, leaving the set was, for a change, a comparatively minor concern. ('James Caan did amicably part ways with this production due to creative differences,' the actor's publicist told the *New York Post*. 'He wished all of the actors and production crew well when he departed.')

In May 2008, the Screen Actors Guild ordered its members to cease working on *Nailed*, after Capitol Films failed to deposit the required salaries into the actors' SAG accounts. That same month, on two separate occasions, the International Alliance of Theatrical and Stage Employees (IATSE) ordered its members not to show up on the film's South Carolina set after employees failed to receive payment. In June, following another instance of non-payment from Capitol, the IATSE imposed what turned out to be the final shutdown. Further complicating matters, the film had secured the use of the South Carolina government's State House to double as Washington DC – a coup that became a burden as production hobbled forward on a week-on, week-off basis.

When production finally petered out in June 2008, the lone scene Russell had to complete was the one the film couldn't do without, in which Biel gets the nail lodged in her head. An unsatisfactory version of the scene had been

NAILED BY GYLLENHAAL

'I don't really know what's happening with that movie. . .' Gyllenhaal (above left, with Biel, right) told Crave Online in 2011. 'I follow my director, not anybody else. So I'm just waiting to hear from David.'

David O. Russell bounced back: the 2010 film he completed while *Nailed* languished – *The Fighter*, a boxing biopic, starring Mark Wahlberg (left) – became the highest grosser of his career and earned him a first Oscar nomination for Best Director. Douglas Wick and Lucy Fisher haven't dipped their toes in independent waters since, instead producing studio efforts *Lawless* (2012) and *The*

Great Gatsby (2013). The stars were still answering questions about the film in 2012. Promoting *Total Recall* (right), Biel summed up the collapse of *Nailed* as 'a major heartbreak' and opined that 'the only person who can save it is David'. Meanwhile, Gyllenhaal said: 'It's weird that a movie you make doesn't come out. But I'm just an actor. It's other people's jobs to put the movie together and sell it.'

shot and the producers calculated that, if they left this crucial do-over until last, David Bergstein would be obliged to see the shoot through to completion.

They thought wrong. And, in summer 2010, by which time he had shot the future Oscar winner *The Fighter*, Russell formally washed his hands of the project: 'Due to a variety of circumstances, I am no longer the writer-director of *Nailed*. This has been a painful process for me. The multiple production delays and stoppages. . . have now spanned two years, and the circumstances under which the film would now be completed are much different on several fundamental levels than when we embarked several years ago. I, unfortunately, am no longer involved in the project and cannot call it "my" film.'

Russell, likening the shoot to a 'stillbirth', resolved to 'stay with the forward moment'. But the financiers weren't done. With the footage in their possession, an edit of *Nailed* was assembled without the director or the producers, and test-screened in 2011. Reactions, unsurprisingly, suggested it was little more than a rough cut, with missing scenes still rendering it unreleasable.

'It's just heartbreaking that so many people put so much work into this particular project only to have it sit there, unfinished. . .' mourned Biel. 'I had an incredible experience with David and the rest of the cast.' It looks like the nail in her head – or lack thereof – may have been the nail in the coffin of this misbegotten production. David O. Russell should make a film about it. **GL**

WILL IT EVER HAPPEN?

3/10 While 2011's test screening suggested the financiers were weighing up the possibility of releasing the film in some form – if only by slipping it onto DVD – the ensuing silence, and subsequent financial tangles and lawsuits involving the now-estranged Bergstein and Tutor, suggest that is off the cards. That's a mercy: *Nailed* certainly isn't Russell's film anymore.

GEMINI MAN

Director Curtis Hanson **Year** 2009 **Budget** $100 million **Country** US **Genre** Sci-fi **Studio** DreamWorks

DARREN LEMKE
While *Gemini Man* failed to launch, writer Darren Lemke helmed *Lost* (2004), a well-received thriller starring Dean Cain. He has latterly carved out a career writing family-oriented movies.

Development hell is a crowded place, and few projects have languished there in more contorted agony than *Gemini Man*. The script – an uncommissioned effort by Darren Lemke (then making a living 'pushing up shopping carts and writing murder mystery dinner theatre') – entered the fray in 1997. 'I've been writing spec screenplays since I was fourteen,' Lemke told StoryLink. 'So by the time I was on my twenty-fifth script, someone finally took notice.' *Gemini Man* is a high-concept sci-fi thriller set in an Orwellian future in which the United States is ruled by a fascistic syndicate known as the Administration. The plot centres on Alexander Kane, an assassin for the Administration's shadowy enforcement agency, the Intelligence Office. Kane is the best-of-the-best, but he's fast approaching his sell-by date and wants out of the game. That, however, is not an option and a decision is made to terminate him. The question is, how do you kill the ultimate killer? The solution – rather than, say, dropping a piano on him – is to set a younger, faster, more ruthless clone of himself on his tail. The clone, called Rye, can anticipate Kane's actions, making him a particularly formidable adversary. Marked for death and desperate to discover why the Administration has turned on him, Kane goes on the run, with Rye in hot pursuit.

JACK RYAN VS. HAN SOLO
It's a setup rich with promise – as the makers of *Looper* (2012) discovered – and was duly brought to Disney's Touchstone Pictures by *Natural Born Killers* (1994) producer Don Murphy. (The *Wall Street Journal*'s Bruce Orwall drily observed that the plot sounded 'remarkably like a violent version of Disney's *The Kid*', referring to a now largely forgotten film from 2000 in which Bruce Willis meets a younger version of himself.) With a 2002 summer release scheduled, the rumour mill began to churn. Sean Connery was an early fan favourite for Kane – his craggy millennial self pitted against a computer-generated, *Goldfinger*-era spectre. Tragically, it never happened. Next up was Harrison Ford, another mouthwatering prospect – think Jack Ryan vs. Han Solo – but again wishful thinking. Ford nixed the rumours himself, claiming in an interview that he had never even heard of the project.

HE'S HERE TO KILL A DANGEROUS MAN... HIMSELF.

GEMINI MAN

A CURTIS HANSON FILM

Then, in May 2000, *The Hollywood Reporter* revealed that test footage of Mel Gibson had been shot, drawing on images from *Payback* (1999) and *The Year of Living Dangerously* (1982). That too came to nothing. It seemed for a while that Nicolas Cage was in the frame (which would have necessitated an older CGI version, or a very good wig). Then, somewhat inevitably, Bruce Willis was tapped to star. However, despite reports that Touchstone had put it on the fast-track and that Shekhar Kapur, who helmed *Elizabeth* (1998) was on board to direct, the film failed to materialize. Lemke's screenplay, now boasting a production polish from *Ali* (2001) scribes Stephen J. Rivele and Christopher Wilkinson, began its descent to the Tinseltown underworld, consoled only by inheriting the dubious epithet of Best Unmade Script in Hollywood.

Why *Gemini Man* didn't get made in 2000/2001 is a mystery. The concept was solid and Lemke's first draft, although in need of work in the character and dialogue departments, has the momentum of a freight train. There are a wealth of action set pieces, most of them fantastically violent. The screenplay also had a terrific third-act plot twist, absent in later drafts, revealing that Kane himself is a clone. The budget, certainly north of $100 million given the special effects, would have been high but not prohibitive given the right star. Perhaps that was the problem – no one with suitable box-office clout fancied going head-to-head with their younger selves, wary of the comparisons that might be drawn. Whatever the case, *Gemini Man* was spiked for several years.

> *'By the time I was on my twenty-fifth script, someone finally took notice.'*
>
> Darren Lemke

Then, in 2006, it seemed a reprieve had been granted. Superstar producer Jerry Bruckheimer, first linked to the project in 2000, came officially aboard. Ensuing years brought rewrites by Jonathan Hensleigh of *Armageddon* (1998) and David Benioff of *Game of Thrones*, and it was slated for production with Curtis Hanson of *L.A. Confidential* (1997) to direct. Hanson seemed an odd choice: the closest he had come to a genuine action movie was the very tame *The River Wild* (1994), with Meryl Streep. Still, with Bruckheimer's formidable weight behind it, *Gemini Man* was, to all intents and purposes, a go project.

KICK CONVINCING ASS

In its favour was the advanced state of CGI, leagues ahead of what had been available earlier in the decade. *The Curious Case of Benjamin Button* (2008) proved that accelerating or reversing the ageing process was achievable. That said, no amount of wizardry would de-crustify the seventy-nine-year-old Sean Connery sufficiently, nor was there a quick computer fix for Mel Gibson's self-inflicted box-office death wish. Again, Bruce Willis seemed to be top of the blogosphere's wish list. The role cried out for an ageing action star who could still kick convincing ass: Willis to a T. (Indeed, Willis proved he could play both older and younger versions of himself in the same year's *Surrogates*, and

NOT TO BE CONFUSED WITH. . .
Gemini Man was a 1976 sci-fi TV show that starred Ben Murphy (above, centre) as a secret agent rendered invisible in a diving accident. Much less painful than an attack of the bends, this also turns out to be a boon professionally, especially after agency boffins come up with a nifty wristwatch that allows him to control his unusual condition. The twist: he can only pull the trick for fifteen minutes each day, lest he vanish for good. Cancelled after five episodes in the United States, the series aired in its entirety in the UK. Two episodes were adapted into a 1976 TV movie called (for reasons unknown) *Riding with Death*. This was spoofed on *Mystery Science Theater 3000* in 1997.

Darren Lemke's script was put back on the Mouse House shelf and everyone concerned moved on. Jerry Bruckheimer busied himself with unassuming arthouse fare like *Pirates of the Caribbean: On Stranger Tides* (2011) and the 2013 reboot of *The Lone Ranger* with Armie Hammer and Johnny Depp. Curtis Hanson returned to surer ground with the 2011 HBO movie *Too Big to Fail*, a dramatization of the 2007 financial crisis. He also had a crack at action, albeit of a different sort, with *Chasing Mavericks* (2012), a biopic of extreme surfer Jay Moriarty that he co-directed with Michael Apted. Following *Shrek Forever After* (2010), Lemke worked on screenplays for the action-fantasy flick *Jack The Giant Slayer* (2013) and *Turbo*, with Ryan Reynolds as a snail with a need for speed.

turned up as a fiftysomething hit man hunted by his younger self in *Looper,* 2012.) Again, though, the project stubbornly failed to coalesce. No cast was officially announced and, just as mysteriously as before, it disappeared.

The project seemed dead in the water. But, just like its titular assassin, *Gemini Man* wouldn't lie down without a fight. In late 2012, writer-director Joe Carnahan (*Narc, 2002*; *Smokin' Aces, 2006*) attempted to breathe new life into the project with a tantalizing sizzle reel that he posted online. The pseudo-trailer features Clint Eastwood as Kane, ingeniously combining footage from various movies to create the impression of old Clint playing a deadly game of cat-and-mouse with Dirty Harry. Whether Eastwood, eighty-two at the time of writing (the same age as Connery), could have pulled off the role of a relentless killing machine is debatable, but it gives an indication of what the film might have been in Carnahan's hands. The director also claimed that tests had been done with Jon Voight to assess the feasibility of a younger, CGI duplicate.

Unfortunately, Carnahan was no more successful than anyone else. No call from Jerry Bruckheimer was forthcoming; no hand hovered over the green light at Disney. The stars, it seems, simply refuse to align for *Gemini Man*. **SB**

GEMINI MAN MEETS HIS NEMESIS
Joe Carnahan's Clint Eastwood-starring *Gemini Man* sizzle reel (above) made pulses race. But Carnahan switched his focus to an adaptation of the Mark Millar (*Kick-Ass*) comic book *Nemesis*.

WILL IT EVER HAPPEN?

3/10 The script is out there and Joe Carnahan's sizzle reel proves it has high-profile interest. But given the broad similarities with *Looper*, it's unlikely that *Gemini Man* will get a green light – and, in any case, clones jumped the sci-fi shark a decade ago. Of course, it only needs one A-lister to take a sniff and it'll resurrected once more. And, with the gimmick of the same actor playing both the older Kane and the younger Rye, it does differ from *Looper* in one crucial respect: in that film, Bruce Willis's younger self was played by Joseph Gordon-Levitt with only basic Brucification make-up.

FRANK OR FRANCIS

Director Charlie Kaufman **Starring** Steve Carell, Jack Black, Nicolas Cage, Elizabeth Banks, Kevin Kline, Catherine Keener, Paul Reubens **Year** 2012 **Country** US **Genre** Musical satire **Studio** Columbia

CHARLIE KAUFMAN

'I don't really have any idea how we're going to do it,' the writer-director told *Time Out*. 'It's important when you're writing to not bridle yourself with pragmatic concerns. . . The scope of it and the world it inhabits is very, very large.'

Hollywood movies about Hollywood are plentiful and varied. At one end of the scale is *Singin' in the Rain* (1952), at the other *An Alan Smithee Film: Burn Hollywood Burn* (1997), a work so unremittingly awful that it actually became an Alan Smithee film when director Arthur Hiller disowned it. Where Charlie Kaufman's surreal Tinseltown satire *Frank or Francis* would have weighed in on the list is something we'll probably never know. But, given Kaufman's typically brilliant, wigged-out script, one suspects fairly near the top.

SKEWED VERSION OF REALITY

'In the broadest possible sense,' Kaufman told *Time Out*'s London edition in 2011, 'it's about online film criticism – but, as usual, the world that I'm writing about is not necessarily the world that I'm writing about.'

The world Kaufman was not necessarily writing about in *Frank or Francis* is a slightly skewed version of reality in which an online blogger and a famous film-maker embark on a bitter feud. Of course, this being Charlie Kaufman – famed for such inspired, mind-bending fare as *Being John Malkovich* (1999), *Adaptation* (2002) and *Eternal Sunshine of the Spotless Mind* (2004) – there is more to it than that. By taking a well-aimed, subversive swipe at both the film biz and the internet, he manages to send up the malaise of modern living. 'There's a lot in there about the internet and anger: cultural, societal and individual anger,' he said. 'And isolation in this particular age we live in. And competition: it's about the idea of people in this world wanting to be seen.'

Steve Carell was lined up to play Frank Arder, a pretentious Oscar-winning screenwriter. Jack Black was his nemesis, Francis Deems, a blogger who hates every film he sees and reserves special scorn for Arder. It was also to feature Nicolas Cage as fading comic actor Alan Modell, desperate to escape the shadow of his biggest hits (*Fat Dad* and *Fat Dad 2: Skinny Dad*); a Michael Bay-style director promoting his latest taste-free blockbuster, *Hiroshima*; a supporting cast including Elizabeth Banks, Catherine Keener and Paul Reubens; and a disembodied robotic head (voiced by Kevin Kline) programmed to write the perfect screenplay – one whose mass appeal is matched only by its complete absence of artistic integrity. And, oh yes, it was also a musical.

directed by charlie kaufman

frank
or
francis

starring steve carell *jack black* nicolas cage *elizabeth banks*
kevin kline *catherine keener* paul reubens

Frank or Francis was scheduled to start production early in 2012. However, in June, Banks told Moviefone.com, 'We didn't get to shoot that movie. It was ready to go and, as many movies do, it fell apart at the last minute.' Kaufman's reps allowed only that the project had been postponed.

Speculation that *Frank or Francis* has been put on hold deliberately to stir up internet traffic, adding a further dimension to the film's twisted universe, is perhaps not far-fetched. Kaufman's screenplay for *Adaptation* (a non-adaptation of Susan Orlean's non-fiction book *The Orchid Thief*) featured a character named Charlie Kaufman, a fictionalized version of himself. It also introduced his identical twin Donald, a talentless (though successful) knucklehead counterpart to Charlie's tortured artiste. Both roles were played by Nicolas Cage. The movie credits Donald Kaufman as screenwriter and is dedicated to his 'loving memory'. Kaufman does not have, nor has he ever had, a twin brother – although that didn't stop the Academy Award panel nominating both Charlie and Donald for 'their' work on the screenplay.

As of late 2012, *Frank or Francis* remained firmly stuck in neutral. The most likely explanation is that money men were nervously eyeing box office receipts from *Synecdoche, New York* (2008), Kaufman's debut as writer-director.

'I wish that it would happen,' Jack Black told vulture.com in 2012. 'We are just about ten million dollars shy of the cost to make it, so if anyone out there reading this can scrape together a cool ten mil, this thing can happen.' **SB**

WILL IT EVER HAPPEN?

5/10 Classified as 'postponed' rather than cancelled, *Frank or Francis* has a better chance than any other film in this book. That said, it faces major hurdles, not least the subject matter. After all, what industry would fund a project that sets out to expose it as shallow, venal and ethically bankrupt?

Poster: Pedro Vidotto

POTSDAMER PLATZ

Director Tony Scott **Starring** Mickey Rourke, Javier Bardem, Christopher Walken, Johnny Hallyday
Year 2012 **Budget** $38 million **Country** US **Genre** Crime drama **Studio** Lionsgate

TONY SCOTT

'It's not a little movie,' the director told comingsoon.net in 2009, 'but it's based on a true story of the Jersey mob and when they tried to take over the construction business in Germany. . . I've got a great cast with Mickey [Rourke].'

After his cracking *Unstoppable* (2010), speculation about Tony Scott's next film abounded. In contention were: *The Associate*, a John Grisham adaptation set to star Shia LaBeouf; *Hell's Angels*, with Mickey Rourke as Angels founder Sonny Barger; the long-mooted *Top Gun 2* and *Potsdamer Platz*, based on author Buddy Giovinazzo's novel. The latter led the pack.

DEADLY MAELSTROM

'Not since *Goodfellas* has there been such a brilliant and unique look into the gangster world,' the book's cover quotes Scott as saying. He had optioned the script, also by Giovinazzo, in 2000 and often spoke of his desire to make it.

Set shortly after the fall of the Soviet Union, the plot involves a New Jersey crime family – the Franchise – with global ambitions. They duly establish a presence at Europe's biggest construction site: Potsdamer Platz – a wasteland once bisected by the Berlin Wall – in the newly unified German capital. With the economy in upheaval and new money flooding in, there are fortunes to be made and the Franchise face competition from Russia, East Germany and Turkey. Into this deadly maelstrom the Franchise send Tony, their youngest yet most ruthless hit man, to make their presence felt. This proves disastrous. Following the accidental killing of an innocent fourteen-year-old girl, Tony suffers a crisis of conscience that severely tests his allegiance to the Franchise. And when he falls for Monica, an East Berlin student, he's forced to choose between the redemption she seems to offer and the security of the Franchise.

It appears that Giovinazzo wrote the novel, published in 2004, after the screenplay, relocating to Berlin to research it. That would explain the book's intensely cinematic tone. It is also violent, sexy and packed with action, just the thing to attract a film-maker with Scott's pedigree. It was announced that he would begin production on it in early 2002. But that didn't happen and, despite his initial enthusiasm, it was relegated to the back burner for ten years while he busied himself with the spectaculars that marked his career in the 2000s – *Man on Fire* (2004), *Domino* (2005) and *Unstoppable* among them.

When Scott revived the project in 2010, the title was dropped and the script, reports said, was reworked by *Sexy Beast* (2000) scribes David Scinto and

FROM THE INTERNATIONAL BEST- SELLER

DIRECTED BY
TONY SCOTT

STARRING
MICKEY ROURKE
JAVIER BARDEM
CHRISTOPHER WALKEN
JOHNNY HALLYDAY

POTSDAMER PLATZ

Louis Mellis. Two New Jersey mobsters are sent to Puerto Rico (presumably more attractive to potential investors) to put the squeeze on their boss's rival by wiping out his operation. Like Tony in the novel, their consciences are pricked when they discover a six-year-old girl hiding in the rival's compound and allow her to live. Big mistake. The girl was the target of the hit: an act of revenge by their boss on a woman he once loved. This act of mercy presents them with the dilemma of hunting down the girl or incurring the boss's murderous wrath.

It was enough to attract a raft of talent. In 2002, Scott had tried to get his *Enemy of the State* (1998) star Gene Hackman interested and, in 2010, he attempted to coax the eighty-year-old out of retirement to rejoin the project. Hackman passed, as did Al Pacino. It was then reported that Mickey Rourke, back from the dead after 2008's *The Wrestler*, was on board, joined by Jason Statham, Javier Bardem, Christopher Walken (who appeared in Scott's *Man on Fire*, 2004) and French singer-turned-actor Johnny Hallyday. It seems Statham subsequently dropped out, but, with a deal in place at Lionsgate, the project – still untitled – looked all set to proceed in 2012. Tragically, it was not to be.

WHAT HAPPENED NEXT. . .
On 19 August 2012, Tony Scott – for reasons unconfirmed – threw himself to his death off the Vincent Thomas Bridge in San Pedro, California. There can be few films that have been cancelled under sadder circumstances. **SB**

 WILL IT EVER HAPPEN?
3/10 It's possible Giovinazzo's novel will be adapted, perhaps from the author's own script. But, in the wake of Scott's suicide, it's unlikely anyone will revive the project any time soon. If they do, it's equally doubtful that Mickey Rourke, Christopher Walken, Javier Bardem or Johnny Hallyday will be involved.

NOT COMING SOON. . . A few more of our favourites

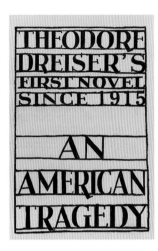

AN AMERICAN TRAGEDY 1930
Sergei M. Eisenstein (director)

In 1930, Eisenstein arrived in the United States to take up the Paramount offer to direct 'films at his convenience'. But the studio shredded his wish list – including an adaptation of Theodore Dreiser's 1925 *An American Tragedy*, about a poor man's desperation to better himself, based on a real murder case. Having read Eisenstein's screenplay, associate director David O. Selznick reported: 'It was for me a memorable experience; the most moving script I have ever read. It was so effective, it was positively torturing. When I had finished reading it, I was so depressed that I wanted to reach for the bourbon bottle. As entertainment, I don't think it has one chance in a hundred.' Selznick concluded it was 'a subject that will appeal to our vanity through the critical acclaim that must necessarily attach to its production, but that cannot possibly offer anything but a most miserable two hours to millions of happy-minded young Americans'. **AE**

IT'S ALL TRUE 1942
Orson Welles (director)

In 1942, RKO stockholder Nelson Rockefeller and President Franklin D. Roosevelt, a friend of Welles, asked the director to make a film in Brazil to foster inter-American relations in the wake of Pearl Harbor. Intended as a four-part travelogue, Welles reformatted it into a trilogy: *My Friend Bonito*, about a Mexican boy's friendship with a bull; *The Story of Samba*, charting the dance from the favelas to the Rio carnival; and *Four Men on a Raft*, a re-enactment of a 2,575-kilometre journey undertaken by four poor fishermen to speak to Brazil's president about the exploitation of fishermen. Welles also planned a segment featuring jazz legend Louis Armstrong, but never shot it. The project was judged too political by both the Brazilian and US administrations, and by RKO – which, already dismayed by a fatal accident during the filming of the raft sequence, halted production. Some footage was used in the 1993 documentary *It's All True* (above). **DN**

ADAM AND EVE 1947
Leo McCarey (scriptwriter)

Famed for comedies of marital disharmony, smart repartee, lush sentimentality, unabashed religiosity and a little sex, Leo McCarey was full of ideas that were never realized. A Hollywood exposé was shelved when producer Howard Hughes backed out. There was a Marco Polo biopic and a horror film with his friend Alfred Hitchcock as the killer. However, the screenplay he pitched most ardently was *Adam and Eve*, a version of the Bible story co-written with satirist Sinclair Lewis and starring (he hoped) James Stewart and Ingrid Bergman. When word got out, a big name silent star showed up at his office to offer her services as Eve. 'It's true, I'm working on a new version of *Adam and Eve*,' McCarey told her. 'But not with the original cast.' Producers were less keen. Nevertheless, in 1955, a weary Bergman reported that McCarey was still plaguing her about playing Eve – this time opposite John Wayne! **AE**

A DAY AT THE UNITED NATIONS 1961
Billy Wilder (writer-director)

In 1960, at the peak of his powers, Billy Wilder (above) came up with an idea for the Marx Brothers. The siblings hadn't made a film together since 1949's *Love Happy*, but Wilder felt the prospect of Groucho, Chico and Harpo running amok in the United Nations was a perfect mix of satire and farce. After pitching the idea to Groucho and Gummo, the brothers' agent, Wilder and collaborator I.A.L. Diamond put together a treatment for *A Day at the United Nations*. 'We want to make a satire on the conditions of the world today,' stated Wilder. 'A satire on the deterioration of diplomatic behaviour, on brinksmanship, wild jokes about the H-bomb, that type of stuff. It's all so dramatic that a few jokes put over by the Marx Bros should alleviate the tension.' Unfortunately, it all happened too late. The brothers were all in their seventies and Harpo suffering a heart attack halted production. When Chico died in 1961, so did the project. **SW**

UP AGAINST IT 1967
Joe Orton (writer)

Casting around for a follow-up to the hit *Help!* (1965), The Beatles's manager Brian Epstein alighted on Joe Orton (above). The playwright had risen to fame with 1964's *Entertaining Mr Sloane*, and his controversy-baiting cynicism seemed a perfect match for the deadpan Liverpudlians. However, the resulting tale of anarchy, assassination and apocalypse proved hard to stomach even by young men on the verge of turning off their minds, relaxing and floating downstream. 'The reason why we didn't do *Up Against It* wasn't because it was too far out or anything,' noted Paul McCartney. 'We didn't do it because it was gay. . . It wasn't that we were anti-gay – just that we, The Beatles, weren't gay.' Other, equally doomed ideas included The Beatles starring in an adaptation of *The Lord of the Rings*. This notion won few favours from mooted director Stanley Kubrick, who told John Lennon that he thought the book unfilmable. **BMac**

THE MERCHANT OF VENICE 1969
Orson Welles (director)

As part of a commission for a CBS television special, Orson Welles (above) wrote a condensed and radical interpretation of William Shakespeare's play to star Charles Gray as Antonio and himself, heavily made-up, as Shylock. His mistress Oja Kodar declined to play Portia, on the grounds that her English wasn't up to the task. Welles duly removed the character altogether, focusing instead on the drama between Antonio and Shylock, and setting the story in the eighteenth century. Shot in Yugoslavia and Venice, the picture was finished by 1970. However, two reels of the workprint, complete with the master sound elements, were stolen from the director's production office in Rome. The negative remained intact (and is still in Kodar's possession), but sound exists only for the one reel that wasn't stolen. The mystery of the theft was never solved and Welles only admitted that the film even existed a decade after it was made. **DN**

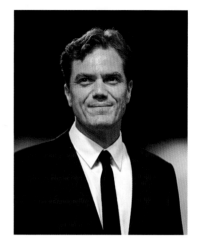

THE DEEP *c.*1970
Orson Welles (director)

Coming off *Chimes at Midnight* (1965), Welles wrote a script based on Charles Williams's novel *Dead Calm*, about a man who has a breakdown after accidentally killing a woman while diving in the sea, then hijacks two boats to escape. The cast was led by Laurence Harvey, with Jeanne Moreau (above, with Welles in *Chimes...*), Michael Bryant, Oja Kodar and Welles himself. Filmed over two years, off the coast of Croatia, the shoot was all but finished when Welles became nervous about the film's reception. He suspended the project, blaming weather at sea and Bryant's commitment to a play in London, and turned to *F for Fake* (1973) instead. All that remained to be shot was an explosive climax, coupled with post-production work (Moreau needed to dub her dialogue). The delay proved fatal: in 1973 Harvey died, making it impossible to complete the picture. Footage, suggesting the film was shot largely in close-up, graces the documentary *Orson Welles: The One-Man Band* (1995). A 1989 adaptation of the novel by director Phillip Noyce used its original title: *Dead Calm*. **DN**

A CONFEDERACY OF DUNCES
1980s–present
John Kennedy Toole (original novel)

A Confederacy of Dunces is cursed. Once film-makers start work on it, they are stricken by calamity. Look at the statistics: John Belushi, John Candy and Chris Farley (actors attached to the project) – dead; Natasha Lyonne (actress attached to the project) – Lohan-esque career derailment; New Orleans (city attached to the project) – decimated by Hurricane Katrina; Jo Beth Bolton (Louisiana Film Commissioner, attached to the project) – murdered; Will Ferrell (actor attached to the project) – made *Blades of Glory* (2007) instead. Most recently in the frame, Zach Galifianakis would be superb – so doubtless it won't happen. It all goes back to the book's tragic genesis – namely the suicide of its author John Kennedy Toole, several years before his mother persuaded a dubious editor to read the manuscript. Perhaps, instead of wasting their time, talent, energy and lives trying to film *A Confederacy of Dunces*, film-makers would be better off trying to make a film about the impossibility of making a film of *A Confederacy of Dunces*. **PR**

EDWARD FORD *c.*1980s
Lem Dobbs (writer)

Written in 1979, *Edward Ford* is Hollywood's most lauded unproduced screenplay. Its writer, Lem Dobbs (born Anton Kitaj), was an unknown, five years away from his first paid gig: an uncredited rewrite of *Romancing the Stone* (1984). But through his father, painter R.B. Kitaj, he knew cinema luminaries including Billy Wilder, so his work passed before talented and influential eyes. The titular character of Dobbs's script is a young man who moves to Los Angeles in the 1960s, hoping to be an actor. Over the next thirty years, he lives on the fringes of Hollywood and befriends actors, but never uses them to further his own career, making do with terrible Christian theatre. Despite the raves it earned from everyone who read it, *Edward Ford* failed to sell. Dobbs, however, has become a successful screenwriter, and believes the reverence afforded to the piece means it couldn't have helped his career any more if it *had* been made. But late 2012 brought the intriguing news that the piece had been adopted by director Terry Zwigoff, with Michael Shannon (above) attached to star. **DN**

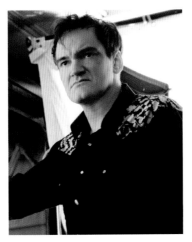

GONE WITH THE WIND c.1985
Sergio Leone (director)

As if *Leningrad* (see page 148) were not evidence enough of his ambition, Leone (above) had high hopes for another epic. A fan of *Gone with the Wind* – both Margaret Mitchell's 1936 novel and its 1939 film adaptation – he announced his intentions for a remake. According to family and friends, he often talked about a version closer to the original novel. Orson Welles had told him he was certifiable, pointing out that, *Gone with the Wind* aside, Civil War movies were box-office poison. Proving Welles wrong – *The Good, The Bad and the Ugly* (1966) was a hit – might have persuaded Leone that a remake was feasible. However, it never took flight, so we were denied the prospect of Southern spectacle à la Leone: a sweeping Morricone score and Clint Eastwood not giving a damn as Rhett Butler (not a prospect that would have thrilled Mitchell, whose first choice for the role was Groucho Marx). When Leone died in 1989, he was working on the script for a Western, *A Place Only Mary Knows*. Set amid the Civil War, it was an homage to, among other works, *Gone with the Wind*. **SB**

DOUBLE V VEGA c.1995 onwards
Quentin Tarantino (director)

Kill Bill fans forlornly hope for a third film ('We'll see,' said Tarantino [above] in 2012. 'Probably not, though') and *Inglourious Basterds* may yet spawn a spin-off ('It would be called *Killer Crow* or something like that'). Another of QT's projects, however, is dead and buried: a movie uniting Michael Madsen's *Reservoir Dogs* psycho Vic Vega (aka Mr Blonde) with John Travolta's *Pulp Fiction* hitman, Vincent Vega. 'We're both on a flight from Los Angeles, having just been released from prison. . .' revealed Madsen. 'Neither one of us know that we're the twin brother of the other one and we're both on our way back to LA to avenge the death of our brothers.' The project even earned a title: *Double V Vega*. 'It's nothing I want to rush into,' Tarantino said in 2003. 'But, bottom line, the studio wants it, the fans want it. I'm sure I can compromise.' By 2010, however, the brothers had bitten the dust. 'Since [the characters] both died, it would have to be a prequel. . .' he observed. 'But now, [Madsen and Travolta] are too old for that. I got to say, it's kind of unlikely.' **BMac**

PINOCCHIO 1995
Francis Ford Coppola (director)

In 1994, Coppola announced plans for a live-action *Pinocchio*. In contrast to the Disney classic, it would be closer to Carlo Collodi's original story, in which Pinocchio kills Jiminy Cricket and is haunted by his ghost. Exactly how faithful it would have been is questionable, as Coppola envisaged a musical set in Nazi-occupied France. Pinocchio, he told *Variety*, 'will be the product of a whole range of the latest technology, from puppet to live action to the computer technology started with *Jurassic Park*'. The director, who intended to play Gepetto, wrote a script and enlisted *The Godfather* (1972) production designer Dean Tavoularis, music producer Don Was and fashion designer Karl Lagerfeld. However, in 1995, Coppola and Warner Bros fell out over budget issues. Coppola sued Warner, asserting it had sabotaged his efforts to shop the film to another studio. Warner claimed it owned the rights to the property; Coppola counterclaimed that, as no contract had been signed, it did not. In 1998, to Hollywood's astonishment, a Los Angeles jury sided with Coppola. **SB**

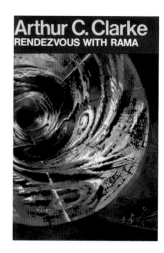

THE ALIENIST 1996
Curtis Hanson/Philip Kaufman
(directors)

Gemini Man (see page 236) isn't
the only high-profile project to slip
through Curtis Hanson's fingers. In
1995 he lost out on an adaptation of
The Alienist, Caleb Carr's novel about
a killer terrorizing New York and the
criminologist tasked with hunting
him. Paramount bought the rights,
envisioning Anthony Hopkins or Sam
Neill as the killer and Emma Thompson
as the first woman to serve with the
NYPD. Hanson was announced as
director, a script was commissioned
from playwright David Henry Hwang,
and a 1995 release was trumpeted.
But Hwang's screenplay was subjected
to numerous rewrites, including one
from Philip Kaufman (see *Star Trek*,
page 106) – who replaced Hanson as
director when, according to *Variety*, the
latter quit over cost issues. Dissatisfied
with the script, Paramount was further
disenchanted by the budget, estimated
to be close to $50 million. In 1996,
Variety reported that the project was in
turnaround. Carr was so disillusioned
that he refused to sell the rights to *The
Alienist*'s sequel to Hollywood. **SB**

THE MAN WHO KILLED DON
QUIXOTE *c.*2001
Terry Gilliam (director)

Orson Welles was not the only one to
struggle with Miguel de Cervantes's
tale (see page 77). Like him, Sergio
Leone wanted to place the knight and
his squire in a modern setting. 'America
would be Don Quixote,' Leone said,
'while Sancho, a European finding
out about that country, would be the
only positive character in the film.' In
2000, Terry Gilliam began production
for *The Man Who Killed Don Quixote*
– the story of an advertising executive
transported back to the seventeenth
century and mistaken for Sancho
Panza by Don Quixote – but promptly
ran into difficulties. A flash flood on
the second day destroyed equipment
and drastically changed the look of
the location they were using. Then
French actor Jean Rochefort, who
had learned English to play Quixote,
suffered a herniated disc that left him
unable to ride a horse. The production
was cancelled and, although Gilliam
has attempted to revive it, the only
fruit of his labour remains *Lost in La
Mancha*, a 2002 documentary about
the disastrous production. **DN**

RENDEZVOUS WITH RAMA *c.*2002
David Fincher (director)

Following 1999's *Fight Club*, Fincher
was attached to a bevy of projects:
Seared, an adaptation of Anthony
Bourdain's *Kitchen Confidential* starring
Brad Pitt and Benicio del Toro; a version
of Frank Miller's ultraviolent graphic
novel *Hard Boiled*; *They Fought Alone*,
a Second World War drama also starring
Pitt; *Chemical Pink*, a twisted tale set
in the world of bodybuilding; the Cold
War thriller *Squids*; *Mank*, a biopic of
screenwriter Herman J. Mankiewicz;
a long-gestating remake of *The
Reincarnation of Peter Proud* (1975);
a remake of Hitchcock's *Strangers
on a Train* (1951); an untitled chef
project starring Keanu Reeves and a
Cleopatra film starring Angelina Jolie.
Among these possibilities, the big one
was *Rendezvous with Rama*. Morgan
Freeman has been attached to star in
the Arthur C. Clarke-penned tale for
over a decade. According to Fincher,
the cost has kept it on hold. 'It's great
but it's just really expensive,' he told
MTV, 'and talk about the bones being
picked by so many other stories. . .'
As of 2012, however, it was still being
reported as a going concern. **SW**

WONDER WOMAN c.2007
Joss Whedon (writer-director)

By the time *Buffy the Vampire Slayer* creator Joss Whedon (above) boarded Wonder Woman's invisible plane, a slew of writers had plummeted to earth. In 1999, Warner Bros hired Jon Cohen to conjure a screenplay for producer Joel Silver and star Sandra Bullock. In 2001, the task fell to *Antz* (1998) co-writer Todd Alcott; then, in 2003, to *Smallville* scribe Philip Levens. With DC Comics presumably wary after another of its femmes fatales, Catwoman, flopped off the big screen in 2004, Whedon started from scratch in 2005. 'I was given license to purely make it my own,' he declared. But, in 2007, he too was out. 'I had a take on the film that, well, nobody liked,' he admitted. As for casting rumours that included Lindsay Lohan, he said, 'I never had an actress picked out.' Warner's focus switched to the now equally mythical *Justice League* film, which would have teamed Wonder Woman with fellow DC heroes Batman and Superman. Whedon's revenge was sweet: he wrote and directed Paramount's *The Avengers* (2012), based on the Justice League's Marvel universe rivals. **BMac**

PHANTASMAGORIA: THE VISIONS OF LEWIS CARROLL c.2008
Marilyn Manson (writer-director)

Manson's depiction of the *Alice's Adventures in Wonderland* author was to star himself as Carroll, with his then girlfriend Evan Rachel Wood, Lily Cole (above, with Manson) and Tilda Swinton. 'A common misconception about *Phantasmagoria* is that it's going to look like a long Marilyn Manson music video. . .' protested the shock rocker's co-writer Anthony Silva. 'This is not the case. Manson and I have set out to create a serious psychological horror film in the vein of Polanski and Bergman.' The project edged towards production, with Manson even being loaned a Future Camera System by James Cameron to shoot in stereoscopic 3D. Then it was reported that mixed reactions to a trailer shown at the Berlin International Film Festival put paid to the movie ('I'm not sure where that rumour started considering most investors saw the trailer several years ago,' argued Silva). However, the Hollywood writers' strike, the end of Manson and Wood's relationship and the star's declining fortunes are more probable causes of its demise. **BMac**

PINKVILLE c.2008
Oliver Stone (director)

As he fought in the war himself, it's forgivable that, despite *Platoon* (1986) and *Born on the Fourth of July* (1989), Oliver Stone hasn't got Vietnam out of his system. In 2007 came news of *Pinkville*, named after the scene of the My Lai massacre in 1968, in which US soldiers, finding no enemy troops, slaughtered women, children, the elderly and livestock. A US helicopter pilot, witnessing the attack, attempted to position his vehicle as a shield for the civilians, imploring his gunners to open fire on their own side if they persisted. Yet only one of the soldiers was convicted of wrongdoing. This horrifying story was ideally suited to Stone, who lined up Channing Tatum, then Shia LaBeouf, to play the helicopter pilot, and Bruce Willis as the general whose investigation into the incident and its cover-up was to form the basis of the movie. Unfortunately, it was derailed by the 2007 writers' strike. Willis jumped ship to *Surrogates* (2009) and Stone to *W.* (2008). However, in a commentary for the DVD of 2010's *Wall Street: Money Never Sleeps*, the director hinted that he might revive the project. **BMac**

CONTRIBUTORS

Robin Askew (RA) was Bristol listings magazine *Venue*'s film editor (his reviews are at venue.co.uk/film). He is now film editor for the *Bristol Post*'s *Weekend* magazine and writes about film and music for anyone offering hard cash. He once graced the *Guardian*'s Corrections and Clarifications column after confusion with Robin Askwith.

Simon Braund (SB) is the author of the definitive history of Alejandro Jodorowsky's failed attempt to adapt Frank Herbert's *Dune*. A British writer living in Los Angeles, he has been a contributing editor to *Empire* for ten years and has written for a range of other titles including the *Sunday Times*, *Q*, the *Observer* and *Time Out*.

Simon Crook (SC) is a former deputy editor of *Total Film* and monthly contributor to *Empire* magazine, where he writes about movies you've probably never heard of. Among those he's interviewed: Jeff Bridges, Mike Leigh, Jack Black and Steven Soderbergh. He lives in London and likes squid. Follow him on Twitter @sicrook.

Angie Errigo (AE) is a contributing editor to *Empire* and an award-winning broadcaster on film, entertainment and arts for radio and TV. She has written for UK newspapers, magazines and books, and conducts on-stage Q&As with leading film-makers and actors. She is the author of *Chick Flicks: A Girl's Guide to Movies* (Orion, 2004).

Ian Freer (IF) is assistant editor of *Empire*. He has interviewed the world's greatest directors, written about movies for publications including the *Times* and *Famous Monsters of Filmland* and has talked about film on everything from BBC Radio 4 to *Good Morning America*. He is the author of *The Complete Spielberg* (Virgin Books, 2001) and *Movie Makers* (Quercus Books, 2009).

Dan Jolin (DJ), features editor of *Empire*, has been a film journalist for fifteen years, during which time he's witnessed the making of two Bond movies and two Batman movies, and visited both Pixar and Ghibli studios.

Guy Lodge (GL) is a South African-born film journalist, whose work regularly appears in *Variety*, *Time Out*, *Empire* and the *Guardian*, and a screenwriter with a master's degree from the London Film School. He lives in London.

Bruno MacDonald (BMac) edited *1001 Songs You Must Hear Before You Die* (Cassell, 2010) and *Pink Floyd: Through the Eyes of. . .*(DaCapo, 1997).

Bob McCabe (BM) wrote the bestsellers *Harry Potter from Page to Screen* (Titan Books, 2011) and *The Pythons' Autobiography by the Pythons* (Orion, 2003). In addition to broadcasting for the BBC, and writing for magazines and newspapers, he wrote *Dreams & Nightmares: Terry Gilliam, 'The Brothers Grimm' and Other Cautionary Tales of Hollywood* (HarperCollins, 2005) and *The Authorised Biography of Ronnie Barker* (BBC Books, 2004).

Ian Nathan (IN), who lives and works in London, has been a writer, producer, broadcaster and magazine editor. He is the author of *Alien Vault*, the bestselling history of the 1979 classic, and *Cahiers Du Cinema*'s *Masters of Cinema: Joel and Ethan Coen*. He is executive editor of *Empire*, and has contributed to the *Times* and *Independent*.

Dominic Nolan (DN) is a novelist and critic.

Cleaver Patterson (CP) is a film critic and writer who has done everything from studying the history of art to selling antiquarian books. A contributor to *Starburst* magazine and *The Big Picture*, his reviews can be read online at Film International, The People's Movies and CineVue among others.

Pat Reid (PR), originally a music journalist, now provides film-related content for the UK cinema chain Cineworld. As editor of the long-running *Cineworld Magazine* – the UK's highest-circulating film publication – he writes about hundreds of releases each year.

Simon Ward (SW) is a writer and editor working in London. He has won awards for his short story work and has written extensively on cinema and comic books. He was a contributor to the bestselling *1001 Movies You Must See Before You Die* (Cassell, 2008).

Owen Williams (OW) is a regular contributor to *Empire*, and has smuggled work into *DeathRay, Rue Morgue, SFX, Film3Sixty* (free with the *Guardian* and the *Evening Standard*) and Yahoo. He doesn't blog and very rarely tweets.

Damon Wise (DW) is a contributing editor on *Empire*. A film writer since 1987, he has had features, interviews and reviews published in the *Guardian, Times* and *Observer*, and magazines such as *Sight & Sound* and the much-missed *Neon*. In 1998 he published his first book – *Come by Sunday* (Sidgwick & Jackson), a biography of British film star Diana Dors.

POSTER DESIGNERS

Paul Burgess is a freelance illustrator, designer, photographer and writer. Paul is also the course leader for BA (Hons) Illustration at the University of Brighton. He has exhibited his work in numerous solo and group exhibitions in both the UK and abroad, and has worked as a freelance illustrator for over twenty years. He is interested in collage, found ephemera and making things by hand. www.mrpaulburgess.com

Isabel Eeles graduated from Central Saint Martins School of Art and Design with First Class Honours in Graphic Design. In 2012 she won a competition to create designs for L'Oreal Professionnel's 'London Addixion' styling products. View her work at www.isabeleeles.com.

Rich Fox is a freelance graphic designer. His projects have included identity, promotion and logos for Universidade Tecnológica Federal do Paraná (Brazil), Wellington University (New Zealand), UNICEF and Partisan Productions theatre company (Northern Ireland). His work can be viewed at richfoxdesign. tumblr.com. He lives in Bristol, UK.

Simon Halfon works as an art director in London and Los Angeles. He has designed album covers and campaigns for acts including George Michael, Frank Sinatra and Oasis. www.simon-halfon.com

Alison Hau studied graphic design in the UK and Hong Kong. Based in London, she designs illustrated reference books. www.alisonhau.com

Tom Howey lives and works in London as a designer of popular illustrated reference books.

Damian Jaques trained in printmaking at Portsmouth Polytechnic and Wimbledon College of Art before becoming involved in graphic design. He was a co-founder and designer of *COIL, Journal of the Moving Image*, and designer of *Mute* magazine from 1997 to 2005. His work has been published in *Typography Now Two – Implosion, Mapping* (RotoVision, 2008), and *magCulture: New Magazine Design* (Laurence King, 2003).

Heath Killen is a graphic designer, art director and design consultant from Newcastle, Australia. Represented by The Jacky Winter Group creative agency, he has worked on numerous high-profile projects for clients as diverse as Smirnoff, Paramount Pictures Art Gallery of New South Wales and Tropfest. He is currently editor of Australian design magazine *Desktop*.

Herita MacDonald is a freelance graphic designer. Her publishing, packaging, web design and corporate identity work also includes illustration, painting, 3D modelling and stained glass. www.heritamacdonald.com

Dean Martin is a London based graphic designer and illustrator. deangmartin@me.com

Roderick Mills is an illustrator based in London. He has worked for various international clients including the BBC, the Design Museum, the National Theatre, Opéra National de Paris and *The New York Times*. Also an award winning film-maker, his films have been screened at London Short Film Festival ICA London, Edinburgh Film Festival, Cork Film Festival and Festival Nouveau Cinéma Montreál, Canada.

Matt Needle runs a freelance design and illustration studio based in Cardiff, UK. He has been working in design for several years on various projects across branding, illustration and editorial design. As well as working commercially in these areas, he also runs Needle Print-store and LYF Clothing.

Jay Shaw is a poster artist based in Broomfield, Colorado. He has been commissioned to create film art for numerous companies, including The Criterion Collection, Paramount, The Weinstein Company and Mondo.

Akiko Stehrenberger began her career in New York illustrating for *Spin, The Source, New York Press, Filter* and other publications. Upon moving back to Los Angeles in 2004, she became an art director and designer for movie posters. She is best known for her award-winning illustrated posters: *Funny Games*, *Casa De Mi Padre*, *Dust Up* and more. Examples of her work can be seen at akikomatic.com.

Pedro Vidotto has a degree in advertising, six years' experience in art direction and four in graphic design and has worked with clients around the world. His artwork has been featured in both national and international publications, as well as highly respected design websites.

Lawrence Zeegen is an educator, designer and illustrator. As the dean of the School of Design at London College of Communication, University of the Arts London, Zeegen leads courses in advertising and branding, animation and games design, interactive design, illustration and typographic design.

SELECTED BIBLIOGRAPHY & WEBSITES

Berg, Chuck; Erskine, Tom et al
The Encyclopedia of Orson Welles
(Facts on File Inc., 2002)

Broccoli, Cubby; Zec, Donald
When the Snow Melts: The Autobiography of Cubby Broccoli
(Boxtree, 1998)

Cocks, Geoffrey
The Wolf at the Door: Stanley Kubrick, History & the Holocaust
(Peter Lang Publishing Inc., 2004)

Estrin, Mark W. (ed.)
Orson Welles Interviews
(University Press of Mississippi, 2002)

Harryhausen, Ray; Dalton, Tony
The Art of Ray Harryhausen
(Aurum Press Ltd, 2006)

Herbert, Brian
Dreamer of Dune: The Biography of Frank Herbert
(Tor Books, 2004)

Hughes, David
Tales from Development Hell
(Titan Books, 2004)

McBride, Joseph
Steven Spielberg: A Biography
(Faber and Faber, 1997)

Quinlan, David
Quinlan's Film Directors
(Batsford, 1999)

Sackett, Susan; Roddenberry, Gene
The Making of Star Trek The Motion Picture
(Wallaby Books, 1980)

Summers, Anthony
Goddess: The Secret Lives of Marilyn Monroe
(Gollancz, 1985)

Mae Brussell – World Watchers International radio broadcast, 21 March 1982

Phil Nugent at the Screengrab (2007–09)

300spartanwarriors.com
aintitcool.com
alfredhitchcockgeek.com
anthemmagazine.com
batman-on-film.com
beatlesbible.com
bestforfilm.com
blastr.com
collider.com
criterion.com
deadline.com
denofgeek.com
duneinfo.com
empireonline.com
english.carlthdreyer.dk
flixist.com
guardian.co.uk/film
horror.about.com
identitytheory.com
ifc.com
ign.com
imdb.com
jigsawlounge.co.uk
jimbelushi.ws
klockworkkugler.com
lynchnet.com
mania.com
philjens.plus.com
powell-pressburger.org
scriptmag.com
sensesofcinema.com
slashfilm.com
superherohype.com
thecityofabsurdity.com
totalfilm.com
uproxx.com
variety.com
war-ofthe-worlds.co.uk
wellesnet.com
wongkarwai.net
writingwithhitchcock.com

INDEX

PICTURE CREDITS

2 Nathan Jones/Getty Images **6** Museum of the City of New York/Byron Co. Collection/Getty Images **12** Topical Press Agency/Getty Images **14 t** NY Daily News Archive via Getty Images **14 b** The Kobal Collection/Warner Bros./Elmer Fryer **15** Everett Collection/Rex Features **17** Bettmann/Corbis **18** Mary Evans Picture Library/National Magazine Company **19 t** The Kobal Collection/Selznick/United Artists **19 b** image courtesy of Elevator Repair Service Theater **20** The Kobal Collection/Otto Dyar **22 t** The Kobal Collection/Mosfilm **22 bl** The Kobal Collection/Mexican Picture Trust **22 br** The Kobal Collection/Mexican Picture Trust **23** Movie Poster Database **25** Everett Collection/Rex Features **26 t** American Stock/Getty Images **27** Jesse Grant/WireImage/Getty Images **28** The Kobal Collection/Warner Bros. **30** H. & H. Jacobsen/Authenticated News/Archive Photos/Getty Images **32** Smith & Haas **33 tl** Dial Press **33 tr** The Kobal Collection/Société Générale de Films **34 c** AGF s.r.l./Rex Features **35** The Kobal Collection/Columbia **37** © The Ray & Diana Harryhausen Foundation **38 t** © The Ray & Diana Harryhausen Foundation **38 b** © The Ray & Diana Harryhausen Foundation **39** Movie Poster Database **41** The Kobal Collection **42 t** The Kobal Collection/Warner Bros. **42 b** The Kobal Collection/Tudor **43** The Kobal Collection/Paramount **47** SNAP/Rex Features **48 tl** The Kobal Collection/20th Century Fox **48 tr** Bettmann/CORBIS **49 tl** The Kobal Collection/20th Century Fox **49 tr** Cat's Collection/Corbis **50** The Kobal Collection/RKO **51** Movie Poster Database **53** Keystone-France/Getty Images **54 t** Sunset Boulevard/Corbis **54 b** The Kobal Collection/Columbia **55** The Kobal Collection/PARC/ARGOS **56** Henri Bureau/Sygma/Corbis **58 t** The Kobal Collection/Lobster Films **58 c** The Kobal Collection/Lobster Films **58 b** The Kobal Collection/Lobster Films **59** The Kobal Collection/Atelier/Continental **60 bl** Henri Bureau/Apis/Sygma/Corbis **60 br** Henri Bureau/Apis/Sygma/Corbis **61** The Kobal Collection/Films Corona/VERA **62** Everett Collection/Rex Features **64** Mondadori Collection/Getty Images **65 t** The Kobal Collection/F.C. Rome/P.E.C.F.Paris **65 c** AP/Press Association Images **67** The Kobal Collection/Universal **68 t** The Kobal Collection/MGM **69** The Kobal Collection/Universal **70** The Kobal Collection/Warner Bros. **72** French Olympia Press **73** Dutton/Signet **74 t** FremantleMedia Ltd./Rex features **74 c** Allstar/Cinetext/Handmade Films **74 b** The Kobal Collection/Channel 4 Films/Mikado Films/Rai Cinemafiction **75** Movie Poster Database **77** The Kobal Collection/Universal **82** Miramax/Everett Collection/Rex Features **85** Mondadori Portfolio/Angelo Deligio/Getty Images **86 bl** STF/AFP/Getty Images **86 br** Express Newspapers/Getty Images **87** Movie Poster Database **89** The Kobal Collection/SACI **90 t** SNAP/Rex Features **91** The Kobal Collection **92** The Kobal Collection **94** The Kobal Collection/Archers/London Films/British Lion **95 bl** Heinemann **95 br** The Kobal Collection/Rock Studios **96** The Kobal Collection/Prods Panic **98** © Chris Foss, courtesy ChrisFossArt.com **100** Luiz Alberto/Keystone Features/Getty Images **101** The Kobal Collection/Universal **102** Hulton-Deutsch Collection/Corbis **104** Tomahawk Press **105** The Kobal Collection/DANJAQ/EON/UA **106** United Archives GmbH / Alamy **108 t** The Kobal Collection/United Artists **108 b** The Kobal Collection/Warner 7 Arts **109 tl** Pictorial Press Ltd / Alamy **109 tr** Photos 12 / Alamy **111** The Kobal Collection **114** The Kobal Collection/Boyd's Co./Virgin Films/Matrixbest **115** The Kobal Collection/Boyd's Co./Virgin Films/Matrixbest **118** The Kobal Collection/Columbia **120** MGM/Getty Images **122** Pamela Juhl / Demotix/Demotix/Corbis **123** Moviestore Collection/Rex Features **125** The Kobal Collection/United Artists **126 t** The Kobal Collection/EMI **126 b** Ron Galella/WireImage/Getty Images **127** The Kobal Collection/Columbia Pictures **128** Express/Getty Images **131** The Kobal Collection/Columbia **132** Didier Olivré/Corbis **134** Hulton-Deutsch Collection/CORBIS **136** Tom Wargacki/WireImage/Getty Images **138** Mansell/Time Life Pictures/Getty Images **139** AF Archive/Alamy **141** The Kobal Collection/Paramount **142** Image courtesy of Karl Shefelman, reproduced with permission by American Zoetrope **143** Movie Poster Database **145** The Kobal Collection/MGM/UA **146** Quartet Books **147** M. Tran/FilmMagic/Getty Images **148** Spia Press/Rex Features **150** The Kobal Collection/Rafran/San Marco **151** Andreas Solaro/AFP/Getty Images **154** The Kobal Collection **156 t** The Kobal Collection/Wellspring Media **156 b** American Broadcasting Companies, Inc. All rights reserved./Getty Images **157** Jeff Kravitz/FilmMagic/Getty Images **159** British Film Institute **160** British Film Institute **161** British Film Institute **162 t** British Film Institute **162 b** British Film Institute **163** The Kobal Collection/Miramax/Dimension Films **165** David Hartley/Rex Features **166** Allstar/Cinetext/Columbia **167 t** © Terry Gilliam **167 c** © Terry Gilliam **167 b** © Terry Gilliam **168** Everett Collection/Rex Features **169** The Kobal Collection/Polygram **170** SNAP/Rex Features **173 l** Movie Poster Database **173 r** Movie Poster Database **175** The Kobal Collection/Carolco/Tri-Star/Theo Westenberger **176** The Kobal Collection/De Laurentiis **177 t** The Kobal Collection/Columbia Tristar **177 b** The Kobal Collection/20th Century Fox/David Appleby **178** Everett Collection/Rex Features **180** HarperCollins **181 l** The Kobal Collection/Touchstone/Cinergi **181 r** The Kobal Collection/Warner Bros./Southside Amusement Co. **182** The Kobal Collection/Miramax/Lorenzo Bevilaqua **184 t** The Kobal Collection/Marv Films **184 b** The Kobal Collection/20th Century Fox/Marvel **185** Movie Poster Database **189** Artisan/Everett Collection/Rex Features **190 t** DC Comics **191** Movie Poster Database **193** AF archive/Alamy **195** Everett Collection/Rex Features **196** The Kobal Collection/Touchstone/Universal/Melinda Sue Gordon **198** The Kobal Collection/Working Title/Polygram/Michael Tackett **199 tl** The Kobal Collection/Paramount/Miramax **199 tr** The Kobal Collection/Working Title/Studio Canal **199 c** The Kobal Collection/Working Title/Studio Canal **201** AP/Press Association Images **202** Movie Poster Database **203** The Kobal Collection/Key Creatives **205** George Pimentel/WireImage/Getty Images **206** The Kobal Collection/Columbia/Block 2/Jet Tone Films **207 tl** The Kobal Collection/Jet Tone Production **207 tr** The Kobal Collection/Fox Searchlight Pictures **207 c** 20th C. Fox/Everett Collection/Rex Features **208** The Kobal Collection/Paramount/Frank Connor **211** The Kobal Collection/Dreamworks/Universal/Jaap Buitendijk **212 t** The Kobal Collection/Surefire Films/First Look Pictures **212 b** The Kobal Collection/Universal Pictures **213 l** The Kobal Collection/Universal Pictures **213 r** Startraks Photo/Rex Features **214** AP/Press Association Images **217** Grove/Atlantic **218** Daniele Venturelli/WireImage/Getty Images **219 l** The Kobal Collection/Twentieth Century-Fox Film **219 r** The Kobal Collection/Focus Features **221** Charles Burns **222** Brian Michael Bendis/Marc Andreyko **223 tl** Jun Sato/ WireImage/Getty Images **223 tr** Charles Burns **224** Andrew Ross/Corbis **226 t** New York Times Co./Getty Images **226 b** Roadside/Everett Collection/Rex Features **227** Everett Collection/Rex Features **228** Pool Catarina/Vandeville/Gamma-Rapho via Getty Images **230** Penguin **231 tl** The Kobal Collection/Warner Bros. **231 tr** The Kobal Collection/Exclusive Films **231 c** AGF s.r.l./Rex Features **233** Stephen Shugerman/Getty Images **234 t** Jon Kopaloff/FilmMagic/Getty Images **234 b** MiB/Splash News Online **235 l** The Kobal Collection/Mandeville Films/Jojo Whilden **235 r** The Kobal Collection/Rekall Productions **236** Mike Fanous/Gamma-Rapho via Getty Images **238** The Kobal Collection **239 tl** Photos 12 / Alamy **239 tr** The Kobal Collection/Dream Works Animation **240** Dave M. Benett/Getty Images **242** Twentieth Century Fox/Regency/Sunset Boulevard/Corbis **244 l** Boni & Liveright **244 c** Movie Poster Database **244 r** The Kobal Collection/Paramount **245 l** Hulton Archive/Getty Images **245 c** Evening Standard/Hulton Archive/Getty Images **246 l** The Kobal Collection/International Films Espanola/Alpine Productions **246 c** Louisiana State University Press **246 r** ITV/Rex Features **247 l** The Kobal Collection/Ladd Company/Warner Bros. **247 c** The Kobal Collection/Universal Pictures **247 r** British Library/Robana/Getty Images **248 l** Random House **248 c** Movie Poster Database **248 r** Gollancz **249 l** Scott Myers/Rex Features **249 c** MJ Kim/Getty Images **249 r** The Kobal Collection/Edward R. Pressman

Thanks to: Chris Bryans for his assistance with *Who Killed Bambi?*; Nick Mason for his assistance with *Dune*; and Dominic Nolan and Simon Ward for setting up this book